In honor of
Dr. Thomas Bailey's
90th birthday 2007.

Ritual, Discourse, and Community in Cuban Santería

CONTEMPORARY CUBA

UNIVERSITY PRESS OF FLORIDA

Florida A&M University, Tallahassee
Florida Atlantic University, Boca Raton
Florida Gulf Coast University, Ft. Myers
Florida International University, Miami
Florida State University, Tallahassee
University of Central Florida, Orlando
University of Florida, Gainesville
University of North Florida, Jacksonville
University of South Florida, Tampa
University of West Florida, Pensacola

Contemporary Cuba

Edited by John M. Kirk

Ritual, Discourse, and Community in Cuban Santería

Speaking a Sacred World

Kristina Wirtz

University Press of Florida

Gainesville   Tallahassee   Tampa   Boca Raton
Pensacola   Orlando   Miami   Jacksonville   Ft. Myers

12 11 10 09 08 07   6 5 4 3 2 1

Chapter 3 contains a revised version of "Santería in Cuban National
Consciousness: A Religious Case of the Doble Moral." *Journal of Latin American
Anthropology* 9, no. 2 (Fall 2004): 409–38.
Library of Congress Cataloging-in-Publication Data
Wirtz, Kristina.
Ritual, discourse, and community in Cuban Santería : speaking a sacred world /
Kristina Wirtz.
p. cm.—(Contemporary Cuba)
Includes bibliographical references and index.
ISBN 978-0-8130-3064-7 (alk. paper)
1. Santeria—Cuba—Santiago de Cuba—Case studies. 2. Communities—Religious
aspects—Santeria—Case studies. 3. Santiago de Cuba (Cuba)—Religious life and
customs—Case studies. I. Title.
BL2532.S3.W57 2007
299.6'7409729165—dc22   2007004257

The University Press of Florida is the scholarly publishing agency for the State
University System of Florida, comprising Florida A&M University, Florida Atlantic
University, Florida Gulf Coast University, Florida International University, Florida
State University, University of Central Florida, University of Florida, University
of North Florida, University of South Florida, and University of West Florida.

University Press of Florida
15 Northwest 15th Street
Gainesville, FL 32611-2079
www.upf.com

#82471784

Kí ikú má ṣe padrino mío, ¡Mo dúpẹ́!

To Ed and Yasmin, with love

Contents

Illustrations

Figures

Table

Preface

In this book I revisit an enduring question of anthropology: how do communities coalesce and persist through time? I pose this question about a specific community of religious practitioners of Santería that I came to know through my fieldwork in the city of Santiago de Cuba in eastern Cuba. Santería is one of several often-overlapping popular religions practiced in Santiago de Cuba, and many religious practitioners combine practices or seek expert services from what scholars represent as ostensibly distinct religious traditions, such as Palo Mayombe, Spiritism, Santería, and even Muertería. Even among those who have been initiated as priests in Santería, different ritual lineages may have distinct traditions—the best known and most visible such distinction separates *santeros* (priests of Ocha) and *babalawos* (priests of Ifá), although some babalawos are also initiated santeros.

These introductory observations suggest the need to demonstrate, rather than assume, the existence and composition of a local religious community of Santería. They also raise questions about how such a community differentiates itself amid the bustle of religious activity and how it regulates its membership by managing relationships across—as well as within—certain ritually established lineages of fictive and genealogical kinship. This issue of how intergroup boundaries of identity are maintained was articulated by Fredrik Barth (1969) in a classic essay on how ethnic groups constitute and maintain themselves. In Santería, no ethnic distinctions are available to naturalize religious community belonging, although Cuban histories of race and its internal differentiations into African *naciones* (ethnicities) during the centuries of Atlantic World slavery permeate local understandings of Santería and other popular religions, albeit in what Stephen Palmié aptly characterizes as "complex and ill-understood ways" (2002b: 197). Santería, for example, clearly derives from what today is known as Yoruba tradition, recreated in Cuba by enslaved West Africans from the region of modern-day southwestern Nigeria and Benin. Santería's modern-day practitioners in Cuba, however, span all racial and other social categories. Without clear racial/ethnic distinctions, and without clear-cut differences in religious practices, how do some practitioners create and recognize links of religious community with one another? As Barth suggests for ethnic groups, processes of competition, cooperation, and what I call discursive polarization among various religious traditions also contribute to maintaining distinctions among religious communities-of-practice. Palmié, for example, discusses how Cuban popular religions are arrayed along a racially polarized moral spectrum, in which Yoruba-derived Santería is juxtaposed as a proper, moral, Christian-influenced religion to the amoral, even exploitative "black magic" of the Reglas de Congo like Palo Mayombe (2002b: 189–200; see also Argyriadis 2000). I aim to show how such distinctions around Santería are maintained through a variety of historical and contemporary discourses.

Such boundary-making discourses interact with ritual practices to create distinctions among what emerge as different religious traditions. They also generate distinctions between religious and nonreligious domains of social life. It is crucial to recognize that what a particular religion is—whether in fact there is agreement that a certain set of practices and practitioners constitutes a "religion"—depends upon observers' perspectives. Consider Santería: even using this name over other available labels involves ideologically charged choices. To call this entity "Lucumí religion," or "La Regla de Ocha," or even just "La Ocha," let alone referring to it as witchcraft, or an Afro-Cuban popular religion, or folklore, or superstitious nonsense (all of which are circulating labels in contemporary Cuba) would signal different directions a book such as this could take and distinct, even irreconcilably different, visions of the topic. By making a choice among these interpretive or *metacultural* frames (Urban 2001), I necessarily essentialize the cultural phenomenon that interests me as a particular kind of entity. Those who come into contact with Santería by any name—practitioners, their neighbors and compatriots, government officials, Cuban folklorists, and not least, ethnographers—construe it through particular and varied metacultural stances toward religion, various ritual practices, things Afro-Cuban, and so forth. Indeed, as Briggs (1996) points out, since some of these actors have more discursive authority than others, some labels ("Santería" for example) circulate more widely than others ("Regla de Ocha," as practitioners prefer). If the predominant opinion is that a social and cultural (that is, discursive) entity called Santería is a religion, then how did this come to be so, and what is the significance of alternative perspectives that continue to circulate?

This book is an attempt to not only avoid presenting an essentialized, normative vision of the religion, but to focus attention on the interpretive processes by which different essentializations, such as those listed above, emerge. My particular interest is in how religious practitioners themselves, through their often conflictual discursive activity, continually bring into being something they largely can agree is Santería. Their vision of Santería bumps up against other construals from other secular and religious vantage points, and out of the ongoing mélange, something called Santería takes shape, like smoke that seems solid from a distance but resolves into plumes of dancing particles when viewed closely.

Smoke metaphors aside, I have come to see that the dominant trope permeating my analysis is one of an almost Darwinian landscape, his "entangled bank" of competing views (Darwin 1964: 489), in what Susan Philips (2004), perhaps channeling Gregory Bateson, describes as a sort of ecological system of ideologies or interpretive frames, in which each strand has its own "niche"— practices, attitudes, identities, relationships, and institutions that sustain it— and multiple ideologies or frames can coexist, even find points of convergence, even though they may also put pressure on one another. Such systems are dynamic, but not necessarily shifting in any inexorable direction (for example, toward secular modernism). The ecological trope undoubtedly holds a certain attraction for me because of my prior training in ecology and evolutionary theory, but it is also a productive alternative to accounts of competing ideologies based on either Marxist models of domination and resistance or "cultural flow" models of globalization, as Philips argues (232–33). Interestingly, Barth (1969) also employs an ecological metaphor to describe the dynamics of competition, borrowing, and interdependence that sustain group boundaries in poly-ethnic societies, an idea that resonates with analyses of complex poly-religious "ecologies" in the Caribbean, such as Houk's account of Trinidad (1995) Austin-Broos' account of Jamaica (1997) and Palmié's account of Cuba (2002b). Most importantly, however, the ecological trope expresses my observations about how discursive dynamics construct social realities. At the macrosocial level, competing discourses (in the broad, Foucauldian sense) clash over the meaning and role of Santería in national life, and at the microsocial level of daily interactions among religious practitioners similar debates over what constitutes "correct" and proper religious practice hammer out a local community, one I will argue is united as much by conflict as by consensus. As Comaroff and Comaroff (1993: xxiii) suggest, rituals may serve to open up "fields of argument," in which conflicting viewpoints are brought into dialogue.[1]

The ecological metaphors underlying how I characterize these dynamics fit with what has been called a constructionist viewpoint on social entities such

as religions and communities. Kay Warren (1992) argues for a constructionist alternative to essentialized identities, which do not exist "except as [they]
are constructed, contested, negotiated, imposed, imputed, resisted, and rede-
fined in action" (205). Although she is describing Mayan and Ladino identities
in Guatemala, her description fits my argument about Cuban Santería. This
brand of constructionism, then, takes a dialogical view of culture that is based
on semiotic understandings of how cultural forms and categories get created,
circulated, replicated, and modified across all sorts of human interactions. As
Tedlock and Mannheim argue in their introduction to *The Dialogic Emergence
of Culture* (1995: 1–32), the seeming cultural totalities we experience as a sort
of gestalt are in fact comprised of circulating signs that are mediated by, and in
turn mediate, interactions among people. In order to understand the semiotic
mediation of cultural forms and social realities, I thus employ methods and
analytical perspectives developed within the ethnography of communication
and more recent semiotic and discourse-centered approaches, which in turn
are chiefly inspired by C. S. Peirce, Mikhail Bakhtin and Valentin Voloshinov,
Román Jakobson, and Erving Goffman.[2] I discuss and illustrate discourse-
centered analysis in chapter 1.

This ethnography of religious community thus pays particular attention to
practitioners' ritual and other discursive practices and how these both create and reflect their understandings of religious experience, consciousness of
belonging to a community, and position within the broader religious and so-
ciohistorical context. Exploring how santeros' local moral community emerges
out of the ritual and interpretive practices of its members raises a set of important issues. First and foremost: what is "community," and how is it best
characterized? In particular, is community necessarily predicated upon commonality, or is there room within community for what Iris Young (1986) calls
a "politics of difference?" What allows an ethnographer or, for that matter,
anyone in a given society, to recognize a religious community or even a religion
as a distinct social entity? As a related issue, how can such social entities be described without being essentialized? That is, how do we capture the discursive
processes as well as the "real" (tangible, seemingly self-evident) social entities
and identities such processes precipitate? And finally, what role do rituals play
in generating community, and what other activities might also contribute? In
the pages that follow I seek to juxtapose these questions in a way that points to
some surprising conclusions about the dynamics of religious community and
ritual life among santeros.

One comment on my "community" terminology: I have come to prefer thinking of santeros' religious community as a moral community (and indeed I use the phrases almost interchangeably). Durkheim (1995/1912) used "moral community" in a broader sense to apply to religion's role in cementing social cohesion in an entire small-scale society. I instead adopt it to refer to a local religious community because the phrase evokes shared concern over religious propriety rather than shared belief. As I will explore throughout the book, santeros hold much in common with other Cuban religious practitioners and at the same time find plenty to disagree about among themselves; it is not shared belief that unites and distinguishes santeros so much as participation in a common dialogue about correct practice and interpretation.

In all honesty, I did not begin my fieldwork among santeros in Santiago de Cuba with the plan of investigating how their religious community is consti-tuted. Rather, I did what it seems most ethnographers of religious communities tend to do without much comment: I assumed that the community of local Santería practitioners would become self-evident as I became familiar with my research setting. I took it for granted that ritual events would most clear-ly embody the religious community and that the structures of ritual lineage produced and reinforced through ritual activities would unproblematically indicate to me who the community's members were. My plan was to attend rituals and follow up on ritual genealogies in order to map out the community and locate those whose experiences and expertise could answer my questions. Identifying the community was not originally an end in itself, but simply a step along the way to my research objectives. Based on my prior reading of the normative accounts of Santería rituals and beliefs that prevail in the literature, I fully expected that a relatively consistent image of Santería would emerge out of explanations provided by the practitioners I worked with. In short, I naively hoped to "land" in a community, establish rapport with its members, and get on with learning about what I had come to learn: Santería's ritual language. In large part, this is what happened, or at least what felt like it was happening. The moral community of Santería felt very real to me, and it became ever more tan-gible and all-encompassing as I delved deeper into the religion, even though I retained my marginal position as an uninitiated outsider.

What I came to realize (and what this book is about) is that Santería's moral community felt most real, most present, and most powerful to me when en-acted in the dense, ever-present interchange of conversation, gossip, planning, reports, complaints, and critiques that comprise practitioners' reflective dis-course about their religion and specifically about rituals they had attended, were planning, and were currently participating in. At first, this background chatter of conversation was so ordinary as to be almost invisible to me, serving simply as the context in which rituals stood out as specially framed, even momentous events. Everyday, naturally occurring discourse, as it is called by discourse-centered theorists, was there to be observed, recorded, and mined for data. However, the background gradually became foreground, as I increasingly recognized this realm of "ordinary" reflective discourse as the real social glue of communal religious life, the force that organized rituals and the way in which the meanings of specific ritual performances were negotiated and woven together into often competing metanarratives of what it meant to be a santero and what the religion itself stood for. While santeros themselves characterized their religious community as being structured by ritually cemented ties of ritual kinship with one another, the ancestors, and the orichas (deities), their discursive activity suggested to me that what enmeshed otherwise distinct, often competing ritual lineages into a cohesive and distinctive moral community was, paradoxically, the often conflictual discourse surrounding, and indeed frequently provoked by, rituals.

Durkheim long ago emphasized the critical role of rituals in bringing people together around symbols of communality and of religion itself as a shared second-order interpretation of the experience of society's power over the individual (Durkheim 1995/1912). My analysis displaces the central role scholars since Durkheim continue to grant rituals in themselves to instead shift attention to the reflective discourse rituals generate as the principal dynamic through which community is reproduced and through which communities manage and police themselves. This book illustrates how a local religious community of Santería takes shape primarily through the critiques, discussions, and controversies surrounding religious rituals. That is, rituals provide the fodder for reflective discourse through which individual and collective religious understandings are negotiated and local notions and perceptions of community are generated.

Recent critiques of the community concept have pointed out a common assumption that community, however it is "imagined" or "represented," is an idealized site of homogeneity and consensus (Creed 2004; Kelly and Kaplan 2001). Such romantic notions of community do not correspond to the everyday experience of social life, which is often rife with conflicts and differences. Nor does idealized community sit well with post-structuralist analyses of how the workings of power can be disguised by projecting the appearance of homogeneity and consensus. Such projections cast conflict as dangerous to community, unless it is a conflict with outsiders around which members of a community can rally, and even then the goal is to bury internal differences under common cause.

I instead suggest that intracommunity conflict, rather than always and everywhere being antithetical to community-building, might sometimes constitute community. This happens when conflict increases the density of circulating discourse that links participants to one another and highlights an ontological common ground within disagreements. Among santeros in Santiago, this dynamic is most visible in how santeros reflect upon and interpret ritual performances, and so I carefully attend to what it is in ritual performances that so grabs santeros' attention and provokes so much reflection. One key role of rituals in Santería is to allow communication with the divine, and it turns out that santeros are preoccupied with evaluating whether particular ritual performances indeed achieved this sort of religious experience. Santeros bring a skeptical eye to bear on the minutest details of ritual preparations, participation, and even motives of their fellow participants. They are passionately concerned with "correct," "proper," and "respectful" religious practices, even though they sometimes equally passionately disagree about whether specific instances were correct, proper, and respectful. Such judgments, in turn, affect whether a particular ritual is deemed successful, whether advice received in a divination is heeded as having divine origin, or whether a relationship with another religious practitioner or lineage is pursued or dropped. That is, all of the gossip, critique, and controversy allows santeros, individually and collectively, to decide whether and how to interpret rituals and other events as religious experiences, and with what repercussions. The local community that encompasses at least some santeros (and others) some of the time, and that has a certain historical continuity through several generations of particular families and neighborhoods, is, I will argue, a by-product of these reflective activities. That is, the local Santería community resolves itself out of fleeting traces of face-to-face interactions, like bouncing particles of smoke seen from a distance.

I have described my major goal as challenging a tendency for ethnographic studies of religious communities, in particular, to take for granted their boundaries, shared tradition, and unity of purpose. I instead ask how such seemingly empirical realities emerge out of the ferment of debate over the meaning of ritual experiences. This question compels attention to the fine-grained detail of real-time, unfolding events and face-to-face human interactions in all of the messiness of the micropolitics of everyday life and the fluid, emergent, not-quite-in-focus understandings participants seem always just on the verge of reaching. Out of this ephemeral stuff, santeros render their religion meaningful and their community real.

With all of this constructionist talk, I hasten to add that there is a "there" there. Santería has recognizable and distinctive forms: rituals, jargon, priestly hierarchies, and historical lineages reaching back at least a hundred years, with clear antecedents in Cuba and beyond, notably among West Africans today known as the Yoruba. This book pays special attention to these cultural elements, too, and especially to how santeros invoke them to generate phenomenological experiences of the sacred. But again, my focus is not on describing the cultural objects-in-themselves (which so many books on Santería already do), but on how their reality, their distinctiveness, their persistence, and their tangible effects on people's lives emerge out of the ferment of discursive activity about what santeros are engaged in. I tell a tale of intrigue, of skepticism, controversy, and gossip, out of which, paradoxically, emerge faith, moral community, and numinous experience. I tell a tale of speaking the sacred.

Ethnographic Prologue

Field site overview

I worked with santeros in the eastern Cuban city of Santiago de Cuba (see figure 1), where I engaged in participant observation during four visits to the city, totalling a year, and including an extended stay of eight months from September 1999 through May 2000. My first visit was in December 1997, and my most recent visit was in April 2002. My fieldwork brought me into extensive contact with religious practitioners of Santería and with Cuban folklorists, both researchers and performers. I worked especially closely with several individuals who are both religious practitioners and researchers.

Santiago de Cuba sometimes strikes Cubanists and Cuban scholars as an odd choice of fieldsite for someone studying Santería, because Havana's working class Regla and Guanabacoa neighborhoods and the nearby city of Matanzas are the accepted "birthplaces" of Santería. It is true that most foreign scholars base themselves in Havana, which is not surprising given that Havana, as the capital, is (and has always been) the political and cultural center of gravity on the island. Likewise, Havana-based Cuban scholars and academic institu-

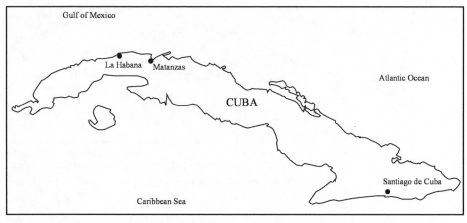

Figure 1. Map of Cuba showing Santiago de Cuba's location. Adaptation by Pamela Rups, Western Michigan University, from *Maps on File* (New York: Facts on File, Inc., 2000).

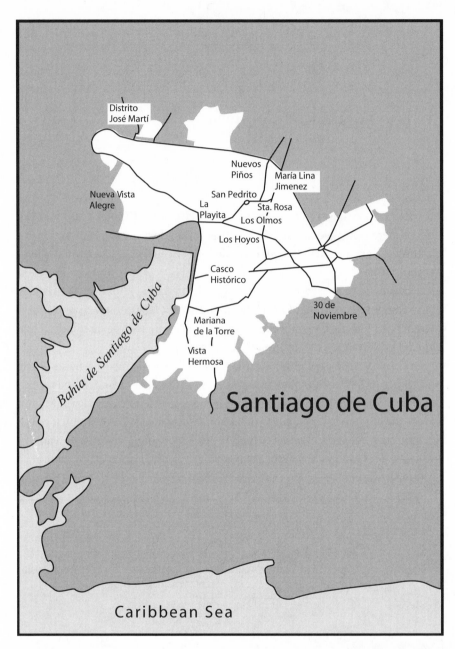

Figure 2. Map of the city of Santiago de Cuba showing principal neighborhoods in which field-work was conducted. Adaptation by Pamela Rups, Western Michigan University, from "Map of Santiago de Cuba," (Cuba: Ediciones GEO, 1999).

tions garner more prestige and resources than do those in the provinces. But I see this as all the more reason to encourage ethnographic work in the rest of Cuba, so as to counter prevailing Havana-centric tendencies. From Havana's point of view, Santiago is very provincial, although it is the second largest city on the island with a population of 478,000.[3] Doing fieldwork on Santería in Santiago thus gives me a very different view from the religious and political margins, amid the dominant voices of Havana-based scholarship.

What is fascinating about Santiago is that its vibrant Santería community is relatively new, by most accounts dating only to the 1930s, and santeros in Santiago are very aware of its relative newness. Unlike Havana and Matanzas, Santiago has few babalawos, high priests of *Ifá* divination, and its Santería community has relatively less visibility and more competition amidst the numerous, self-styled "santeros" who practice related popular religions. At the same time, Santiago is a much more Afro-Cuban city, and, despite its proud history as the cradle of revolutions and revolts, is far from the center of political power.

Although Santiago has hundreds of initiates in Santería, I was able to develop a general sense of the Santería community and its power centers, major personalities, fault lines, and oral history, as well as how Santería fits into the Cuban religious mosaic. I also developed strong ties with several ritual families and lineages and thus was able to participate in numerous and varied rituals and in-depth conversations and interviews. Despite the famed secrecy shielding much ritual activity, I was allowed access to a number of private rituals. I also found that there was an abundance of public rituals and talk about rituals available to a noninitiate.

My fieldwork took me into many neighborhoods of the city, and especially into the traditionally Afro-Cuban areas of Los Hoyos and San Pedrito and other neighborhoods to the north of the historic city center, or *casco histórico*. I also found myself in the newer neighborhoods of the Distrito José Martí and Nueva Vista Alegre, further west of San Pedrito. I have labeled the neighborhoods in which I conducted fieldwork with santeros in figure 2.

Methods

I did much of my fieldwork in the company of a few key field consultants who were both santeros and folklorists. They gave me entrée into events and introduced me to many other santeros. The benefits of working closely with key consultants were that we developed a strong working relationship over several years and that these expert consultants gave me in-depth tutorials on various topics. I also sought to branch out and meet other religious practitioners independently of my key consultants, especially by following up on a wide variety of other contacts and invitations, in order to achieve a more representative view of the local religious scene.

The principal types of ethnographic data I collected were ritual events, naturally occurring conversations, and interviews.[4] In addition to writing fieldnotes, I also made extensive audio recordings and, when able, videorecordings, of many events in which I participated.[5] I also recorded elicited and naturally occurring autobiographical narratives of religious participants, normative accounts of how to conduct rituals correctly, evaluations of particular rituals, and discourse concerning religion, identity, religious adherence, and types of religious participants. Some of these discourse events occurred in the course of informal visiting or during ritual proceedings. In other cases, I conducted semiformal interviews, played back ritual recordings or discussed field notes, or received classes (privately or with others) from secular and religiously involved folklorists who study religion.

It was in comparing how highly educated folklorists and younger santeros talked about Santería versus what older santeros had to say that I first glimpsed some of the ideological buttresses behind typical and often-repeated depictions of Santería. As I listened to more people, including Christian and nonreligious Cubans whose views on Santería presented additional facets, I came to detect certain fault lines in who would be referred to as a santero and in what alternatives santeros and Santería were collocated with or contrasted to. Patterns emerged in which labels were used, who used them, and whether Santería was described as "Cuban" or "Afro-Cuban," "religion" or "witchcraft," "syncretic," "popular," or "Yoruba"—my scare quotes here indicate how ideologically charged these labels all are. Amid these competing visions of Santería, santeros navigated their religious lives and negotiated the membership, boundaries, and norms of their moral community.

Acknowledgments

I am humbled by how many people contributed to making this book possible and only hope they can forgive me the errors that surely remain. Ethnographic research is above all a highly collaborative and cooperative enterprise that depends upon the goodwill of those whose home becomes one's field site. First and foremost I thank my hosts, consultants, and teachers in Santiago de Cuba for their tremendous support and forbearance: particular thanks to Ernesto Armiñán Linares; Maruchi Berbes and her household; Abelardo Larduet; Teresita Reyes Guerrero and her husband Carlos, mother Ena, and sons Karel and Carlitín; Veronica Gebra Nash and José Alberto Aguilera, their son Guillermo and granddaughter Loreta Aguilera; Kathy, Marta, and Manuel Pérez; Merceditas Causse Cathcart; Olga Portuondo Zúñiga; Rafael Soler (now tragically deceased); Miguel Matute; Reina Hechavarría; Ana María Fernández de Hierreguelo; Nurina Salas Ribero; and Carlos Labrada. Marisela and two other friends who will remain anonymous were dedicated and meticulous transcribers. Warm thanks also to the members of the Conjuncto Folklórico Cutumba and bobo iworo coggua ilé—all the santeros and other religious practitioners of Santiago who helped me and tolerated my research, and so many of whose stories are retold anonymously in these pages. ¡Kí ikú má şe! (May death spare you!) All of these people, their lovely families, and so many others unnamed here, helped make Santiago home for me and my husband and enveloped us in the bonds of *socio-lismo* (camaraderie) that sustained us through many trials and tribulations. In addition, I thank a number of Habaneros, and especially Manuel Agustín García, Sergio Valdés Bernal, and Jorge Ramírez Calzadilla of the Centro de Investigaciones Psicológicas y Sociológicas, which generously allowed me access to its wonderful library. I am also profoundly grateful to the institutions and talented staff of the Universidad del Oriente, the Casa del Caribe, and the Casa de Africa in Santiago, which provided me with institutional homes and intellectual communities during my research trips, and I applaud their openness to foreigners and U.S. citizens, particularly in the face of an unjust and cruel U.S. embargo.

I must thank the highly effective, long-term "moral community" of my writing group, whose incisive feedback on various drafts challenged me and kept me honest, and whose own incredible scholarship gave me so much food for thought: Çati Coe, Jane Cowley, Hilary Parsons Dick, Clare Ignatowski, Yoonhee Kang, Catherine Newling, and Lorrin Thomas. Matt Tomlinson and Trevor Stack helped from afar, and many other friends at Penn helped me clarify my thinking over the years. My dissertation advisor and committee were true mentors, and the stamp of each one's highly original thinking is everywhere in my work: heartfelt gratitude to Greg Urban, Asif Agha, Sandra Barnes, Nancy Farriss, and Rebecca Huss-Ashmore, as well as to my informal mentors, Stanton Wortham and Lee Cassanelli. Yiwọla Awoyale patiently turned his expert ear to deciphering possible Yoruba derivations in my Cuban Lucumí texts. The faculty of the African and Asian Studies Department of the University of Lagos taught me as much Yoruba as they could during my summer in Lagos. Norman Whitten provided valuable advice about getting several chapters into shape for publication. My colleagues at Western Michigan University have been wonderfully supportive during the revision process. Many thanks to the University Press of Florida, especially to John Byram for encouraging me to publish this book, and to my acquisitions editor Amy Gorelick and two anonymous reviewers for support and constructive critique.

This research was funded by a Brody-Foley Grant for summer research from the University of Pennsylvania, an International Predissertation Training Fellowship from the Social Science Research Council and the American Council of Learned Societies with funds provided by the Ford Foundation, and two U.S. Department of Education Foreign Language and Area Studies Fellowships.

A Note on the Text

Several linguistic codes are relevant to this examination of Santería in Cuba. First, Spanish (Castellano) is the language of Cuba and therefore of most of my fieldwork. Santería's ritual register, most often called "Lucumí," derives from the West African language called "Yoruba." In some rituals, a nonstandard variety of Spanish that Cubans call "bozal" is also used. For ease of reading, I represent bozal and Lucumí in standard Spanish orthography, except when my field consultants' representations of Lucumí words parted from standard Spanish. For example, I represent [w] in [agwa] as "agua" (water) in Spanish but as "awa" (we) in Lucumí. When all of these codes appear and I need to distinguish among them, I label Lucumí phrases with underlining and bozal phrases with an asterisk at the end. Readers familiar with Spanish will also recognize "errors" of grammar and "eye-dialect" that I use to capture pronunciation differences that differentiate bozal from standard Spanish.

In cases where a putative Yoruba derivation of a Lucumí term is noted, I use standard Yoruba orthography. Yoruba vowels are similar to Spanish vowels, except that ẹ is pronounced "eh" as in English "egg" and ọ is pronounced "aw" as in English "all." Yoruba ṣ is pronounced "sh" (which is usually assimilated to Spanish "ch" in Lucumí). Note that Yoruba has three tone phonemes, so accent marks that indicate stress in Spanish and Lucumí words (like "Lucumí") instead indicate high or low tone in Yoruba words.

The English translations I provide in longer transcript excerpts sometimes retain Lucumí words (underlined) because they were unintelligible to my field consultants and to me. When I wish to distinguish between what my field consultants understood of a Lucumí utterance and what I learned it to mean in broader context, I place my consultant's gloss in quotes and my gloss in parentheses.

Even in cases like quoted interview excerpts where the original utterance was in unproblematic standard Cuban Spanish and only the English translation is presented in the text, I always provide the original in an endnote. This is a compromise between my goal of providing thorough linguistic evidence of my interpretations, as befits a linguistic anthropologist, and my desire to keep the text as readable as possible.

I have also tried to strike a balance in my transcription conventions between providing the necessary information and keeping transcripts readable. I use the following conventions whenever I deem the information they code to be relevant to my analysis or the reader's ability to evaluate my analysis:

Word . word	A period separated on either side by a space denotes a single beat pause or hesitation in an utterance that does not correspond to normal phrasing indicated by standard punctuation.
Word .. word	Two periods separated on either side by a space denote a double beat pause or hesitation in an utterance. In like manner, three periods indicates a triple-beat pause. Longer pauses are marked by duration (for example, 1 second).
A: [speaks B: [speaks	Lined up square brackets indicate overlapping speech.
A: speaks— B: —speaks	Em dashes indicate no break between utterances.
A: speaks-	A hyphen indicates an incomplete utterance or false start.
Wo:rd	Colon following a vowel indicates prolonged vowel, as in "wooord."
Word	Bold type indicates emphasis, unless otherwise noted.
/ // /	Slashes indicate finger-tapping on a table by the speaker.

1

Introduction

Telling Moments

In this book I seek to describe the textures of religious life that generate community among practitioners of Santería in Santiago de Cuba. In doing so, I wish to show how *santeros*' (initiated practitioners') ritual and reflective practices produce a shared set of religious experiences and a distinct moral community. Religious life, as I experienced it in my admittedly agnostic but open-minded role as ethnographer, is marked by a series of telling moments. By "telling moments" I mean both noteworthy moments themselves and their narrated representations as they are retold and mined for religious meanings. Numinous experiences, it seems, continue to circulate in narratives that may express awe and hold out the promise of more such experiences, as in the words with which one santero began to recount a "telling moment" to me:

> I have [had] incredible experiences "in the saint." That's why I believe so much in my saint. And I have so much respect, because these are experiences one has had. It seems like a lie, it seems like one of Aladdin's tales.[1]

Practitioners do not simply engage in ritual practices that produce religious experiences by some automatic, invisible mechanism. Upon closer inspection (and not surprisingly), they are constantly engaged in reflection about what they and other practitioners are doing, about how the *orichas* (deities) might respond, and about what the consequences of their actions will be or were. Much of this reflection enters into circulation, whether as private or public discourse, as santeros evaluate, critique, compare, commemorate, condemn, or celebrate particular events, be they ritual moments or other religiously significant events.

Consider the santero who blamed a bad divination sign on his ritual godfather's earlier mistake. His godfather had tried to save money by purchasing one sheep to offer to two orichas. When the sheep died before it could be properly sacrificed, those present in the ceremony confirmed that the godfather had made a mistake. When, later in the ritual, the godchild—call him Emilio—received a dire warning in divination, he came to interpret the warning as a consequence of the orichas' ire at his godfather—a case of the (god)father's sins being visited upon the (god)son.[2]

By focusing their reflective attention on particular events, santeros render them telling moments—moments that reveal something about causality and about whether or not the sacred is present, and why. Such moments get represented in discourse as narratives that, as I will show, can be embedded in many other types of activities, circulate across many contexts, and serve many purposes. This particular event was related to me several years after it occurred, in a context I will more fully describe later in the chapter.

In a sense, such reflective discourse is simply one particular cultural manifestation of Weber's two religious "problems of meaning," which Parsons paraphrases as human frustration over events we cannot control and our corresponding lack of certainty that our endeavors will be successful (Parsons 1979: 62–63; Weber 1963/1922: 138–50). Weber's corollary, the question of theodicy, poses the ultimate test of faith: if there is/are divine power(s), why do bad things still happen to good people? In practice, religious adherents also pose the practical question: what can I do to impose order on events? Santeros' answers to these basic religious questions vary with the situation, but usually invoke central ideas such as respect for the religious code, called the Regla (Law), and strict adherence to correct ritual procedure, topics that saturate even ordinary conversations among santeros.

For example, a decade after the event, Emilio still told the story of his godfather's error. He would emphasize that the sheep died dramatically, dropping stone dead at the threshold of the room where it was to be sacrificed. As a result, someone had to rush out to buy two more sheep so that the ceremony could continue. Instead of saving money as intended, the error cost him an extra sheep. Each time he repeated the story, Emilio would conclude that the saints are blunt in reinforcing their Regla.

Ritual performances and events of everyday life—both the extraordinary and the mundane—provide the experiences that become the fodder for reflection, and such reflection frequently enters into discourse. For example, santeros weave telling moments into long-term and often stable narratives about themselves, their beliefs, and their moral community. These narratives serve as one important form of data for describing what it means to be a practitioner of Santería and to participate in local religious life. Whether such narratives are told as entire, complete autobiographical stories or whether they are more briefly referenced in the course of other kinds of discourse, the characters that populate them (and their relationship to those present at the telling) also trace the outlines—the inclusions and exclusions—of a local religious community, past, present, and future.

For example, Emilio shared many such stories with me as moral parables from which I should learn as I, too, entered into the religion. On other occasions I heard him refer to these stories to variously teach other neophytes, reinforce ties with some interlocutors, and even imply that others, usually not present, should be sanctioned for their breaches of religious propriety.

I have referred to the reflective function of such discourse, but the community of santeros is no idealized contemplative order: santeros express as much skepticism as faith in their narratives. One paradox is that the skepticism and mutual suspiciousness so characteristic of santeros' interpretations of putatively sacred events nonetheless serve as a focal point for delineating a moral community of Santería.

One occasion on which Emilio repeated his story to me was when he was in the midst of critiquing another santero, Roberto, whose ceremony we had attended together. He cataloged the many ritual errors Roberto had made, imputing a crass motive of saving money at the expense of showing respect for the saints. He expressed his surprise that the divination results that day had all been positive, then told the story of his godfather's mistake to illustrate that what goes around comes around. Sooner or later, Roberto would be called to task for flouting the Regla. Until then, I should be wary of his motives. Emilio also made a point of repeating his critique of Roberto's shoddy performance for several other santeros in his own ritual lineage, who would invariably shake their heads and bemoan the crass commercialism into which their religion was sinking. Together, through the story of the other santero, they reaffirmed their own commitment to "respecting the religion."

It is through the retelling of telling moments—the debate over the occurrence and meaning of ineffable experiences—that the moral community of Santería emerges. In the very process of disagreeing, of offering contradictory readings of what experiences mean, santeros construct individual and collective religious understandings that recreate, moment to moment, what their religion is.

We more typically look to rituals to serve as the glue of communal solidarity and shared meanings, and indeed they do at least in part serve these functions in Santería. But I suggest that santeros' apparently skeptical and divisive reflective discourses also serve as a sort of communal glue, insofar as such discourses envelope interlocutors in dense networks of "speech chains" (to use Asif Agha's term [2003]) about religious matters, and insofar as santeros who participate in these speech chains agree to disagree with reference to a common sacred orientation. Thus, the skepticism of santeros is of a different epistemological order than secular skepticism about Santería, which throws into question the entire religious enterprise. Instead, santeros' skepticism—indeed, their overall tendency toward reflection and retelling—is the process by which they construe some experiences as religious and construct their religion itself as a tangible moral force.

In the ceremony Emilio critiqued, a young man was initiated as a santero. After the divination ceremony, the young initiate told me, with tears in his eyes, how incredibly moved he was by the divination results, which had revealed things he knew to be true. He attested that Roberto could not have known the private details the divination revealed, so clearly the saints had spoken directly to him. Meanwhile, Emilio later gave a devastating analysis of that very same divination, arguing that Roberto had used the divination, consciously or not, to produce results based on his own beliefs. Emilio thus implied that the saints had not spoken at all!

Emilio, Roberto, the new initiate, and I myself were all interconnected not just because of having attended the same ritual event, but perhaps more importantly because we continued to interact and discuss the ritual long after it had ended, seeking to interpret what had happened. The ritual lived on in our retellings, as did we, not only as narrators and audience, but as figures populating our firsthand accounts, in spite of the fact that each of our retellings might conflict with the versions told by others. Was the divination a profoundly moving experience of divine omniscience or an error-ridden fraud? The ritual event even came to have importance to people who had not been present for it, in the case of others who heard Emilio's account of Roberto's errors. For them, the ritual existed only in its narrated form, much as Emilio's story of his godfather's error also does for us.

It should be apparent that the layer of conscious reflection among santeros is as much a set of cultural practices, a product of circulating cultural forms and norms, as are ritual practices. Rituals understandably attract the ethnographic eye because their very characteristics as rituals make them stand out as identifiable, often vivid and extra-ordinary events—this feature is what linguistic anthropologists, following Bauman and Briggs (1992) and Silverstein (1992), would call their high degree of entextualization. Indeed, rituals in Santería have this attention-grabbing effect on all of their participants. But I will argue that anthropologists of religion have paid too little attention to more amorphous, often quotidian activities surrounding rituals. I mean not only the preparations and clean-up, but more importantly the rich but ordinary discourses in which rituals are discussed: the negotiations that go into planning, the "backchanneling" chatter that occurs during most of the Santería ceremonies I witnessed, and the after-the-fact reports, gossip, evaluations, critiques, and even reminiscences that continue to enliven memories of long-past rituals and show their continuing relevance in conversants' lives.

That is, it is not rituals in themselves that generate moral community, but rather rituals together with the discourses they provoke that embody and thus bring into tangible being a moral community of Santería. After all, ritual events may be attended by non-santeros, newcomers, visitors, neighbors, and other incidental curiosity-seekers and casual onlookers who have little or no additional contact with santeros. However, rituals often provoke participants to reflect upon and discuss them, and those ritual participants who also take part in persistent circuits of reflective discourse, I argue, do tangibly coalesce as a community. The metaphor of an atomic nucleus and orbitals provides one image of the relationship I propose between these different categories of discourse events: rituals comprise a nucleus of religious activity around which swirls all of the surrounding discourse about rituals and religious life, like a cloud of electrons. To push the atom analogy further, Santería emerges as a religious activity comprising both ritual nucleus and informal discourse cloud, even when some of that discourse seems to be merely gossip, calumny, or storytelling, and not purely about sacred matters. Demonstrating how such seemingly peripheral clouds of discourse envelop some practitioners into a stable and tangible community is the goal of part 3 in particular, although an example later in this chapter will lay out some of the groundwork.

My argument for decentering ritual's primacy in producing religious community suggests a need to also re-examine ritual's assumed (and undertheorized) primacy in producing religious experiences. We can ask, for example, how and why Emilio and the new initiate reached such different interpretations of the divination they both experienced, a question phenomenology alone cannot address. Whereas the phenomenological approach favored in the psychology of religion tends to conceive of religious experiences in terms of private, transcendent sensations localizable in brain physiology, and to look for ritual stimuli that directly produce certain physiological responses, I suggest that phenomenological experiences are subject not only to framing during rituals, but also to ongoing reinterpretation and social negotiation of their consequences through "retelling" (Hood 1995; Newberg et al. 2001). That is, rituals and their surrounding discourse bring together phenomenology and interpretation as two poles of culturally mediated activity.

Within anthropology, tacitly phenomenological approaches to religious experience have followed the philosophical and psychological emphasis on individual, even private, constructions of experience built directly on sensory being-in-the-world (Berhenn 1995; Eliade 1959; James 1922/1902; Merleau-Ponty 1989/1962; Proudfoot 1985). But recent critiques, especially within the anthropology of the senses, challenge us to examine how culture mediates phenomenological experience, and in particular, its articulation in discourse (Crapanzano 2003: 11–14; Csordas 1994; Geurts 2003; Jackson 1996). In line with these critiques, I consider how cultural forms like rituals offer certain sorts of experiences whose meanings get negotiated in publicly circulating discourse. I examine experiences as fluid, intersubjective constructs of discourse and memory that are seldom fixed but rather are open to new tellings and new interpretations. Interpretation, then, is the complement of phenomenology—the way in which culture mediates the senses.

Anthropologists have long focused on the role of rituals in shaping religious experience with good reason. Rituals serve to generate distinctive phenomenological experiences in participants by enveloping them in lush sensoria and bodily praxis that make symbolic configurations tangible, imbue them with emotion, and enforce them, at least temporarily, as normative. The tangible, sensible aspects of speech and song in themselves may produce memorable experiences of a particular metaphysical order—the poetics of ritual speech being one example.[3] That is, successful rituals persuade participants to enter into structures of participation that may even violate social roles or expectations of the physical world: in Santería's rituals, for example, orichas take possession of participants' bodies, cowrie shells "speak" during divinations, and the etiquette of the priestly hierarchy prevails over other, quotidian social identities. Rituals as events distinguish themselves from everyday life by offering distinctive phenomenological experiences and hints for interpreting them as religious experiences. Santería's rituals are also discursively rich events. They pose special problems of intelligibility for participants, in part because they so heavily rely upon an esoteric ritual register called Lucumí. These rituals, in a sense, cry out for interpretation, because they simultaneously enable tangible communications with the divine and render those communications only partly intelligible.

This brings us to the interpretive pole of cultural activity. Rituals, the saying goes, are both models of and models for the world, which is to say that they set people into distinctive configurations or frames of participation that set up particular expectations about how the event will unfold (Geertz 1973: 93–94; Goffman 1981).[4] Something about these participant configurations then carries over into life outside of ritual, so that even when people are not engaging in ritual-like activities, they can draw upon notions of relation and causality learned in ritual or through ritual and inhabit those same footings developed in rituals. Participants, in their reflective discourses, in turn, may (often unconsciously) replicate the alignments learned through ritual participation and in doing so draw upon those rituals as models for causality or social relations. For example, santeros often attribute problems they face in everyday life to the handiwork of the orichas, an explanatory model of events that is heavily reinforced through frequent rituals of divination. Divination also provides the avenue for solution: once one identifies orichas as the actual source of a problem, one need only figure out which oricha to appease and by what means.

But the relationship between ritual models and other situations is neither direct nor automatic, because people are constantly engaged in interpretive work, in which they may take up alignments learned in one context and embed them in more complex frames that recontextualize their apparent meanings.[5] Urban (2001) refers to this interpretive work, and the sometimes durable cultural forms it generates, as metaculture, because it is culture reflexively focused on itself. Book reviews, for example, are a well-defined metacultural genre that bring a book to our attention by reflecting upon it and characterizing it as an exemplar of a certain type of recognizable cultural form—books of a particular genre, for example. After-the-fact commentaries on ritual performances in Santería are a different form of metaculture, one that has its own canon and its own pattern of circulation among Santería practitioners. The significance of attending not only to ritual events, but also to patterns of interpretive activity triggered by rituals is that these are how participants make sense of their ritual experiences—to render them intelligible, whether as moments of numinosity or of human blunder. The almost incidental consequence of these dense webs of retelling and meaning-making is that the people they envelop are brought into communion (if not agreement) not only as ritual participants, but also as participants in reflective discourses, which is to say as members of a moral community.

Metaphysical reflections on religious ethnography

In a sense, ethnography, too, consists of seeking to render one's experiences intelligible by weaving together a series of telling moments that reveal something about an underlying order. During my fieldwork, I participated in the rituals and reflective discourses of santeros as a temporary and peripheral member of their moral community. I am necessarily adding my own layer of reflection and interpretation onto theirs (and therefore doing my part to construct Santería as a recognizable cultural entity of a particular sort), even as I try to reveal how santeros go about interpreting their experiences. It is only fair that I say something about my own (admittedly complicated) metaphysical stance before representing those of my field consultants.

I first became interested in Santería in the mid-1990s when I learned the dances of the orichas in an African dance class. I was entranced by the complex rhythms of the three *batá* drums, whose rhythms blend like a running brook over rocks, compelling the body to move polyrhythmically. Even in the secular context of a Seattle dance studio I felt the power of these dances! Surely they were mnemonics for all the esoterica of the Yoruba pantheon; the dances performed each orichas' personality, preferences, attributes, and special associations with the natural world: Ochún's coquettish vanity, Yemayá's billowing ocean waves, Ochosí's cocked bow, Ogún's fierce machete. It wasn't until I first visited Cuba in December 1997 (as a beginning graduate student in anthropology) that I experienced the music and dance as practitioners perform it in ceremonies to praise and call down the orichas. I went on one of the increasingly common "folklore" study tours of the 1990s, choosing Santiago de Cuba in eastern Cuba as my destination because of its history as an Afro-Cuban city. On that trip I first heard Santería's ritual songs, captivating and unintelligible, sung as they are in Lucumí. Then and now, I always find myself singing along in the chorus in the call-and-response that layers over the tumbling, thumping, ringing drums.

My first visit to Cuba also occasioned the first of many divination rituals I received or witnessed. I found the ritual process of making cowrie shells speak or reading divine responses into coconut shell pieces compelling in the way such divinations provided a direct and personal message, as if calling up God on the phone. The messages received were, I noticed, sometimes cryptic, demanding interpretation, and sometimes simple and direct, demanding action. As I eagerly participated in rituals and willed myself to let go and believe, I wondered whether Cuban participants felt the same visceral response to ritual speech and song that I did. Over the course of my field research during longer stays in the summer of 1998, much of the fall of 1999 to the summer of 2000, April 2002, and up to the present, I find myself vacillating between captivation with the drama of rituals and the visceral quality of divine messages I and others received and frequent bouts of skepticism about whether particular events and performances—particular messages—are truly of divine origin. Although I remain uninitiated, I have been unwilling to categorically reject the religious worldview of practitioners: honestly speaking, I want to be convinced. Perhaps my own skeptical open-mindedness attuned me to a dynamic tension between skepticism and faith that was present in so many conversations I witnessed or participated in. Certainly, attending to this tension helped me make sense of much that was initially puzzling to me, such as santeros' insistence that they always followed orichas' commands to the letter at the same time that, by their own admission, they were very selective in disregarding or discounting a great deal of what orichas putatively said in divinations or possession trances. Although I did not "get religion," I did find my research project.

I have to admit to a certain quandary in which I found myself. Religious people immediately interpreted my research interest as spiritually motivated, as indeed it is, but in complicated ways. They understood my doubts, if not my agnosticism, often telling me that they, too, had once harbored such doubts, and that I was right to be skeptical of the religious activities of some who purported to be santeros. They were confident that the saints had brought me into my line of research for a reason and that the saints would find ways to convince me of their importance in my life.

As a result of a consultation during my very first visit to Cuba, a santero who quickly became one of my key consultants and mentors did a ceremony for me that cemented a bond of godparentship between us. This santero and folklorist, Emilio, also took me under his wing as a student of folklore. I was and am Emilio's godchild and his student, and he would introduce me as such when he took me to meet other santeros around Santiago de Cuba. I have no doubt that my identification as a godchild and thus as one-potentially-on-the-path-to-initiation facilitated my access to information and ritual activities from which a noninitiate would usually be barred. It also generated its own momentum, because diviners and mediums were quick to discover further evidence of my future spiritual trajectory: the spirits of the dead who surrounded and protected me; the same oricha, Obatalá, who was repeatedly identified as my "Angel," guiding my destiny. Although I respect Santería and its practitioners and feel an energy during certain rituals that I have experienced nowhere else in my life, I can never quite overcome my agnosticism. I resist committing myself to any creed, even while I seek out the energy, the *aché* of religious experience in Santería.

My mentor, godfather, and field consultant extraordinaire, Emilio, has pointed out parallels between his own one-time professed atheism and my state of disbelief. In chapter 4 I present his conversion story and discuss how he used this narrative to position me on a religious trajectory just like his, in which events will sooner or later compel me to be initiated as a santera, just as he, a decade ago, could no longer ignore the presence of the orichas in his life. Emilio and other santeros often retold narratives about compelling ritual events in their lives to me and to each other, and many of these stories reappear here. I will argue that the circulation of these narratives—and many related forms of reflective discourse about rituals, including what would more accurately be characterized as evaluations, critiques, and controversies—is what maintains the moral community among santeros in Santiago and ratifies (or denies) membership in that community.

At the same time, my very marginality in the religious community, my uninitiated status and open-minded skepticism also facilitated my interactions with others on the blurry margins of Santería. A telling moment of my own from my final night in Cuba during a trip in April 2002 will illustrate this. My hostess in Havana, Soledad, and I got onto the topic of my research. She was intrigued and asked me many questions about my own beliefs. I was honest, saying that I feel a great affinity for Santería and even have a godparent in the religion, but that I can't help falling too easily into skepticism and agnosticism. Perhaps too many years of scientific training (while first soaking in and later sparring with a highly opinionated and devoutly Catholic grandmother) had spoiled my ability to commit wholeheartedly to any religious practice. My admission opened the floodgates. She told me that she consults with two different santeros but that as a biochemical engineer she finds it hard to set aside her skepticism. But what they tell her in consultations is always true. Once, one advised her to say good-bye to her grandmother and prepare herself, because her grandmother would die in fifteen days. There was nothing to be done to save her. Sure enough, her grandmother died about fifteen days later. "Frightening," she concluded.

Seeing my sympathetic response, she launched into a number of other stories in which the santeros' drastic predictions came to pass. Most recently, the santero had told her that her husband would leave her, either moving out or dying. This really frightened her, and she begged her husband to go to a doctor or get a consultation himself with the santero. At this, her husband, who had come into the room and was listening, abruptly left for the kitchen. He doesn't believe any of it, she sighed. And her? Well, she remains skeptical.

One way of reconciling her stated skepticism with her testaments to uncannily accurate predictions is to understand that Soledad was skeptical not of the santeros' *ability* to read the future, but of their *motives* in, as she said, "putting themselves in the middle" of intimate family matters. Ever curious, she returns for more consultations because she finds the weight of many true predictions hard to ignore.

How do people come to interpret some experiences as religious, and how do the reflective discourses through which they reach religious interpretations help bring into being a moral community and a sense of Santería itself as a cultural entity? The next section introduces the discourse-centered approach I will use throughout the book to address these questions by examining one of Emilio's most often repeated telling moments. Along the way, I also introduce some key ethnographic information about Santería's rituals, religious hierarchy, reflective discourse, and moral community.

The warning

During the same year that Emilio initiated as a santero, his younger brother, always healthy, died suddenly of a fever. Of course the death was devastating to his family. Emilio explained to me with regret that he had been divinely warned during his initiation that someone in his family might die, but that it had not occurred to him that his brother would succumb. After receiving the chilling divination results foretelling of death, he had ritually protected himself and also three elderly, infirm relatives, but this had not been enough. In telling this narrative, Emilio wove together a ritual experience that shook him up and a shattering event several months later, showing a causal relation:

Divine warning → Warning not heeded → Event comes to pass

Here is the complete narrative in translation, as he told it to me in 1998, after I had become his godchild, but when we were just beginning to work together: [6]

1   Emilio: It is not fanaticism. It is not fanaticism, it
2   is reality because I am not a fanatic. I, yes,
3   have my, I am religious and I have my belief but
4   I am not a fanatic.
5   I told you that when in Itá [divination] what
6   came out for me, it was necessary to give me

7   Olokun urgently, on my day of Itá. Or that is,
8   the third day [of initiation], when they told me
9   everything, that among the things that they told me,
10   they told me, the grave is open. The grave in
11   the cemetery is open for one of your family. And
12   rapidly, to save the iyawó [initiate], that is,
13   to save me, they had to give me Olokun [an
14   oricha]. Because Olokun is a dead one, Olokun
15   protects from the dead. Since he is a dead one,
16   he protects from the dead. Or that is, my
17   godfather had to leave rapidly to find me Olokun,
18   to do the ceremony at the ocean, because to do
19   the ceremony at the ocean far away, to find all
20   the tools, to find all the things, all the cloths
21   of Olokun, all the things, and to give me Olokun
22   so that the grave would not be open for me. When
23   there is an open grave for the family in the
24   cemetery, [it is] because someone is going to
25   die. When they gave me Olokun, that they looked
26   for everything rapidly. Everything, everything,
27   everything, to look for a car, rapidly, to the
28   ocean, to find all the things. Well, we saved
29   the initiate. That is, they saved me.
30   So then it wasn't me, now it was someone in the
31   family who is, who was going to die. It is
32   necessary to investigate who it is, and they
33   began to ask but they didn't say who it was.
34   [It] didn't say. The saint didn't say at any
35   point who it was. It is someone in the family,
36   but it didn't say who it is. And, well, what
37   decision was taken? To protect the family
38   members who were the most ill: my mother, my
39   brother Pedro, who always was sick. And an uncle
40   of mine who always was, who since he drank so
41   much, always was ill also. We began to take care
42   of those people, even by me, their medicine, if
43   they had something, rapidly (taking them) to the
44   doctor
45   KW: They had, were able to go to—?

46 E: —to my ceremony of the saint?

47 KW: yes, or to, ah, some—

48 E: —place to protect themselves? No. The saint

49 didn't say it would protect the entire family.

50 To take care of the famil-, of the people who

51 were the most sick within the family. And that

52 was what we did to be careful about my mother, my

53 brother Pedro, and my uncle Marcos, who are the

54 people who, because Pedro was always sick, who

55 drums in [a local folklore troupe]? K: Uhm-hm

56 E: He always had gotten an operation, and my

57 mother has hypertension and always had high blood

58 pressure, and always, like this, very elderly.

59 Now she is 89 years old. Very old, very old, and

60 my uncle Marcos, since he drank so much, always

61 was on the street. He stayed there sleeping, he

62 got hit, he fell, a car hit him one time. So, we

63 thought that one of these three people would be

64 the death because I was well with it. Until they

65 returned, it didn't close.

66 So we began to take care of these three people,

67 and the one whom we least considered was my

68 brother Jorge. It was he who died exactly three

69 months later. They had told me, three months

70 exactly. A downpour fell on him, he was drunk,

71 he got soaked. He went home and went to bed wet,

72 with wet clothes. He threw himself on the bed

73 and went to sleep. The next day he woke up with

74 a raging fever, and he didn't go to the doctor.

75 He began to take medicine himself, and he didn't

76 go to the doctor. A sudden, rage- raging

77 bronchopneumonia got him. In two days he died.

78 It was like that, so fast, like that, so fast. The

79 person we least considered. (pause) Three

80 months later. (pause) That death really was

81 there, and it was my family, one of my family

82 [that] they took away, my brother. Terrible,

83 terrible, the case. And [it] warned me. The

84 saints warn of that.

How does one know when the orichas have, indeed, intervened in one's life? For Santería practitioners, deciding what counts as a divine message or a sacred experience and how it should be interpreted is problematic. Such hermeneutic questions may be deeply personal, but they rely upon shared criteria that circulate according to social processes. That is, the religion one professes has at least something to do with the nature of the religious experiences one seeks and perhaps has. I am reminded of Durkheim, who explained religious experience as a product of "collective effervescence" in which "religious force is none other than the feeling that the collectivity inspires in its members, but projected outside the minds that experience them, and objectified" (Durkheim 1995/1912: 227–28, 230). Without accepting his atheistic assessment of religion at face value, we can apply his insights to ask how what he called a moral community can shape its members' metaphysical experiences (see Durkheim 1995/1912: 42).

At first blush, Emilio's intensely personal story does not seem to tell us much about moral communities or collective effervescence. But in fact, when he recounts how he received the warning, he refers to ritual events that involved a number of actors. In the first part of the narrative in which he receives the warning (lines 5–29), Emilio alludes to various ritual acts: he received a special divination called the Itá on the third day of his week-long initiation ceremony. During the Itá, a divination sign was interpreted to foretell of an "open grave," and so those present decided to protect Emilio from the bad sign by hurriedly doing a ritual called "giving Olokun." With Emilio saved, those present did another divination to investigate who else might be in danger from the open grave. They apparently did not get clear results, and so the decision was made to ritually protect the most vulnerable members of his family.

Who are the actors in the ritual drama he describes? This turns out to be an essential question for understanding the significance of this narrative for creating a local moral community. Emilio's narrative is peopled with characters and voices—"figures"—who inhabit what Asif Agha calls "roles," which are established through various footings or alignments relative to one another and to the narrator and audience (Agha 2005; Goffman 1981: 124–57). In bringing all of these figures together in this narration, Emilio is creating a discursive representation of one local part of his moral community, which encompasses other santeros, ritual and genealogical kin, and divine beings. In doing so, he is not simply representing reality, but rather helping to create that reality through the indexical relationships between the figures in his narrative and the people he knows (Wortham 2001). Some of these indexical relationships are highly presupposed—for example, he is present as a character in his own narrative in the role of a new initiate. Other indexical relationships, such as the unspecified plural, sometimes "they" and sometimes directly quoted "we," are less presupposed and more creative in his narrative—these unspecified pronouns represent the segment of religious community that was faced with interpreting a troubling divination sign.

Just who are "they?" In lines 9–10 "they" tell him the grave is open; "they" then do a ritual for him called giving Olokun. He then quotes "them" saying, "we saved the initiate" (lines 28–29). Finally, "they" unsuccessfully investigate who else in his family might be in danger. Most of these "theys" likely refer to Emilio's ritual elders, who would have been conducting his ceremony: his godfather and godmother, an officiating priest (or *italero*), and other senior santeros invited to the initiation by his godfather. We can surmise that the assembled santeros were the ones to interpret a bad divination result into a course of action. Emilio experienced the ritual events as a close call on his own life—he was "saved" from the grave by timely ritual intervention.

The success of the ritual intervention, however, is ultimately due to other actors: the "saints" and the "dead." In lines 9–10, it is ambiguous whether he attributes the quotation "the grave is open" to the santeros or to the saints who speak through divination: either entailment, in my experience, is possible. What is not ambiguous is that the oricha Olokun protects Emilio from death as a result of a ritual, and "the saint" does not say who else in his family might be in danger, in spite of a ritual (lines 33–34).

All of this is to say that Emilio did not arrive at his assessment of events alone: his narrative makes clear that a group of santeros collectively engaged in ritual and reflective activity in order to reach a consensus about what a bad divination sign meant. We might say that that small group representing the religious community gave voice to the orichas, with whom they shared responsibility for the ritual acts and interpretations they imposed on Emilio. Altogether, living practitioners, spirits of those deceased, and orichas comprise the "imagined" moral community of Santería. Cross-cutting networks of ritual lineage and, sometimes, regular genealogical lineage unite santeros into overlapping circles of mutual obligation and concern that ultimately encompass the spirit world as well. Santeros may become ritually empowered to speak on behalf of the orichas, or even to speak as orichas, through divination and possession trance ceremonies.

It is useful to briefly consider the normative model of ritual kinship, which was the idiom through which santeros explained to me who was included in the local Santería community. Figures 1.1 and 1.2 diagram the connections of ritual kinship that link santeros to other santeros and orichas. Through initiation, the santero is permanently linked to a principal oricha, or "angel," whom the santero will refer to as his or her "mother" or "father." A second oricha of the opposite gender becomes the other "parent" of the initiate. Special protector spirits—a deceased relative or ancestor, for example—may also be identified. The identities of these orichas and spirits may or may not already be clear to a person prior to undergoing initiation, but in any case the initiation process confirms them. Initiation also links the santero into a ritual lineage through his or her godparents, and through them to a line of ritual ancestors and ritual "siblings"—one's godparents' other godchildren. The santero incurs obligations as well to the principal orichas of the godparents, which ritually "gave birth to" his or her angel. Finally, the santero may initiate his or her own godchildren, thus producing new links in the ritual hierarchy. Santeros draw upon their ritual networks whenever they engage in ritual activity, thereby continually reestablishing the links that comprise their moral community. They also reinforce these links each time they retell narratives like Emilio's that are peopled with divine and human members of their ritual kin.

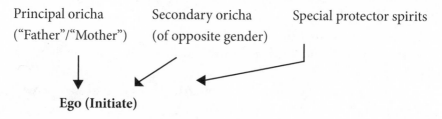

Figure 1.1. Diagram of human-divine kinship connections in Santería.

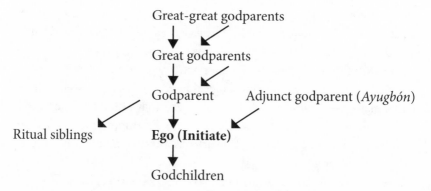

Figure 1.2. Diagram of ritual kinship connections in Santería.

Emilio's narrative makes clear that even in ritual, and even with as dramatic an event as seeing the divination cowries fall into a foreboding pattern and hearing the dire prognosis, "a grave is open," religious experience is more complicated than simply hearing divine voices or sensing something transcendent in a ritual. Phenomenological experience is certainly part of the equation, but we cannot leave matters there. People engage in interpretations, private and public, of their sensory experiences, and these interpretations often surface in discourse. Phenomenological experience and interpretation are intersubjective, which is to say that they are culturally embedded activities. The ideas of bad signs, warnings, and spiritual protection are all in circulation among santeros, ready to be invoked in order to demonstrate divine interventions in events.

Nor is it a given that divination results will be taken at face value. As I witnessed countless times, dire divination results do not always lead to frantic countermeasures. Sometimes the recipient apparently accepted the result at the time, then later expressed doubts about whether the saints had really been speaking or whether the diviner was somehow in error. After hearing so many narratives of close calls like Emilio's, I was puzzled to discover how rarely religious practitioners actually followed through on what they had been told to do in a divination. This seeming apathy was even more surprising when the person had urgently sought the divination. What I eventually came to understand was that santeros typically identified religious experiences—truly divine messages, for example—with hindsight, after subsequent events confirmed divination results. Only then would they begin to publicly narrate an event as a religious experience.

Indeed, religious Cubans are deeply concerned with seeking *la comprobación* (proof) to evaluate whether particular acts have succeeded in triggering the deities' involvement and whether rituals and other events have transcended human interests and errors to communicate with the divine. Adherents to Santería, in particular, engage in intense reflection that evaluates particular ritual performances, critiques other santeros, and evinces skepticism, not about the existence or power of the deities, but about whether they are present or have acted in any particular moment. To address how religious practitioners interpret religious experiences, we will need to consider all of these types of experiential and interpretive activity.

One important aspect of santeros' emphasis on proof is that it demands that people revisit their experiences and reconsider them with hindsight. Emilio's narrative exemplifies the retrospection that allows santeros to redefine an experience as sacred or not based on later events. How does Emilio narrativize the links between the ritual events described above and the later fact of his brother's death in lines 67–77? He builds the case that he had been warned of his brother's death by adding the detail that the divination had specified that a family member would succumb in three months. He emphasizes that Jorge died "exactly three months" after the ritual. He then recounts how his brother died: he was careless after catching a chill and died from something preventable because he would not go to the doctor. But, in a distinction Evans-Pritchard (1937) made long ago in discussing witchcraft among the Azande, the chill and fever are only the proximate reasons for the brother's sudden death; Emilio's entire narrative suggests that the saints had already marked Jorge, and so it was, in some sense, divine will that Jorge died. Tragically, in Emilio's estimation, the death could have been preventable because the saints had warned Emilio. If only he had understood who needed protecting, he could have ritually protected his brother. Emilio has retold this story many times—I recorded versions of it or references to it at least a half dozen times over several years.

Considering the narrative in its totality once more, it becomes clear that Emilio conveys through it his religious stance toward the world, in which the saints give warnings, rituals can protect one from death, and people live or die because divine beings will it to be so. Emilio's narrated experience illustrates that it is only prudent to carefully attend to the orichas—no religious fanaticism is necessary when such wrenchingly vivid proof is before you. Emilio's narratives accomplish something else, in addition: as they circulate, they draw our attention to the cultural forms that comprise Santería. Through my retelling of his narrative, you the reader learn something about how divinations work and how santeros ritually respond to the messages they receive. For that matter, Emilio borrows some idioms of ritual forms of speech, such as the use of Lucumí jargon (for example, "Olokun," "Itá," "iyawó") and the typical pattern of describing divination results as if quoting and then elaborating on divine speech (lines 10–16, for example). Such trappings of ritual speech genres, borrowed into the narrative, convey a certain mystical or esoteric flavor and perhaps also a sense of "being there." If compelling enough, such narrativizations of ritual activity may encourage future ritual participation. Emilio's interlocutors may become curious to experience a divination for themselves, or at least to know more about how such rituals work.

If retellings of rituals generate interest in rituals, the reverse is also true: rituals in many ways provoke retellings. Emilio's narrative is a product of a memorable ritual event in which he participated. And so there is a sequence—an interlocking chain, to again borrow Agha's metaphor (2003)—of cultural forms promoting one another across instances of interaction among religious participants: rituals provoke retellings and reflection that circulate representations of the ritual beyond ritual events themselves, and these retellings may provoke renewed participation in future rituals. Even when the reflection on the ritual performance is negative, it may still generate a sort of momentum. Consider the earlier example in which Emilio critiqued Roberto's shoddy ritual work. He created a buzz by gossiping about the errors Roberto had made. In doing so, Emilio and his interlocutors reinforced their shared criteria for proper ritual conduct. This book considers many variations on such chains of events through which culturally conditioned experiences get retold and reinterpreted. The paradox is that individuals move through these recognizable types of cultural activity to arrive at subjective understandings of the most personally significant and phenomenologically gripping events in their lives.

Overview of chapters

In the following chapters I examine how santeros engage in Santería's formal ritual practices and intense reflective practices in search of experiences of the sacred and how their discursive activity interacts with other discourses about religion in Cuban society to produce Santería as a recognizable and distinctly positioned religious community. One consequence is that a tangible sense of, and indeed, consensus on what and who is "inside" or "outside" Santería is constantly emerging through this activity. Of course, the construal of Santería from "within," by practitioners, encounters other "external" construals of Santería, including secular perspectives that write off religion as superstition or refashion it as folklore, religious perspectives that share aspects of Santería's religious orientation or borrow bits and pieces from it, and so on. These interpretive interactions are the subject of part 1, "Religious Histories," which examines the social and historical context in which Santería arose and persists. Chapter 2 situates Santería in the landscape of competing religious and secular orientations prevalent in contemporary Cuban society, in which santeros strive to maintain Santería's distinction as the folkloric emblem of Cuba's national ideology of hybridity.

Chapter 3 traces the history of competing secular and religious discourses about the value of markedly Afro-Cuban cultural forms to show how Santería emerged and continues to be situated within the Cuban nation. In the course of their religious and quotidian lives, santeros find themselves in various sorts of double binds, in which they must negotiate different, even conflicting, interpretations of Santería. The examples in the current chapter of two ways in which Emilio opened his narratives—by distancing himself from the figure of the religious "fanatic" (lines 1–4 of his narrative), and by comparing his experiences to "Aladdin's tales"—hint at ways in which negative societal images of Santería creep into santeros' own reflective discourse about their religious experiences.

In part 2, "Religious Experience," two chapters explore the meaning of "religious experience" and ask how religious discourse mediates the metaphysical experiences of Santería's practitioners. Chapter 4 develops the argument introduced in this chapter that religious experiences cannot be accounted for simply as individually experienced sensations. Rather, putative religious experiences are intersubjectively recognized and interpreted through being retold as "telling events," in which participants mobilize cultural forms, including figures or types of people, in order to interpret experiences by, in effect, representing a sacred world. As this chapter's brief introduction to Emilio's narrative of the warning indicates, such narratives cannot simply be analyzed for content, but must be considered as complex choreographies of figures and footings through which narrators convey explicit and implicit understandings of their experiences.

In chapter 5 I ask on what evidence people ascribe particular metaphysical interpretations to their experiences. Presenting an in-depth analysis of a compelling possession trance later judged to be "false," I focus on how rituals enact participation frameworks that model the "proper" religious orientation for interpreting experience. I go on to examine some of the implications of religious practitioners' tendency to apply a general attitude of skepticism and seek proof in their evaluations of ritual experiences.

In part 3, "Religious Community," two chapters build upon the stage set in part 2 to examine the ferment of discussion, critique, and controversy surrounding ritual performances that I argue creates the moral community of Santería. Both chapters probe how rituals can both exacerbate and resolve the tensions between collective aims and shared meanings on the one hand and individual skepticism and agendas for personal advancement on the other. In chapter 6 I explore the paradox that critical discourses highlighting skepticism and individual interpretation also serve to build shared understandings and a common sense of community in an otherwise decentralized religion with little institutionalization. Chapter 7 analyzes several cases that reveal how even apparently divisive conflicts actually serve to reinforce the boundaries of the local moral community. My conclusions challenge the received notion in anthropology of community as an entity best characterized by homogeneity and consensus. What if internal conflict and controversy actually serve to reinforce a local moral community?

Chapter 8 considers how the dialectic between ritual performances and the reflective, critical discourse they provoke promotes an ever-wider circulation of discourses about Santería rituals, even beyond the bounds of the local moral community. That is, how do ritual structures and interpretive frameworks promoted by Santería induce even somewhat reluctant participants like Soledad, the biochemical engineer mentioned earlier, to interpret their experiences as religious? This concluding chapter traces the surprisingly global circuits of one particular semiritual genre known as the "promise," from a family emergency to a nightclub performance to a novel interpretation of the 1950s North American sitcom, *I Love Lucy*. This chapter brings together threads of argument from earlier chapters to explore how Santería's influence has recently expanded and with what consequences for the local religious community in Santiago de Cuba.

I

Religious Histories

"All the Priests in the House"

Defining Santería

Moyubá todo los omo ocha y babalocha, bobo iguoro cogguá ilé.
(I give homage to all the children of the oricha and fathers of the oricha,
all the priests in the house.)
—*Typical ending to santeros' moyubá invocation*

One hundred years ago, the signifier "Santería" did not exist. Its referent—
those cultural practices originally linked to Afro-Cubans of Lucumí (Yoruba)
origin—was not delimited in the way familiar today, but was part of a different enunciative order of marginalized social practices that were most often
labeled *brujería* (witchcraft). Recently Santería has become the most visible,
most recognizable, and most emblematic Cuban popular religion. Santería the
religion and its decontextualizable elements of dance, music, and iconography
are promoted as emblems of Cuba's national folklore by the state, a process of
"folkloricization" that began long before the Cuban Revolution, as I describe
in chapter 3 (Daniel 1995; Hagedorn 2001: 11–12, 67–68). This visibility arose
despite the crowded religious field, in which Santería's adherents number only
perhaps 8 percent of the population, and despite what ethnomusicologist Robin Moore accurately describes as a national ambivalence toward Afro-Cuban
cultural expressions (1997: 220).

In part 1, I lay out the intersection of race, religion, and nation in which
Santería has been and continues to be constructed as Cuba's emblematic syncretic Afro-Cuban religion. In this chapter I introduce contemporary Cuba's
complex religious landscape and argue that Santería's social valorizations
emerge from how it gets positioned relative to other religious practices by religious practitioners themselves and others. Then, in chapter 3 I consider the
historical question of how Santería emerged out of *brujería* to take its current

place of honor. To begin, I must problematize the question of what this entity called Santería is. Taking a constructionist view, I argue that all possible definitions of a cultural form like Santería are ideologically charged in that they cannot help but ascribe particular social values to (and therefore essentialize) Santería, whether explicitly or implicitly. Santería, as such, exists most tangibly as it is continually reinvented in the dialogical interactions among the discourses and other practices that frame it, including scholarly texts like this book (see Warren 1992: 204–6).[1] As David Brown says in discussing the very issue of how "Lucumí religion" has been represented, "the narratives that ethnographers and practitioners tell, and have told, are mutually constituted in a kind of intertextual hall of mirrors. . . . Theology and historiography seem to be inextricably intertwined and mutually defining" (2003: 19).[2]

The interpretive act of definition

I am intentionally working against the way Santería too often gets described in the scholarly and popular literature, which is in abstract, structuralist terms as a homogenous, discrete, completely explicit and coherent worldview centered on a "pantheon" of Yoruba deities and informed by a fixed set of oral texts known as *patakines* that convey parable-like stories of the deities and other set characters. Its roster of rituals, songs, prayers, and herbal lore are often presented in prescriptive terms (and indeed sometimes such books serve as how-to manuals).[3] This manner of defining Santería, which certainly rings true for many santeros, clearly does metacultural work by presenting Santería as a neat, complete, and almost fully decontextualized package. There is no hint of debate over labels like "religion," no hint of overlap with other Cuban religions, and no hint of disagreements or struggles over meaning and membership within the ranks of practitioners, although I will show that these, too, are critical to understanding Santería. To fully understand such portrayals of Santería it would be necessary to trace their origins in genres such as religious manuals written by practitioners, early Cuban folkloric studies, and structuralist anthropological accounts of non-Western religions, and to think about how the authors and consumers of these works align themselves toward their materials, an analysis I return to in chapter 3.

How to define Santería

The standard thumbnail definition of Santería, available in many books, describes it as an Afro-Cuban religion that syncretizes Catholicism and Yoruba beliefs.[4] This definition, used by practitioners and scholars alike (myself included), carries indexical baggage that links to a particular view of Santería's place in the racialized hierarchy of popular religions in Cuba. Instead of simply accepting and transmitting this standard view of what Santería is, I wish to deconstruct it to reveal its underlying assumptions. I will then present an alternate view of what Santería is by focusing on its social and specifically religious context in Cuba and on what santeros, in their ongoing boundary-making efforts, promote as Santería's distinguishing features amid the various boundary-making and boundary-blurring activities of santeros and others. Doing so, I hope, will lay bare the semiotic processes that continually give shape to Santería and other popular religions of Cuba.

That is, the entity described variously as Santería or La Regla de Ocha coalesces as a tangible cultural form with these labels through interpretive activity by santeros themselves in interaction with more broadly circulating discourses that assign value to particular cultural practices or kinds of people, as manifested in everything from everyday conversations to ethnographies. These processes can be traced historically, with the goal of linking unfolding moments of everyday interaction to larger-scale and longer-term social phenomena.

The term "Afro-Cuban" is problematic because it serves as both the label of a marked identity category (that is, for Cubans of African descent) and a descriptor of cultural elements deemed to have African origins. Santería is clearly Afro-Cuban in the second sense because of its cultural roots in West African practices and cosmologies. However, many Cubans would call Santería Afro-Cuban in the first sense as well, because they identify Santería's practitioners as Afro-Cuban, which is to say black, even though the evidence is that Santería is today and has for a long time been practiced by Cubans spanning racial groupings and social classes. As Palmié says, "*Africanity* and *blackness* are not coterminous in the world of Afro-Cuban religion. Nor have they, for what must surely be a long time, more than partially overlapped in complex and ill-understood ways" (2002a: 197). Calling Santería "Afro-Cuban," as most people would, lumps it together with other "African"-derived Cuban religions like Palo and Vodú in opposition to "European"-derived popular religions like Spiritism, although in both senses of the word, Spiritism appears to be as Afro-Cuban as these other practices, a point I return to below. A few Cuban folklorists, in contrast, insisted to me that Santería was simply "Cuban" because "all Cubans are Afro," a clear extension of the national ideology captured in Fidel's description of Cuba as an "Afro-Latin nation" (Martínez Furé 1979; C. Moore 1988; Wedel 2004: 33). Ayorinde (2004) describes a current debate in Cuba about whether Santería is "a black, an African, or a national religion" (173), one that parallels Santería's politics of identity among Cuban Americans and African Americans in the United States (Brandon 1993; Palmié 1995).

As to Santería's (by now well-established) status as a religion, Ayorinde (2004: 7–8) and Palmié (2002b: 203–10) comment on the ideological weight of labels in the contrast set of religion, magic, witchcraft, and science. Santería, as Palmié compellingly argues (2002a: 159–68), became a religion in part as it was morally differentiated from what continued to be regarded as less religion-like, more magic- or witchcraft-like Reglas de Conga.[5] I say more on this below, but note that these labels themselves are highly problematic because of their power to grant or deny legitimacy to the practices they describe. While there are ethnographic examples of people in Puerto Rico and the United States reclaiming pejorative labels like "witchcraft" and "magic" to positively describe their practices, in Cuba these terms continue to be negatively charged, and "religion" is the preferred label (Drufovka and Stanford 1996; Pike 2001; Romberg 2003). I take people's usage of all of these labels as important ethnographic facts to consider, especially since they can be applied to ostensibly the "same" actual practices, but I follow Cuban scholarly practice in using "religion" as my default descriptor, precisely because "magic" and especially "witchcraft" are such negatively loaded terms in Cuba.[6]

There is another important bit of baggage to be unpacked in defining Santería as a religion. The naive notion of a "religion" still seems to imply a cohesive, coherent, and more or less homogenous system, however much anthropologists have problematized such understandings. In fact, Santería, much like what today gets glossed as "Yoruba traditional religion" in Nigeria, remains a decentralized network of lineages, cults, and disparate public and private ritual practices that readily intermingle across definitional boundaries with other religions (Barber 1990; Matory 1994a, 1994b). Among Yoruba people in Nigeria, worship of the orisha often coexists in complementary tension with Islam and Christianity (Matory 1994b), just as Santería forms one strand of Cuba's equally complex religious landscape.[7] But the image of a strand implies a more unitary and centralized system than actually exists in practice. The most fundamental division separates santeros, who initiate into Santería (Ocha) proper, from *babalawos*, who initiate specifically into the cult of Ifá and become specialists in Ifá divination. There is some debate among practitioners themselves, and among scholars, about whether Ifá is part of Santería or is a separate religion. Certainly, there is evidence for both views and the question of same versus different religion gains a political edge in the often-fraught relations between santeros and babalawos, which are in equal measure competitive and complementary (see Ayorinde 2004: 179–80; Dianteill 2000; D. H. Brown 2003: 143–57).

Santería (with or without Ifá) has traditionally been described as a syncretic amalgam of Catholicism and Yoruba orisha cults forged in the crucible of New World plantation slavery, a characterization with strong ideological connections to Cuba's national origin myth. However, an examination of ritual practices reveals closer affinities to the Yoruba, with only a thin veneer of Catholic iconography that tends to accompany, rather than replace, Yoruba religious aesthetics (Bascom 1971).[8] Much of the Catholic influence has been filtered through, and thus mediated by, popular cults of the saints, since the institutionalized Church with its clergy, catechism, and services never fully penetrated Cuban society, especially in rural areas (Brandon 1993; Ortiz 1995/1906; Portuondo Zúñiga 1995). What did come to permeate popular religious practices were the Iberian Catholic calendar of saints' days and the iconography and intense veneration of an entire pantheon of Catholic saints. Santería also bears the influence of Spiritist and Congo notions of the dead, which Gonzalez-Whippler (1995), Palmié (2002b: 192–93) and others have argued largely supplanted West African rituals for the ancestors (known in Santería as *eggún*).

As for Santería's Yoruba connection, before a "Yoruba" people existed, people from modern-day southwestern Nigeria and eastern Benin were known to European slavers and slave owners as Lucumí (Castellanos 1996; Lachatañeré 1992: 149–64).[9] Santeros still sometimes refer to Santería as "Lucumí religion" and continue to label its ritual language "Lucumí" more frequently than "Yorubá." Santería developed as the religious practices and devotions to the Yoruba orisha spread beyond the relatively small proportion of the population that re-created African orisha worship practices on Cuban soil (D. H. Brown 2003; Otero 2002). Other Africans and creole children of Africans would have been first to come into contact with the reconstructed oricha cults, divination practices, and cosmology of their Lucumí kin and neighbors, and in short order the religion ceased to have clear ethnic associations, especially as African ethnicities overall faded in importance after the end of slavery (see Cabrera 1993; Palmié 1993; 2002a). Although historical evidence about the early circulation of oricha cults in Cuban society is limited, in modern times the western Cuban city of Matanzas and certain neighborhoods of Havana (Regla and Guanabacoa in particular) are renowned as strongholds of Yoruba tradition (D. H. Brown 2003). According to santeros themselves, Santería is a more recent, less historically deep tradition in the Oriente (eastern Cuba).

Rather than emphasizing the "classic" syncretisms between Catholic saints and Yoruba orisha, it is more accurate to understand Santería to be a relatively recent invention that coalesced out of diverse religious practices of African-born residents in particular urban areas of western Cuba around the end of the nineteenth century (D. H. Brown 2003; Castellanos and Castellanos 1988; Ortiz 1995; Otero 2002; Palmié 2002b). In any case, the name "Santería" seems not to have come into wide usage until after Cuban folklorist Rómulo Lachatañeré first proposed it in the late 1930s (Barreal 1992: xvii–viii; Dianteill 1995: 44–50; Lachatañeré 1992: 90, 197). Then and now, practitioners of Santería have preferred to call their religion "La Regla de Ocha," meaning the "Law" or "Order of the Orichas."

The popular religious complex in Cuba

It should now be clear that any attempt to define Santería without sinking into oversimplifications and essentialisms must make reference to Cuba's fuller religico-magic landscape and to the ideological work that produces its internal differentiation according to a calculus of race, tradition/syncretism, and morality. In particular, Santería's relationship to other so-called popular religions, some of which I have already mentioned in passing, is particularly salient to its social valorizations. Table 2.1 compares the major religious traditions of Cuba according to the popular and scholarly consensus on their names, provenances, and popular connotations. One potential side effect of the table is to imply that all of these practices appear as discrete choices or affiliations, which is somewhat misleading. In fact, there has likely always been a good deal of cross-pollination and of movement among them, much as we see today (Argüelles Mederos and Hodge Limonta 1991; CIPS 1998; James Figarola 1999). The so-called popular religions of Santería, Spiritism, Palo, Muertería, and folk Catholicism are in an especially close relationship to one another because they have to a large degree emerged and developed alongside one another, and they continue to mutually define each other.[10] An emerging body of scholarship focusing on their interactions suggests that they are most productively understood to be elements of a single popular religious complex, a view supported by my discussion below of commonalities, divergences, and crosscutting tendencies toward both combination and differentiation (Argyriadis 2000; James Figarola 1999; Palmié 2002b).[11]

Many Cubans combine elements of several ostensibly distinct traditions in complicated and often idiosyncratic juxtapositions. For example, many religious practitioners in eastern Cuba combine practices from Spiritism and Palo

Table 2.1. Overview of Major Religious Traditions in Cuba

Name/Alternate Names	Provenance	Regional Stronghold	Spirits/Deities	Stereotypical Social Valorization
Palo Monte, Palo Mayombe, Regla(s) de Congo, *brujería*	Congo or Bantu (16th–19th C.)	Oriente	Ngangas, Mpungu, Nzambi (God)	Witchcraft; the most African, dangerous, and deadly practice
Vodú, Religión Haitiana	Haitian/Fon-Dahomean (1920s)	Oriente (rural)	Loas	Potent religion of small, isolated Hatian communities
Santería, Regla de Ocha, Religión Lucumí	Yoruba (since 19th C.)	Western Cuba (Matanzas, La Habana)	Orichas or Santos, Eggún, Olofi (God)	Syncretism of Yoruba and Catholic practices
Spiritism, *or when combined with Palo,* Muertería	United States (since late 19th C.)	Oriente	*Los muertos*, *Las ciencias*	Kardecian (European), with many ties to Catholicism
Catholicism	Spain (since 16th C.)	Urban areas	*Santos*, Dios Supremo (God)	Few churchgoers; many more practice popular cults to the saints
Protestantism (Most sects are present in Cuba)	United States (20th C.)	Minor presence everywhere	Dios Supremo (God)	Keep separate from other "idolatrous" religions

into an amalgam that Cuban scholars have referred to as "Muertería" or *muer-terismo* (where *muertos* means the dead and *muerteros* are those who work with the dead) (Millet 2000; James Figarola, 1999). Early in my fieldwork, I was confused when acquaintances would introduce me to a "santero" they knew who turned out not to be an initiated priest of Ocha but someone whose religious practices seemed to inventively combine Spiritist and more generalized African elements in ways that seemed very idiosyncratic. These practitioners are probably best described as muerteros, although they and others might apply different labels to their practices. In many cases, initiated santeros also worked with spirits of the dead and would sometimes be better known for their expertise as muerteros than as santeros.[12]

Santería (and its Yoruba antecedents in Cuba) has certainly been mined as a

Figure 2.1. Altar to a *muerto* (spirit of the dead) named *Ma Rufina*.

Figure 2.2. Altar to San Lázaro, a popular Catholic saint, incorporating Spiritist elements.

source of practices and beliefs that generally can cohere with bits and pieces of other ostensibly distinct traditions. To cite a few examples, one *muertera* friend who worked with an African spirit and moonlighted from her professional job to provide consultations for clients was eager to have me teach her Lucumí words and songs used by santeros that she could incorporate into her rituals.[13] Many other Cubans I knew drew upon the iconography and lore of Santería's orichas in their religious understandings and practices. My observations are in keeping with survey results by the researchers of the Havana-based Centro de Investigaciones Psicológicas y Sociológicas (1998: 17), who argue that a greater percentage of Cubans engage in private or family-level, autonomous, and highly syncretic religious practices (30 percent) than commit to congregations or other formalized groups of all of the organized religions of Cuba together (15 percent).

The most widespread institutionalized religions in Cuba are numerous Christian denominations (Pérez Jr. 1995a, 1995b).[14] While self-defined Catholics may worship saints in ways that overlap with Spiritist and even Santería practices, Protestants typically will have nothing to do with any of these "idolatrous" practices. Nonetheless, I encountered many households in which different members subscribed to different religions: santeros and Jehovah's Witnesses; Spiritists and Catholics.

Measures of Cuban religious affiliation

Data on religious affiliation in Cuba are notably spare for two reasons. First, the Cuban government controls all demographic studies. Second, if it even keeps them, the government has not made census statistics on religious participation available.[15] What *is* available are two more limited surveys by Cuban scholars. The first was conducted in the city and neighborhood where I did much of my fieldwork.

Millet, Brea, and Ruiz Vila (1997) collected data on 133 households in the traditionally Afro-Cuban neighborhood of Los Hoyos, a stronghold of Santería in the city of Santiago de Cuba. They cite census figures showing that Los Hoyos has a total population of about 20,000 across 4,476 households.[16] In Los Hoyos and similar neighborhoods, I noted that people take pride in their Afro-Cuban heritage and are therefore more likely to be open about their religiosity than residents of higher-status, traditionally whiter neighborhoods.[17] Nonetheless, Millet's group recognizes that even in Los Hoyos people are reluctant to completely confide in anyone taking official statistics, so their procedure for identifying religiosity was to note whether or not signs of such were visible on persons or in their homes.[18] The researchers assumed that their procedure would undercount religious participation, identifying only 70 percent of those who are, in fact, religious. They found that 73 households, or 54.9 percent of their sample, manifested some sign of religiosity and so estimated that as much as 80 percent of households in the neighborhood were religious (54–55).

As to how applicable their results would be to other neighborhoods with different demographics, Millet and fellow researchers *do* provide data on the correlation between race, educational level, and visible religiosity: they found that around 73 percent of blacks and 71 percent of Chinese-Cubans were visibly religious, whereas only 43–44 percent of those they identified as white or mulatto were visibly religious. Results were similarly divided between those with less than a secondary school education (63–66 percent were religious) and those who had completed at least secondary level training (40–44 percent were religious) (55–56).[19] Despite these significant differences, we note the overall high levels of religious participation in Los Hoyos, which suggest how prevalent religiosity is in Cuban society.

Although there are no statistics reporting overall participation in various religious traditions, one official Cuban study (CIPS 1998: 17) mentions in passing that 15 percent of Cubans belong to some organized religion, 15 percent are not religious, and the remaining majority fall into the categories of "vacillating" (20 percent), "elaborating only a low level of religious belief"

(20 percent), and practicing privately and intermittently (30 percent). If we simplify these rather underdetermined categories into "religious" and "not religious," it appears that as much as 85 percent of the Cuban population is to some degree religious, a finding that seems to validate the estimates made by Millet's group.

Unfortunately, Millet, Brea, and Ruiz Villa do not attempt to specify type of religious adherence, although their study's implicit assumption seems to be that residents of Los Hoyos practice "popular" rather than institutionalized religions. By comparison, Argüelles Mederos and Hodge Limonta (1991) give at least a partial view of relative participation in Afro-Cuban traditions and Spiritism. They collected data across ten provinces from 3,283 applications for licenses to conduct home-based religious ceremonies (251–53). This sample, of course, did not allow them to state overall numbers for religious participation in the total population, but from the applications they identified 2,939 santeros, 35 paleros, and 202 adherents to more than one religion (211–12, table 7).[20] A separate study of rural areas in six provinces showed that of 1,135 interviewees, 37.5 percent identified themselves as Spiritists, 8.3 percent as santeros, and 2.7 percent as adherents of Vodú (212–13). These proportions have at least face validity for the situation I observed in Santiago, in which Spiritism and Muertería seemed to be most widely practiced, followed by smaller numbers of (presumably initiated) Santería and Palo practitioners, with only a tiny fraction of small, rural communities practicing Vodú. Interestingly, the total percentage the authors give for respondents who self-identified as religious in Spiritism, Santería, or Vodú is about 50 percent—in the range of the 54.9 percent of households that Millet, Brea, and Ruiz Villa identified as religious in their 1997 study.[21]

What of the total number of santeros? If, keeping in mind all the preceding caveats, we accept Argüelles Mederos and Hodge Limonta's estimate that somewhere around 8 percent of the total population practices Santería, then practitioners in Cuba number 800,000 to 900,000 out of a population of 11 million, a not unsubstantial number. If we further add that, despite some clustering by region, neighborhood, and even socioeconomic stratum, Santería practitioners do occur throughout the island's population and that many more people participate in ceremonies or consult santeros than actually undergo initiation, then it is not surprising that most, if not all, Cubans know something of Santería either directly or through a family member, neighbor, or work associate. Certainly, these generalizations coincide with my experience.

Commonalities across the popular religious complex

I have suggested that Santería is best understood as part of a popular religious complex. Going on, I wish to explore two opposing tendencies in how
practitioners and scholars treat the traditions comprising this complex. One
tendency differentiates traditions based on their particular European, African,
or syncretic origins (much as I did in table 2.1), while the other, long tacit in
practitioners' combinations but which has emerged only recently among scholars, seeks parallels and underlying commonalities that unite them. Argüelles
Mederos and Hodge Limonta, whose statistics I cited above, are a classic example of "splitters"; they devote a chapter of *Los llamados cultos sincréticos y
el espiritismo* (1991) to the unique origins and distinguishing characteristics
of each "syncretic cult" and to Spiritism, then nod at the "lumper" position
by providing tables of correspondences between particular orichas, Catholic
saints, Arará deities, and Palo *kimpungulu* (singular *mpungu*, Congo deity).[22]
James Figarola (1999) and Palmié (2002b) instead emphasize the commonalities and common history that unite these magico-religious systems.

Among the many important commonalities, the Yoruba and Catholic notions of a Supreme Creator god (called Oludomare in Yoruba and Olofi by
santeros and corresponding to the Congo Nzambi or Sambia) have converged
in popular belief to produce a generalized belief in a Supreme Creator who
leaves the running of the universe to a lesser pantheon of saints, orichas, and
spirits (Díaz Fabelo 1960; Idowu 1962). Ways of conceptualizing and contacting
these entities, especially the spirits of the dead, have intermingled to the extent
that they seem to draw upon a common metaphysic, which James Figarola
(1999) refers to as "Deep Cuba." Central to these deep commonalities is the
notion that humans and supernatural beings form intensely intimate, personalized, and symbiotic bonds, in which the spirits, saints, or deities repay human attention (in various forms of devotions, offerings, or manipulations) by
directly intervening in people's lives and problems. Karin Barber's now-classic
discussion (1981) of how "man makes God" among the Yoruba applies broadly
to the fluid, ever-shifting hosts of saints, spirits, and orichas that fall in and out
of favor in Cuba.

These commonalities on the deep, cosmological level produce convergences
at the level of ritual practice. Practitioners of the popular religions maintain
home altars—often more than one—which they lavish with offerings on special occasions or when they wish to request spiritual help. Ceremonies of festive worship, which typically feature drumming, singing, and dancing, are also

Figure 2.3. A Spiritist altar, one of several altars kept by a santera in her home.

Figure 2.4. An altar to the same santera's *africanos* or African spirits, each represented by a doll and kept on top of her television set.

Figure 2.5. The *casita* (little house) of the oricha Eleggua, "who opens and closes the door," is next to the main door in the house of the same santera as in figures 2.3 and 2.4.

widespread, even though the spiritual focus of worship may be a saint, a spirit of the dead, or an oricha.

We find another commonality among all of the popular religions in their technologies for two-way communication with spirits and deities, whether through divination, mediumship, or possession trance. Santería, for example, claims three methods of divination, although only priests initiated as babalawos can practice the most intricate form, called "Ifá," which has direct continuities with Yoruba Ifá divination in West Africa.[23] David Brown argues that the second method of divination, using cowrie shells, was elaborated in Cuba as a more readily available adaptation of Ifá divination that santeros, rather than babalawos, could practice (2003: 132–33, 339 n.52; also see Bascom 1980). The third and simplest divination method, using coconut shells, is quite similar to coconut shell divinations I have observed by practitioners

Figure 2.6. A *muertera* gives a client a *consulta* (consultation) with her *muerto*.

of Palo.[24] Spiritists and Muerteros practice mediumship or divination with cards (either a regular deck or Tarot cards) or even with a glass of water and a candle or a mirror. People facing health problems or a wide variety of other personal, familial, economic, or legal difficulties often seek spiritual help and herbal remedies by shopping around across ostensibly distinct traditions (Wedel 2004).

Even those who commit to initiation into Santería, for example, encounter ritual requirements to be initiated (*rayado*) in Regla de Palo; to hold Spiritist masses and otherwise work with spirits of the dead that have an affinity for them; and even to attend Catholic mass and venerate particular saints. Emilio told me that a santero must have been baptized in the Catholic Church. But

Figure 2.7. An altar to the orichas, accompanied by a statue of Santa Bárbara, framed by popular symbols to ward off evil.

note that this ecumenical approach does not diminish distinctions among traditions so much as highlight their complementary strengths in providing a person with a sort of complete package of spiritual protection, undergirded by a shared *cosmovisión* (cosmological vision).

Like an optical illusion in which two contradictory images shift back and forth before one's eyes, the traditions of the popular religious complex are both highly distinctive and highly convergent. I suggest that deep commonalities and deeply rooted pragmatic tendencies toward borrowing encourage convergence at some levels of practice, while an overarching interpretive framework based on Cuban ideologies of racial difference and African-European cultural syncretism encourages practitioners to maintain distinctions at other levels.[25]

Social valorizations of "popular" religions

However much the beliefs and practices of ostensibly different religious traditions overlap and converge, they remain distinct at the metacultural level through a process of discursive polarization that is separate from the processes of practical blending I have already described. Their social valorizations are based on a longstanding opposition of European "civilization" to African "backwardness" that affects both how Cubans typify practitioners of each religion and who admits to practicing them. Each tradition is valorized primarily based on its presumed European, African, or syncretic origins, and thus where it falls on an axis from moral religion to immoral (or at best, amoral) witchcraft. Folk Catholicism is imagined to be the most European of the "popular" religions, followed by different varieties of Spiritism. At the other end of the spectrum, Vodú and Palo are presumed to be the most African traditions, and Palo in particular is generally viewed as morally suspect if not tantamount to witchcraft. Santería and Muertería fall in the middle, which makes their moral status more ambiguous and more contested.

At the same time, by virtue of being intermediate between the European and African poles, Santería (and the less widely recognized or discussed Muertería) have become the prime exemplars of religious syncretism, although in truth all of the traditions across the popular religious complex represent syncretizations or hybridizations of various sorts. As the prototypical syncretic religion of Cuba, Santería has come to signify the creative amalgamation of African and European cultures that is fundamental to Cuba's national origin myth. Thus, Santería has come to play a key role in the politics of national identity, which in Cuba as elsewhere in Latin America revolve around a discourse of racial hybridity that has been labeled the "myth of mestizaje."[26] Of all the religions recognized in Cuba, it is Santería that has become most visible in Cuban society and Santería that has captured the lion's share of international attention and commercialization. This is true even though its adherents probably account for less than 10 percent of the population. But as I will explore from a historical perspective in the next chapter, Santería's importance in the "myth of mestizaje" produces its own difficulties for practitioners and does not erase other more pejorative evaluations of it.

Not surprisingly, religious Cubans may vary how they represent what they or others are doing according to how they wish to align themselves relative to particular audiences and contexts. Román (2002) examines these dynamics by comparing the career trajectories of two Spiritist healers at the turn of the twentieth century, one of whom successfully built a reputation by aligning himself with the Eurocentric drawing rooms of elite Cuba in which Spiritist seances imported from France and the United States became acceptable eccentricity, while the other healer's practice among more humble clients, including many Afro-Cubans, was read by elites and police as criminally dangerous Afro-Cuban sorcery. Román's analysis parallels the dynamics of religion a century later: namely, that social actors distinguish, compare, and judge religious alternatives not only on practical or metaphysical merits, but in terms of other social and political criteria of the larger arena of society (see also Lago Vieito 2001).

Palmié develops a similar argument, suggesting that European Spiritist, Yoruba, and Bantu religious practices became polarized on a spectrum of symbolic valences, from Spiritism, which was the most civilized, white, and pure, to Bantu practices known as Palo, which were the most barbaric, black, and dangerous. The former are characteristics that Cubans, like most European-influenced societies, gloss as proper, moral "religion," whereas the latter are understood to be characteristic of "magic" or "witchcraft." Santería occupied the middle ground, tilting slightly to the moral, religious side, depending on the particular observer. Despite the "practical integration" of Yoruba and Bantú practices, Santería and Palo underwent a "division of cultic labor" in which Santería became a proper "religion" with proper deities and proper morality, while Palo became "magic"—dealing with darker, more exploitative, and decidedly less moral relations with spirits (Palmié 2002a: 190–93). Argyriadis (2000) also explores the contrast between Santería and Palo, but explains it as a juxtaposition between Santería as a representation of a pure and authentic "idealized" African civilization and Palo, which is characterized as "cacophonous" sorcery that represents the backward and disorganized result of improper syncretization. This, however, is probably only part of the story, since many Cubans emphasize Santería's symmetrical syncretism of Catholic and Yoruba traditions.

As Argyriadis also observes, practitioners frequently boost their own place on the spectrum of propriety by describing more "African" practices as "witchcraft" in contrast to their own "religion." For example, on several occasions I got into discussions with santeros concerning the potential to use one's orichas for evil purposes. They typically insisted that the orichas would not allow such activity and that it would backfire onto the santero. But, they inevitably continued, Palo practitioners (*paleros*) could and did do witchcraft. In similar conversations I had with paleros, they would insist that their own practice was "only for good," but that other paleros who practiced the more sinister forms of Palo were the ones doing witchcraft.[27] Somehow, like Clifford Geertz's endless layers of turtles, one never met the actual evildoers, only a succession of

Figure 2.8. A *muertera*'s altar, with Spiritist elements on the shelf above and Palo elements on the ground below.

pointing fingers. My Spiritist friends, in turn, sometimes expressed mingled fear and admiration for the more dangerous and exciting "African" practices. My Spiritist host family on one visit would alternately warn me against the dangers of attending Santería ceremonies and pump me for information when I returned from one.

Practitioners themselves, then, participated in discourses differentiating religious traditions and, alongside their willingness to borrow and blend, engaged in boundary-maintaining practices, such as maintaining different altars for each tradition.[28] One muertera I interviewed proudly showed me her altar, which was neatly divided into a Spiritist part on the mantle and a Congo (Palo) part on the floor below. She explained that the Spiritist part of her practice was light and pure and could only be used for "doing good," which was why it was up high on the altar. The more earthy Congo part of her practice was morally ambiguous and dangerous, but also more powerful. It gave her the potential to help clients by harming those who caused them problems, something the Spiritist practice could not do.

I have suggested that there is a tension in understandings of religions in the popular religious complex between tendencies to blend or lump traditions and tendencies to maintain distinctions that carry moral valuations. This tension is similarly evident among both religious practitioners and scholars. This discussion should make clear why Santería cannot be defined or discussed in isolation from its counterparts in the popular religious complex and that any widely accepted definition is best understood as the precipitate of ongoing, ideologically charged discourses about religion, magic, and witchcraft in Cuba.

Boundary-maintaining practices of Santería

Santeros, those who embrace La Regla de Ocha, face a problem, which is to differentiate their religion from other, similar popular religions at the same time that they, and other religious practitioners, liberally borrow from and blend ostensibly distinct religious traditions. What is at stake at the local level is the cachet and security of belonging to a well-defined moral community, and what is at stake more broadly is Santería's increasingly privileged role as Cuba's exemplary popular and folkloric religion, with all the benefits (and complications) that accrue to its practitioners as a result.

Religious alternatives like Spiritism, Santería, and Palo emerged, exist, and continue to resist blending because of their practitioners' and others' (folklorists, ethnographers, historians, et cetera) boundary-making activities. Having unpacked the essentialisms in the standard, shorthand description of Santería as a syncretic Afro-Cuban religion, I will close the chapter by examining a few of the ways in which santeros mark the boundaries of their moral community. While some boundary-marking occurs overtly in discourse, as when santeros talk about the need to stick to tradition or compare their practices favorably against those of other practitioners, santeros also engage in practices that implicitly convey their claims to insidership.

One easy example is the *moyubá* invocation with which santeros open almost all ritual activity. The title of this chapter, "bobo iguoro cogguá ilé" (all the priests in the house) is a common closing phrase of santeros' moyubá invocations, after they have named all the individual santeros, living and deceased, who are part of their ritual lineage or otherwise important to them. The phrase is a catchall to cover any santeros whose names might inadvertently have been left out of the invocation. For santeros, the phrase and the entire moyubá invocation of which it is part are ways of ritually representing the most salient parts of their religious community, subdivided as it is into ritual lineages, which are traced according to relationships of godparentage sanctified during initiation. The phrase itself is in the esoteric liturgical register santeros call "Lucumí," which santeros regard as the divine language of the orichas and the ancestral language of Santería's Lucumí (Yoruba) ethnic origins. Knowing the proper uses and meanings of Lucumí words and phrases—like those of the moyubá invocation—is as important a mark of insidership in the Santería community as being named in the moyubás of other santeros. These details tell us something of santeros' normative understanding of who, precisely, is part of the local religious community of santeros.

This example also illustrates three crucial features of Santería that santeros highlight in reflective discourse and practice as particular hallmarks of Santería, although none of these features in itself is unique to Santería. Paradoxical as this seems at first glance, santeros find ways to differentiate their way of doing things from other, ostensibly similar practices. The net effect of santeros' interpretive activity is to represent Santería as secretive, closed, and markedly African.

First, santeros point to Santería's exclusive ritual hierarchy that requires initiation to join. Initiation is a lengthy and expensive endeavor that inducts participants into a host of newly cast social relationships and ritual responsibilities (see figure 1.2). The first step of initiation requires a week-long ceremony in which the new initiate undergoes classic rites of passage to be metaphorically reborn into a ritual lineage as the child of an oricha. Santeros emphasize that they had to be initiated because their principal oricha compelled them to. Many are deeply suspicious of those who would be initiated simply because they want to, in the absence of divine pressure. Although initiation rituals are not unique to Santería (Palo has a similar though less elaborate initiation, generating somewhat looser ritual lineages [see Larduet Luaces 1999]), being initiated into Ocha serves a gate-keeping function, distinguishing those with a right to call themselves santeros and participate in even secret ceremonies from all other practitioners.

Second, santeros emphasize their religion's secret and esoteric knowledge, which is gained only by participation in the ritual community and its traditions and not through personal inspiration or invention. Coupled with this is an emphasis on one correct way of doing things in rituals, a way whose logic presumably would be understood only by those with access to secret religious meanings passed along as sacred (and secret) tradition. In contrast, Spiritists encourage individuals to cultivate their natural abilities as spirit mediums, and many religious Cubans pray and make offerings to their saints, orichas, and spirits within their own households, without engaging in communal religious rites. Palo shares with Santería a more secretive orientation, but presumably the secrets differ. Santeros agreed in telling me that the central secret of Santería was the secret shared in initiation, although it was clear that most rituals and types of ritual activity were understood to have increasingly deep layers of occult meaning that were supposed to remain inaccessible to all but the experts (Wirtz 2005, 2007).[29] The moyubá is no exception. Indeed, its Lucumí sections serve to obscure semantic levels of meaning, which raises another key feature of Santería.

Third, Santería's esoteric ritual register, Lucumí, heightens the mystery and insidership of rituals and provides a partly unintelligible code for conveying occult knowledge and religious insidership. Again, consider the phrase "bobo iguoro cogguá ilé" in the chapter epigraph. Lucumí utterances publicly signal the authoritativeness of ritual performances, the focus of which is communication with deities and spirits. Initiates describe Lucumí as the language of the gods, necessary for communication between humans and oricha. Although the language is not secret, it is highly esoteric, even among initiated santeros. To speak in Lucumí is to simultaneously display and disguise one's secret knowledge and to signal one's authority to mediate communication with the sacred. It adds to the veil of secrecy that Lucumí utterances are often not semantically transparent even to religious specialists, who focus on Lucumí's pragmatic force as a magical language (Wirtz 2005). Many santeros would not be able to provide a gloss for even as common a phrase as "bobo iguoro cogguá ilé," as evidenced in the version given in the chapter epigraph, in which the more readily understood "todo los omo ocha y babalocha" (all the children of the oricha and priests) in a sense glosses the more opaque version. Lucumí contributes much of the distinctive pattern of ritual speech that gets taken up and replicated not only in later rituals but also in talk about rituals. Lucumí is key to how Santería is understood by religious participants and outsiders alike, especially in how it reinforces santeros' projected vision of Santería as an exclusive, select religious community whose power resides in its control of occult knowledge deriving from African tradition.

Since Lucumí derives from Yoruba, an African language, it carries all of the complex valences of things African in Cuba. As a result, its interpretation oscillates between being a potent, magical mode of divine communication and being a signifier of Africanity in a society still struggling with racism and other legacies of slavery. To the extent that ritual performances shape social attitudes and allegiances, the former interpretation prevails. But the interpretive frame promoted by rituals is always in competition with other circulating characterizations, such as those anchored in official, folkloric, and commercial representations of Santería and other "Afro-Cuban" elements.

An anecdote will illustrate this point. One of my transcribers, who was not religious, had been working hard at home in the evenings, trying to complete transcriptions of several interviews and a divination ritual before I was to leave. When she came to drop them off, we discussed how the transcribing process had gone. Just fine, she said, although she was very tired from working so hard, and some of it was quite difficult to understand. In fact, her husband had caught her talking to herself, repeating what she heard as she wrote it down. He teased her for "speaking Mandinga," meaning that she was speaking like an enslaved African might have spoken: "Mandinga" refers to an African language and ethnic group (a "*nación*" in Cuban terms) that was well known in colonial times. The word has survived as a playful way of referring to someone or something Afro-Cuban, as in the nonsensical chorus of a well-known *son* (genre of popular music related to salsa) that praises the beauty of a black woman, "Quiquiribú, Mandinga."

African-sounding wordplay has a well-established place in Cuban music and literature (consider Cuban poet Nicolás Guillén's famous sonorous and nonsensical refrain, "sóngoro cosongo," or the equally unintelligible opening of his poem "Canto negro": "¡Yambambó, yambambé!" (1972: 105, 122). But it is decidedly marked speech, not least for its unintelligibility, because it invokes the imperfect speech of enslaved Africans who learned Spanish as a second language. Although my transcriber's husband used the ethnonym "Mandinga," the more commonly heard term is "bozal," which in colonial times referred to both African-born slaves and to their attempts to communicate in pidginized Spanish (Alonso and Fernández 1977; Isabel Castellanos 1990; Laviña 1989; Lipski 1998; Schwegler 2006). Bozal speech still carries the derogatory connotations of being rural, provincial, uneducated, and black. Although there are no longer any bozal speakers, there remain what Cubans and linguists alike call "bozalisms," remnants of a pidgin or semicreolized sociolect (Ortiz López 1998). Cubans who are uninvolved in African-derived religions like Santería are likely to refer to religious jargons such as Lucumí as bozal speech, whereas religious participants do not confuse liturgical language with what they, too, may regard as bozalisms. Palo also has a religious jargon derived from Bantu languages like Kikongo (Barnet 1995; Fuentes Guerra and Schwegler 2005; González Huguet and Baudry 1967; Valdés Bernal 1987).

Conclusion

Just as religious outsiders looking in conflate religious jargons like Lucumí with bozal, they are also likely to conflate Santería with other, more "African" religious traditions and to gloss all of them as witchcraft, *brujería*. Practitioners and outsiders alike understand Santería according to this general matrix of social value that itself perpetuates a racialized social order. Based on the observer's perspective and choice of social alignments, Santería gets glossed variously as religion, witchcraft, "backward" superstition, or African-European syncretism in action, and the meaning of Santería emerges at the epicenter of conflicts among these competing interpretive stances for reasons that trace back to differing historical visions of Cuban identity.

I have demonstrated how Santería as an entity emerges through the pragmatic and interpretive activities of practitioners and others—what Palmié fittingly calls an "indigenous sociology of religious forms" (2002b: 162)—to show how they construct both convergences and boundaries among the practices of the popular religious complex (and between those and other more institutionalized forms of Christianity as well). In doing so, they (inadvertently, unconsciously, necessarily) draw upon—and thus reinscribe—particular orders of race, culture, religion, and nation. All of this has been a perhaps long-winded way of showing the inadequacies of the "easy" definition of Santería as a syncretic Afro-Cuban religion based on Yoruba traditions. Or rather, thumbnail definitions having their uses, of unpacking the inner workings of the social order conjured up by the definition.

I have also provided an introductory sampling of the sorts of interpretive work accomplished by santeros' own activities. The ways in which they prioritize ritual lineage, ritual language, and religious secrets will saturate the examples described in later chapters. In this chapter I have illustrated how these prioritizations link to the broader religious landscape in which santeros seek to demarcate themselves as a moral community. What remains for the next chapter is to show how santeros' activities of self-definition have also interacted with secular, especially elite and official state, views of them. Chapter 3 takes up an historical view of how Santería gained its current stature, amid competing, clashing, and sometimes converging visions of it.

3

Competing Histories
and Dueling Moralities

A tourist in Havana these days would have little difficulty encountering emblems of Santería amid a general proliferation of things Afro-Cuban offered for
tourist consumption: Paintings and postcards in art galleries and stores present
images of the orichas, sometimes Catholicized as "saints" and sometimes "Afri-
canized"; batá drum rhythms entice spectators to view authentic performances
of oricha dances; white-clad "santeras" draped in colorful beaded necklaces
roam the tourist areas of Old City offering consultations to tourists, while their
similarly dressed dolls and ostensibly religious bead necklaces are ubiquitous.
There are books and CDs about Santería in most tourist shops. The relatively
new Museo de la Asociación Cultural Yorubá de Cuba, prominently located
across from the Capitolio in a beautifully renovated building in Central Havana, is easy for tourists to find. Visitors to the museum can wander a gallery
featuring huge sculptures of orichas, each on its own altar, realized in an imagined "African" rather than Catholic aesthetic, and set against lavishly painted
murals that evoke a tropical forest. Many of the items and performances listed
here can also be found, along with the oricha sculptures, in the museum or its
gift shop and art gallery.

Santería is highly visible in contemporary Cuba. The story I will tell in this
chapter traces in broad strokes how something called Santería emerged around
the turn of the twentieth century out of a tumult of popular religious and magical practices—brujería—to become the most visible entity in Cuba's complex of
popular religions. I show how ongoing interactions among different interpretive discourses circulating in Cuban society during the twentieth century and
into the twenty-first have given shape to Santería, both in contradistinction
to other practices, as described in the previous chapter, and as a multifaceted
entity in itself—one that projects different meanings when seen in different
lights.

Underlying my analysis is the notion that multiple interpretive stances in dialogic interaction generate culture—a religion in this case—as an emergent phenomenon (Tedlock and Mannheim 1995: 1–4).[1] That is, relatively stable stances can be distilled out of how people express their alignments toward (or against) Santería and similar practices in particular moments of interaction. This ongoing, moment-to-moment activity of deploying interpretations of people, objects, and events during everyday interactions is what ultimately allows social norms and values to emerge (Agha 2003; Silverstein 2003). Tedlock and Mannheim in their discussion of this dialogic view of culture (1995), cite James Clifford's contention that all culture be "reconceived as inventive process or creolized 'interculture'" (1988: 15), a notion Homi Bhabha echoes in saying, "it is the 'inter'—the cutting edge of translation and negotiation, the *in-between* space—that carries the burden of the meaning of culture" (1994: 38). I will explore how competing stances can produce tremendous tensions or can sometimes almost converge in the alignments they generate toward Santería.

One quite literal, physical interspace is the magnificent and strange Museum of the Yoruba Cultural Association, introduced above. I visited the museum in April 2002 not long after it had opened. The guard who collected my entrance fee, noticing my camera, explained that I was entering a *museo-templo* (museum-temple) and so photos were forbidden, just as some practitioners forbid filming of their private altars. The bulletin board by the door caught my eye. One announcement informed "all practitioners of the Regla Ocha and Ifá" that they could bring their iyawó (new initiates) between 9 and 10 a.m. to ritually present them to their orichas at the altars in the exhibits. Another very formally called upon practitioners of all "Cuban religions of African origin" to follow religious "commandments" (*mandamientos*) to keep all vessels of standing water on their altars clean, so as to help "eradicate the mosquito *Aedes aegypti*, vector of dengue," in order to "preserve the health of our people." The museum was part sacred space, part public space and revenue-generator, and part headquarters for an officially recognized religious association.

In filling these multiple roles, the museum encompassed multiple interpretive stances toward Santería. Even its description as a museum-temple straddled touristic, folkloric, religious, and even bureaucratic functions. As an institution on the main tourist circuit of Havana, the museum collected admission fees in dollars and exhibited religious altars as aestheticized Afro-Cuban "folklore." Indeed, upon entering, one first encountered the Asociación's art gallery, featuring paintings with strong Afro-Cuban religious symbolism.[2] The gallery (not to mention the gift shop and café) suggested a "typical" museum experience. However, other signs, like the first bulletin board notice and the ban on photographs, pointed to the museum's double existence as a religious temple. As an institution under the aegis of a religious association, the museum space and exhibits also permitted (indeed seemed to expect) ceremonial uses, although only before and after hours. As a clearinghouse for communications between the state and a religious organization, the museum and Asociación Cultural Yorubá operated only with the state's official sanction, as the Asociación president had stressed to me during an interview in April 2000. One sign of this official relationship was the second museum bulletin board announcement, which invoked both sacred writ and science to request that religious practitioners help the state's efforts to improve public health. The undercurrent of this seemingly reasonable if officious announcement, as I discuss later in the chapter, echoed a long history of official suspicions of Afro-Cuban ritual practices as unhygienic and counter to the public good.

I wish to push the metaphor of the "interspace" beyond actual physical spaces to consider how Santería has been continually constituted and reconstituted at the juncture of three competing metacultural stances, which for shorthand I call the sacred, the suspicious, and the folkloric. I also examine some of the consequences for santeros who must negotiate their religious and other (racial, national) identities according to fault lines drawn among these different stances. Although similar interpretive processes have shaped all of the religions of Cuba's popular religious complex, my focus in this chapter is on Santería and the particular stances that have been most crucial in its emergence.

The first of these stances is the view from within the religion santeros still prefer to call "the Law of the Orichas" (La Regla de Ocha). This sacred stance is generated by ritual practices that manipulate sacred power and establish communications between humans and deities. Santeros' commentaries on rituals make clear that they place a high premium on obedience to divine authority and, secondarily, to anyone higher in the religious hierarchy. The sacred stance embodies santeros' distinctive historical consciousness, in which ritual lineages link contemporary santeros into a chain of ritual elders, ancestors, and deities that stretches back across enslavement and the Atlantic to an almost mythic African homeland. A major theme of this historical consciousness is the struggle to stem loss—loss of ritual knowledge, loss of memory, loss of language, loss of tradition.[3] Practitioners are understandably obsessed with remembering (and debating) the details of "correct" ritual procedure and are quick to criticize each others' performances in rituals. They guard their knowledge as ritual secrets, lamenting all they no longer know and deploring the deterioration of a once tight-knit religious community.

Loss is a constant danger for marginalized practices and oppressed groups, and indeed, Santería's sacred stance is not as easily recoverable in the historical record as are the dominant stances. What is available are santeros' oral historical narratives, which are an important expression of santeros' historical consciousness. My subsequent discussion of the dominant stances tells the story of how the sacred stance has continued to be marginalized. For example, practitioners' emphasis on secrecy—occult knowledge and practices—has served to protect them under the regime of the second evaluative stance, which is suspicion.

The suspicious stance toward Santería has existed as long as the sacred stance, but it embodies an oppositional, outsider perspective on Afro-Cuban religious practices, one rooted in the denigration of Africans that accompanied their subjugation in plantation society. Santería, under this interpretation, demonstrates a primitive mentality—premodern, superstitious, unscientific—that has been perpetuated by poor living conditions: slavery, social marginalization, poverty. I frequently encountered Cubans, especially educated professionals, who would refer to religious practitioners as "gente sin alto nivel de cultura" (people without a high level of culture). They saw practitioners of Afro-Cuban religions as adherents to an outmoded magical and superstitious worldview. This interpretive stance also ascribes danger and criminality to Afro-Cuban ritual practices, and indeed these same acquaintances expressed fears about my safety in attending ceremonies. The historical consciousness embedded in this stance is one of linear, scientific progress according to elite, Eurocentric norms, a progress threatened by the corrupting influence of what white elites generally understand to be anachronistic practices.[4]

The third interpretive stance is the most recent, emerging fully only in the early twentieth century. It is the folkloric stance that understands Santería to be part of Cuban folkloric heritage and a marker of Cubanidad (Cubanness). The historical consciousness projected by this stance is also one of progress, albeit a unique trajectory of progress achieved through cultural synthesis and hybridization. This is a sense of history that social scientists largely share: African cultures—with an anthropological lower-case "c"—contributed to the *ajiaco* (Cuban stew) that is creole Cuban culture. The ideology of Cubanidad consists in conceiving of Cuban national identity in terms of idealized racial and cultural fusion (de la Fuente 2001; Wright 1990). As a popular Cuban expression about Cubans' shared African heritage observes, "él que no tiene Congo tiene

Carabalí" (he who isn't part Congo in his heritage is part Calabari). That is, all Cubans are a little bit African, whether their ancestors came from the Congo or Calabar. Similar expressions can be found throughout Latin America (see for example Whitten 2003: 61). National ideologies of *mestizaje* often function to further marginalize black or indigenous citizens by marking them as insufficiently hybridized and assimilated while simultaneously downplaying ongoing racism (Rahier 2003: 42; Wade 2001: 849; also see Whitten 2003 and Stutzman 1981). In the historical consciousness embedded within the folkloric stance, Santería and other embodiments of Afro-Cuban culture have folkloric value because they represent a past African influence on Cuban culture that has produced the mestizaje or hybridity of the present. Cuban folklorists often emphasize the syncretic nature of Santería and the multiracial composition of its adherents, even while its roots in Yoruba culture fascinate them.

The sacred, suspicious, and folkloric appraisals of Santería construct very different visions of what Santería is and what its continued presence means for Cuban society. That is, Santería turns out to be significant within very different types of historical consciousness—here understood to be how individuals or groups align themselves toward the past and its role in the present (see Ohnuki-Tierney 1990: 8–9). In particular, my analysis contrasts an historical consciousness grounded in sacred practice to secular modes of historical consciousness that are promoted by Cuban elites and circulated in official and scholarly discourses.

Ritual genealogies in Santiago de Cuba

Santeros talk about their history and the importance of the past in the present most frequently through the idiom of ritual kinship. Relationships of godparentage tie Santería's initiates into ritual lineages that reach back several generations and unite living practitioners into "ritual houses." The requisite ritual invocations that open each and every type of ritual activity, known as the moyubá, require santeros to recite the names of those they consider to be part of their ritual lineage. Other sections of the invocation list deceased and living links in the santero's ritual lineage, all of whose cooperation is necessary for proper communication to occur with the orichas.

Santeros are not only concerned with ritual lineage during ceremonies. As I observed, they also frequently refer to ties of ritual kinship or differences across ritual lineages in everyday conversation. Santeros sometimes tacitly acknowledged the responsibilities incurred by ritual kinship when they called in favors, demanded respect or attention, asked for help or advice for a ceremony, or decided to teach someone something. I often heard them explicitly mention such links, as when a godfather reminded his godchild to respect him as a godparent or when a santero told a senior santera that he named her in his invocation because she had been present for his initiation. To cite another typical example, one friend with a young son often reminded him to refer to her godmother as *madrina* (godmother), as well. On a later occasion, when he misbehaved while the godmother was babysitting him, she pulled him onto her lap, admonishing him to behave with her because she was his godmother. "Who am I?" she demanded, until he answered that she was his madrina. Two years later, when I returned for a visit, the little boy had undergone initiation, formalizing his connection to his madrina.

From discussions of such everyday ritual relationships, santeros frequently move on to mention or discuss more distant ritual relations. Two santeros meeting for the first time may thus establish a common ground in a shared ritual ancestor or a more competitive stance by emphasizing that they belong to distinct (and usually competing) lineages. Or one may privately conclude that the other's religious credentials are dubious because his ritual lineage is unfamiliar. That is, even when santeros do not know one another's godparents, they will frequently recognize some prominent ancestor widely known among Santiago santeros.

I also found that santeros frequently indulged in genealogical reminiscences. In Santiago de Cuba, local santeros understood Santería to be a recent phenomenon in the city, and most santeros recognized the same small group of "founders" who either came from western Cuba or had traveled there to be initiated (Millet 2000: 110–11). Santeros would recount a familiar set of names, always naming Reynerio Pérez first. Reynerio Pérez seems to have come to Santiago from western Cuba as early as 1910–1912 (Millet 2000: 115; see also Larduet Luaces 2001). He was renowned as a muertero for his work with spirits of the dead. Reynerio was initiated as a santero in 1933 (Millet 2000: 117). A charismatic figure, he had an enormous influence on religious practice in the poorer Afro-Cuban neighborhoods of the city. He eventually initiated hundreds of godchildren into both Santería and Palo.

In that same era spanning the 1930s and 1940s, there were a number of other Santiagueros and migrants from other cities who had initiated in Havana or Matanzas, always the mainstays of Santería in Cuba. Santiago santeros inevitably mentioned Rosa Torres in the same breath with Reynerio, as well as others such as La China (Aurora Lamar), Amada Sánchez, and Cunino (for an oral history, see Millet 2000). Such conversations, or reminiscences, if the santero was old enough, were easy enough to start. Sometimes, during interviews, santeros would begin to tell me or others present about this early era of their own accord. Santeros would inevitably also include details about other firsts in Santiago: so-and-so senior santero was the first Eleggua initiated by Reynerio, or the first Obatalá in Santiago, or the first female Ogún. They would explain that the founders either came from western Cuba or were Santiagueros who went to Havana or Matanzas to be initiated there. Most would sooner or later repeat the famous phrase uttered by one of the founders to justify starting initiations in Santiago: "Is there no river in Santiago? No plants? So then, why aren't santeros initiated here?" Interestingly, this famous phrase was attributed to several different santeros, depending upon whom one asked.[5]

According to local oral history, Reynerio and Rosa presided over the golden age of Santería in Santiago when everyone got along. In dozens of interviews and conversations about the good old days, santeros would shake their heads about how things had gone downhill since that time. Such nostalgia for the good old days is hardly rare, but in this case it accompanied fears about ever-increasing numbers of santeros.[6] Prominent elder santeros, especially, worried about the explosive growth of the religion, and their resulting lack of control over such large numbers of santeros who all have their own ideas about what is correct and what is permissible in the religion.

The story most commonly told to illustrate Santería's early rise to glory in Santiago and its subsequent long descent into current chaos involves Reynerio and his large family, most of whom have been initiated. Reynerio's family continues to be prominent in Santería. It includes highly regarded *oriatés* (officiating priests) and singers and has a large role in the unique saint's day procession through his old neighborhood in honor of Saint Bárbara's day, December 4th (see figure 3.1). Reynerio was a son of Changó, who is identified with the Catholic Saint Bárbara. The procession stops at several houses of Reynerio's kin (figure 3.2), and large portraits of Reynerio and his wife are carried in front of the platform bearing a large statue of Saint Bárbara (figure 3.3). Through such observances, Reynerio's and all the founders' legacies are keenly remembered.

Despite (or perhaps because of) the prestige Reynerio's descendants continue to hold, most other santeros would with alacrity recount the fall of the family. The family's gradual decline, according to one story I heard repeatedly, began while Reynerio was still alive. No one in the family possessed the spiritual authority of Reynerio, who seems to have been a powerful, larger-than-life figure. Indeed, upon his death, when his saints were asked in a final divination

Figure 3.1. Procession through the neighborhoods of Los Hoyos and Los Olmos for Santa Bárbara's Day, December 4, 1999.

where they wanted to go, they refused to go with any other family member. According to another often-repeated story, the cowries refused child and godchild alike, until Reynerio's youngest godchild was named. It was he, Vicente, who received into his care Reynerio's saints.[7] For some santeros, Reynerio's mandate from beyond the grave censured his own family.

Spun out of gossip, such morality tales of Reynerio's family vividly illustrate santeros' fears about fallen religious ideals. When prominent santeros like Reynerio, and more recently, Vicente, passed away, santeros lamented the loss of ritual knowledge, because no powerful santero ever shares all of his secrets with his godchildren. The community loses a pillar and also his expertise. Indeed, with santeros rushing to initiate as many godchildren as possible, cutting corners left and right, many santeros expressed fear that the growing population of santeros would mean ever more dilute ritual knowledge.

Figure 3.2. The procession greets the Changó kept at the house of one of Reynerio Pérez's descendents.

Figure 3.3. Portraits of Reynerio Pérez and his wife are carried in the procession by young drummers initiated to his family's consecrated *batá* drum set.

At the same time, local santeros also recounted their progress in making Santiago, by their account, the most vibrant religious community on the island. Whereas in Reynerio's day there were no consecrated batá drums in Santiago, forcing people to hire consecrated batá from western Cuba, there are now several sets in the city. Some santeros also made reference to increasing religious openness in contrast to past repression. Indeed, wearing the bead necklaces and bracelets of Santería had become practically a fashion fad among the young. Some santeros would also make reference to increasing religious openness in contrast to past repression. This state of affairs contrasts with earlier eras in which santeros often practiced in secret. Now, despite a lingering social stigma among the educated and white elites, most santeros I met did not seem to fear expressing their religiosity openly.

Nonetheless, older and younger santeros alike expressed distaste for the controversies, crassness, and blatant commercialization into which they suggested Santería has fallen as it gains in popularity. As evidence of current decadence, they cited numerous "violations" of ritual propriety, escalating ritual fees, and bad blood between lineages whose founders had always cooperated.

Along with other lacunae of historical memory, Santiago santeros spoke of the golden age of the founders as if there were no Santería prior to Reynerio's arrival. They have little to say in answer to the question of what came before Reynerio. Was there really no Santería in Santiago before the late 1920s or early 1930s? While I cannot give a definitive answer, Santiago-born folklorist Rómulo Lachatañeré, writing in the late 1930s and 1940s, mentioned Reynerio Pérez as the founder of Santería in the city (1992: 211–13). In Lachatañeré's account, Santiagueros at the time understood Reynerio to be introducing something new and different.

In the same passage, Lachatañeré mentions that Reynerio's religious practices were novel in his use of Santería's Yoruba-language liturgy. Even today, santeros and folklorists recognize a distinction between the canon of Lucumí songs performed in Santería ceremonies and an older corpus of songs that are still performed in similar *bembé* ceremonies (festive drumming ceremonies) in the city. In contrast to the mostly unintelligible Lucumí songs of Santería, the old bembé songs are mostly in Spanish, even when they name the same Yoruba deities.[8] Likewise, the rhythmic accompaniment of bembé songs may not necessarily use batá drums or Lucumí rhythms. Santeros and folklorists recognize a distinction between the two types of songs, although santeros differ among themselves in how strictly they interpret what is an appropriate song to accompany a ceremony. The old bembé songs add weight to the oral history evidence, suggesting that prior to Reynerio's era there were indeed Yoruba influences present in Santiago, but that Santiago's religious practitioners did not differentiate something called Santería or perhaps even Regla de Ocha out of the mix of religious practices.

In nineteenth-century colonial Cuba, during the slavery regime, Yoruba orisha worship survived in colonial-era urban *cabildos* (Afro-Cuban religious fraternities) and in pockets of religious activity among plantation slaves (Barnet 1994; Brandon 1993; Martinez Furé 1979; Ortiz 1973/1921, 1995/1906). The 30 years of struggles for independence from Spain between 1868 and 1898 were a period of turmoil and population movement that resulted in slave emancipation in 1886 (Ferrer 1999). Ex-slaves joined the struggle for independence; civilians fled battles; political and economic exiles sought refuge outside the country, then reentered as conditions shifted. During newly independent Cuba's First Republic after 1902, as the new nation recovered from war and built its economy under the watchful eye of U.S. interests, social unrest and labor demands led to internal migration as well as new immigration from abroad (de la Fuente 2001; Fernández Robaina 1994). Religious practices we now distinguish as Spiritism, Palo, and Santería were likely on the move during these decades of the late nineteenth and early twentieth centuries (Román 2002). Spiritism in particular became popular among all social classes, proliferating in many forms, often in combination with Catholic and African practices (Argüelles Mederos and Hodge Limonta 1991; Brandon 1993: 85–90; Lago Vieito 2001). There was undoubtedly a religious ferment at the turn of the twentieth century, including the commingling of practices with distinct origins, much as continues to occur today.

Perhaps just as significantly, dominant voices in the media represented all such practices not as religions but as suspect primitive superstitions and witchcraft. With the occasional exception of Spiritism, which because of its European origins more visibly attracted upper-class clientele and practitioners, these religions were otherwise closely associated with Afro-Cubans, although whites, including elites, had participated in "Afro-Cuban" practices since colonial times (Lago Vieito 2001; Palmié 2002a: 148, 197–98; Urrutía y Blanco 1882: 311–70). Nonetheless, elites of the early republican era regarded people and practices deemed Afro-Cuban with deep suspicion. It was in this climate that Afro-Cubans struggled to be accepted as full citizens of the new Cuba (de la Fuente 2001; Román 2002).

Los Negros Brujos, 1906: Suspect witches in the new Cuban Republic

Fernando Ortiz, pioneer of Afro-Cuban folklore, was a seminal figure representing the nation-building ethos of the first republic. His early work captures elite preoccupations with scientifically defined national progress and exemplifies how dominant sectors of society viewed Afro-Cuban "witchcraft" as dangerous because it was "antimodern." Born into wealth and privilege in Cuba to a Spanish father and a Cuban mother, Ortiz spent much of his early life outside of Cuba, aside from a few years studying law at the University of Havana. He was much influenced by positivist scholars of criminology under whom he studied in Spain and Italy, including the Italian criminologist Césare Lombroso (Dianteill 1995; Riverend 1973). Ortiz's first book, *Los Negros Brujos* (*The Black Witches*), was, in the terms of the day, a "criminal ethnology" (Ortiz 1995/1906: 1). In it he took up Lombroso's theory of criminality as evolutionary degeneracy and followed the model of Bernaldo de Quirós's 1901 study, *La mala vida en Madrid* (*Delinquency in Madrid*) (Bronfman 2002).

What makes Ortiz's work stand out is not his association of the Afro-Cuban occult with the criminal, which was common enough (see for example Israel Castellanos 1926 and Urrutía y Blanco 1882; also see Hagedorn 2001: 199). Nor was Ortiz's work much of an ethnography in the modern sense: he culled his data on contemporary practices from police and newspaper reports and confiscated ritual objects (see Mullen 1987: 115). Nevertheless his historical scholarship on Afro-Cuban experience was groundbreaking and eventually transcended his initial racist framework. I discuss Ortiz's work in some detail in order to explore the valences of the suspicious stance and to show how a folkloric stance slowly emerged alongside of it.

In essence, Ortiz distilled prevailing elite opinions about the "crime" of being black. He wrote *Los Negros Brujos* as the first in what was to be a series of "scientific studies" of "el hampa afrocubana" (the Afro-Cuban underworld). In his view at the time, just about any manifestation of Afro-Cuban volition was an "atavism"—a throwback to a primitive stage of ignorance and criminality. Such atavisms, to quote his 1917 prologue to a later edition, "hold back the progress of the black population of Cuba" (Ortiz 1995/1906: 16).

Progress was a major concern for the new Cuban nation after 1898, emerging as it was from the disarray of civil war and into a new arena of volatile domestic politics amid intervention from the United States. In this era of nation-building, Afro-Cubans who had fought Spain for independence were now demanding a political role in the republic (Ferrer 1999: 7–10; Helg 1995: 3–4).

Afro-Cuban elites, especially, mobilized politically by networking among local associations, forming political parties, and starting newspapers (de la Fuente 2001: 51–52, 55–78; Fernández Robaina 1994: 46–109; Helg 1995: 35–39; Montejo Arrechea 1993: 80–104; Rushing 1992: 326–32, 335–37). Out of this political activity emerged the Partido Independiente de Color, whose demise at the hands of the entrenched white elite culminated in the brutal massacre of several thousand Afro-Cubans in 1912 (Aguirre 1974: 337–53; Fernández Robaina 1994: 208–9; Helg 1995: 209–25; Portuondo Linares 1950). Everything about the rhetoric leading up to the massacres echoed the familiar colonial refrains about the "black peril."

In this context, Ortiz's suspicious stance toward the Afro-Cuban sectors of society reprised long-standing racial tensions. But it is also emblematic of a newer historical narrative of progress, in which the modern nation was threatened by its most backward constituents, Afro-Cubans (de la Fuente 2001: 50). Interestingly, Ortiz faulted the Cuban social environment for holding Afro-Cubans back as much as he did an intrinsically inferior African "cultural level." He expressly rejected the biologized scientific racism of his time, resorting instead to what we might call "cultural racism." Afro-Cuban criminality, in Ortiz's mind, was "understood not as a political act [of resistance], but as a lack of 'culture'" (Dianteill 1995: 19). His theory that a degrading environment causes mental and moral underdevelopment among society's oppressed precluded any interpretation of Afro-Cuban activities as intelligent, let alone political, responses to repression. Deemed the products of ignorance, criminalized practices and associations among Afro-Cubans delegitimized Afro-Cuban struggles for justice and equality, instead legitimizing their oppression.

Within the context of heightening racial tensions, however, black witches were more than a symbol of Afro-Cuban ignorance and more than a symptom of social ills. Ortiz portrayed black witches as a real and direct criminal threat to all Cubans, as we see in his sensationalist descriptions of witches murdering children for "black" magic (Ortiz 1995/1906: 83, 104–7, 151–52, 164–66, 172). He additionally argued that their influence could corrupt "vulnerable" lower-class white or almost-white populations, who also lacked mental development. Steeped in ignorance and superstition, these parts of the population would hold back national progress. Thus Ortiz claimed that "witchcraft is an obstacle to civilization" (185).

The metaphors he invoked to explain the threat posed by black witches counterposed superstition to science, which promised to lead the march of progress. In one telling statement, he asserts that "witchcraft is the petri dish for the development of the criminal microbe contained in the psyche of the witch" (182).[9] His metaphor blends the novel sciences of criminology and microbiology, both of which promised to cure ills of the individual and the social body. Because Ortiz considered crime as much an epidemic as yellow fever, he maintained that crime could be similarly cured by isolating the infectious agents to prevent further contagion (187–89). Indeed, he used the metaphor of social hygiene in describing how to rid society of crime and superstition (185–87).

Ortiz was not alone in turning the threat of witchcraft into an epidemiological issue.[10] As Bronfman documents, police in the early republic relied on public health and sanitation laws to prosecute witches, who were ostensibly protected by new constitutional guarantees of religious freedom (1998: 5–6). Ortiz took on the definition problem posed by the law, first acknowledging that African religions exist in Cuba, then writing them off as primitive, amoral stages of religion, in which the so-called priests also engaged in witchcraft (see for example 1995/1906: 64, 128). In his early criminological analysis, black witchcraft threatened modern progress in Cuba, which could be achieved only by educating the populace to accept scientific advances.

The power of the hygiene metaphor derives from its links to the well-established metaphor of contagion. Colonial and now republican elites feared the contagion of too many black bodies on the island, the threat of contagious diseases such as cholera and yellow fever among those black bodies, and the contagion of insurrection among them, too. One proposed solution to what elites called the island's "Africanization" was to "whiten" the collective Cuban body by encouraging only white immigration. Discriminatory immigration policies for this purpose were renewed in the early years of the republic, although the demand for cheap labor soon brought an influx of Antillean laborers to parts of the island where Haitians in particular were scapegoated and demonized as newcomers and for being black (de la Fuente 2001: 47–50: Helg 1990: 101–4).

Ortiz proposed a different sort of whitening in *Los Negros Brujos*. He called for de-Africanization of the Cuban population through education, together with police efforts to isolate, prosecute, and reform those most intransigently African figures, black witches (180–200). His lurid accounts of their antisocial activities left no doubt that they were a plague on society: murder, sexual deviance, vengeance, mutilation and abuse of women and children, even necrophagy are featured in his accounts. By mobilizing the metaphor of contagion, he could argue that these practices would not disappear on their own, but would require scientifically driven efforts to eradicate them. Moreover, the historical logic embedded in his suspicious stance made national progress incumbent upon success in de-Africanizing the population.

Black magic becomes folklore, 1920s–1940s

Denied equitable participation in mainstream Cuban society and persecuted for activities deemed too African to assimilate into a new, modern nation, Afro-Cubans nonetheless continued to struggle for self-definition and social advancement by both assimilative and markedly African means. Afro-Cuban religions continued to be practiced secretly much as they were during the colonial era. The tragedy of 1912 effectively quashed national Afro-Cuban political organizing in the ensuing decades.[11] The smaller-scale, local, and often underground struggles were also masked by the nation's strengthening ideology of racial equality through mestizaje: the idea that the defining character of Cubans is precisely their unique racial and cultural hybridity (de la Fuente 2001: 176–92).[12] Cubans reacting against U.S. imperialism mobilized this mestizo Cubanidad in opposition to the *yanquis*, even as some Cubans imported virulent U.S. models of racism (de la Fuente 2001: 204–5; Fernández Robaina 1994: 134–35, 141–46).

The ideology of mestizaje demanded that the African as well as the European contributions to Cubanidad be revalorized as positive contributions. Indeed, the 1920s are marked by the Cuban elite's discovery of the treasure of Afro-Cuban folklore. Inspired by the new nation's ideology of a creolized national identity, there arose a folkloric stance toward Afro-Cuban religions. Fernando Ortiz emerged as the spokesperson and protector of what his continuing research, now with actual practitioners, led him to reinterpret as the value of African contributions to creolized Cuban culture. He continued his historical research on African-derived religions, ritual societies, and festivals, as well as on the Cuban language, and later, Cuban music (see for example 1973/1921, 1981/1951). He tracked the African words that had come into the Cuban lexicon and helped differentiate Cuban from other varieties of Spanish (1922, 1924, 1991/1924). The national language, like the citizenry, was a little bit "Congo" and a little bit "Carabalí." Out of his wide-ranging historical studies, Ortiz developed his Cuban answer to Herskovits's theory of acculturation (1970/1947). Whereas acculturation focused on the survival of some African cultural elements in the face of an overwhelmingly dominant European cultural system, Ortiz's notion of transculturation emphasized a more equitable situation in which both sets of cultural influences could recombine to form new hybrid forms, like Santería, that fused African and European religious principles.

Instead of displaying confiscated ritual objects and mug shots of criminals, Ortiz now arranged for folkloric performances of Afro-Cuban sacred music and dance and organized journals dedicated to Cuban folklore and history. In his wake, musicians, artists, and writers of the 1920s and 1930s self-consciously incorporated Afro-Cuban elements into their own work in the movement known as "Afrocubanismo" (Matibag 1996; R. Moore 1997; Mullen 1987; Rodríguez 1994). While the movement paralleled the Harlem Renaissance, Garveyism, and the rise of *négritude* elsewhere in the Black Atlantic, Afrocubanismo was primarily an artistic movement among (mostly white) Cuban elites. Scholars of Afrocubanismo have noted its nationalistic political overtones, which are apparent in its focus on black artistic and cultural contributions to an overarching Cubanidad (de la Fuente 2001; R. Moore 1997; K. Y. Morrison 1999). Indeed, as Robin Moore argues, Afrocubanismo was highly ambivalent toward Cuban blacks and contemporary Afro-Cuban cultural expressions, and middle class black Cubans were highly critical of its stereotyped and exoticizing depictions of them (1997: 210–13, 220–21).

The lasting impact of Afrocubanismo has been to delineate an Afro-Cuban folklore that encompasses all cultural forms marked as African and to locate these forms in a nationalist historical narrative of progress through racial and cultural hybridization. Markedly African cultural forms in this brand of historical consciousness are emblems of the past. The narrative's present is the moment of harmonious fusion of different cultural elements: Ortiz called this the Cuban *ajiaco* or stew, while Afro-Cuban poet Nicolás Guillén stated "the spirit of Cuba is mestizo" (1972: 114, v.1; see also K. Y. Morrison 1999 and Ortiz 1973: 154–55).

Construed as an historical anachronism, Afro-Cuban religion came to have value primarily as a "signifier of otherness" in Cuban culture, as its "nationalist alter/native" (Matibag 1996: 94). Living religious practices and practitioners were transformed into icons of the past that could be comfortably encountered through folkloric performances, such as those first organized by Fernando Ortiz himself (Hagedorn 2001: 197), or by reading works like folklorist Lydia Cabrera's *El Monte* (1993). Even ritual objects confiscated in police raids were placed on display in the University of Havana's anthropology museum (Bronfman 1998: 8–9). Meanwhile, the generation of African-born ex-slaves and *mambises*, Afro-Cuban independence fighters, died out, and memories of whose grandmother was Congo and whose grandfather was Carabalí began to fade. The African presence became the stuff of museums, scholarly histories, literary flavor, and folkloric performances that informed elite imaginings of a homogenous, mesticized present, in which racial problems were ignored or relegated to the past.[13]

It was within this developing folkloric stance toward Afro-Cuban cultural expression in general that the word "Santería" gained currency as a name for a specific religion, initially among scholars and only later among practitioners. In folklore studies circles, Lachatañeré was the first to advocate the term "Santería." In his book *¡Oh, Mío Yemayá!*, first published in 1938, he initially defined Santería, "in its discriminatory sense" as "witchcraft," thus echoing the suspicious stance Ortiz had held (1992: 90–91). Lachatañeré pointed out that the word's embedded reference to the *santos*, or Catholic saints, suggested the "disfigurement" of the original Yoruba beliefs in contact with Catholicism. In almost the same breath, he described the "perfect harmony" of Santería's Yoruba and Catholic blend—transculturation in action (1992: 90–91).[14]

By emphasizing Santería's status as a creolized form and as a full and proper religious system, Lachatañeré located it in the present, less a historical anachronism than a syncretic symbol of a true and current Cubanidad. Like Ortiz before him, Lachatañeré began to isolate out of the general background of popular religion and magic those Santería and Lucumí practices conforming most closely to European models of religion. One powerful rhetorical move was to deploy properly religious labels such as "priests," "pantheon," and "deities," in contrast to negatively valued terms such as "witches," "spirits," and "black magic." The folkloric project of classifying and describing Afro-Cuban cultural forms—not just Santería, but Palo and Abakuá (a men's secret society deriving from Calabar-area Efik/Ibibio societies), and the herbal lore, ritual languages, music, dance, social organization, and ceremonies that characterized them—also served to create the polarizations, described in chapter 2, that eventually differentiated Santería as the most perfectly syncretic and most properly religion-like form among those comprising the popular religious complex.

Although the label "Santería" did not immediately catch on, other scholars and practitioners contributed to the sanctification of Lucumí practices as superior among popular Afro-Cuban cultural forms. Some, including Havana santero Nicolas Angarica in the 1950s, continued to refer to the "Lucumí religion."[15] Angarica wrote several books on Lucumí religion with the stated goal of differentiating it from what folklorists like Ortiz and Cabrera (at least initially) had depicted as an undifferentiated tangle of Afro-Cuban folk beliefs (see for example Cabrera 1993/1954).

The very fact that Angarica, an Afro-Cuban santero, sought to enter into scholarly discourse about his religion, and that he emphasized his credentials as an actual practitioner in doing so, demonstrates how much the new folkloric discourse on Santería in the 1930s–1950s differed from the "criminal ethnology" era of Ortiz's *Los Negros Brujos*. And yet, at no point did the folkloric stance toward Santería fully supplant the suspicious stance. Angarica himself recounts the persecution that forced practitioners to fiercely guard their religious secrets (n.d.b: 81). An examination of Angarica's books in light of works by other folklorists allows us to consider the interactions among the three evaluative stances toward Santería during the latter part of Cuba's second republic in the 1940s and 1950s. The intercultural space generated by their interactions was rife with tensions, especially where partial congruence between two stances provided new opportunities but also opened up new contradictions. The sacred and folkloric stances might agree that Santería had value, but for rather different reasons. Although the folkloric stance gave Santería a new cachet, it did so at a cost to the sacred stance. Santeros found themselves squeezed between ongoing repression and the tantalizing, but secularizing, potential of folkloricization. This double bind arose in part because santeros and folklorists increasingly jostled to control how Santería's sacred stance would be portrayed in folkloric accounts and performances.

Competing interpretations of Santería

The emergence of folklorists with claims to religious insidership had a significant impact on the sacred stance. On one hand, the folkloric stance could augment public acceptance of the sacred stance by giving voice to actual practitioners. However, the folkloric ethos of disclosure and secular explanation came into conflict with tenets of the sacred stance, not least by reducing what santeros understood as living worship practices with profound spiritual consequences into quaint, decontextualizable components: dances, songs, divinations, altars. Let us examine how the emblematic folklorists Ortiz, Lachatañeré, Cabrera, and Angarica straddled the metacultural divides before them.

Angarica, an Afro-Cuban autodidact of humble origins, was a santero in Havana (Dianteill 2000: 218–20). Lachatañeré, a mulatto from Santiago, apparently resented his exclusion from the elite, white academy that embraced Ortiz, but turned that outsidership into a virtue by claiming an insidership-by-racial-association in Santería. It is unclear whether Lachatañeré, who came from a prestigious family in less color-bound Santiago de Cuba, was actually a practitioner.[16] Certainly, there would have been social distance between mulattos from politically connected families and black residents of poor neighborhoods where Santería first took root in Santiago. Meanwhile, a new generation of folklorists from the white elite, epitomized by Lydia Cabrera, touted their connections among poor, Afro-Cuban practitioners, even as they projected a certain ironic distance from their informants' beliefs.[17]

These various degrees of "insider" folklorists raised authenticity as a new concern of the folkloric stance. Consider how Ortiz opens a 1937 article entitled "The sacred music of the Yoruba blacks in Cuba." Ortiz originally presented the article as an introductory talk at a performance of sacred Yoruba music. He begins with a Lucumí invocation, as if opening an actual religious ritual. He does not translate the Lucumí words, but instead switches to an exegetical voice to explain their religious function:

¡Aggó Ilé! ¡Aggó Ya! ¡Aggó Olofi! ¡Olóum mbaa!

These phrases and ritual gestures are a simple invocation to the Yoruba gods, so that, in reproducing their chants, the spirits do not take offense and stop treating us with pious benignity.[18]

Note the multivocality of his voicing, somewhere between believer and folklorist. By voicing what he then glosses as the authentic religious opening to a "real" ceremony, and by including himself and those present —"us"—as the beneficiaries of the spirits' goodwill, Ortiz is playing along the boundaries between sacred and folkloric performance. His gesture promises that the performance will be authentic, because the great folklorist does what any santero would do, even if we are left suspecting that his delivery is primarily tongue-in-cheek and theatrical. That is, he momentarily inhabits the sacred stance, but within the larger frame provided by his now-solidly folkloric stance toward Santería.

Fernando Ortiz's transition from what I have called the suspicious to the folkloric stance toward Santería is well known. Indeed, both Cuban and international scholars have lauded his role in revalorizing Afro-Cuban cultural forms by bringing them to the attention of the mainstream (Hagedorn 2001: 173–74, 193–94). However, Ortiz's personal transition does not indicate a complete social transformation, as Hagedorn suggests when she concludes that "the criminalization of sacred practice was gradually replaced with 'spectacle-ization'" (197). The folkloric stance toward Santería never fully supplanted the suspicious stance in broader society. Instead, both secular stances continued (and continue) to coexist, each carving out a distinct discursive space associated with the distinct institutions to which each anchored (police brotherhoods on one hand and folklore societies on the other, for example) and holding distinct versions of historical consciousness. Their coexistence alongside the sacred stance of practitioners produced a rich, complex interspace for negotiating Santería's social value, one permeated by dynamics of social power. Thus could Angarica enter the scholarly debate of the 1950s to critique Cabrera's understanding of Afro-Cuban traditions at the same time that he reported suffering recriminations for his beliefs as recently as 1944. Santería practitioners continued to experience police harassment and to keep their practices underground throughout the republican era, and few were in a position to enter into the scholarly discussion. I suspect that they attended Ortiz's folklore lectures and demonstrations only in their capacity as authentic performers.

If Ortiz's work transitioned between two very different secular stances toward Santería, Angarica straddled the sacred and folkloric stances in his books. The prologue writer for two Angarica books, Dr. José Roque de la Nuez, signs off with his ritual name, which suggests that he, too, straddled interpretive stances. In his prologue to the first book, *Lucumí al alcance de todos* (*Lucumí within everyone's reach*), Roque de la Nuez decries those "modern writers" who have shaped public opinion by creating "a state of make-believe" (un estado de Confeccionismo) contrary to anything professed by practitioners of African religions, who "never have put into practice HUMAN SACRIFICE, as has been erroneously circulated" (Angarica n.d.a: 3). Roque de la Nuez refers here to ongoing sensationalist journalism about black witches ritually murdering children (echoes of Ortiz)—journalism that insidiously played to an entrenched suspicious stance.

Angarica's books themselves have had a double trajectory, serving as contributions to folkloric understanding and as instruction manuals intended for religious practitioners. Angarica addresses "commentators and lecturers" in his introduction, but writes to *Iguoros*, a Lucumí word meaning "priests"—religious insiders—throughout the main text.[19] Santeros then and now have certainly taken up Angarica's work in the tradition of "libretas de santo" (sacred notebooks), which León has described as "written oral tradition" (1971: 139). Indeed, many santeros have copied entire portions of Angarica's books into their personal notebooks. Santeros simultaneously decry his willingness to publish secrets and eagerly consult what have gained the status of canonical texts within Santería.

Why was Angarica, a santero, willing to publish religious secrets? Perhaps his motives are evident when he explains how santeros were often afraid to teach even their own children for fear of being discovered. Rather than lose the precious knowledge or see the religion further distorted, he may have decided to ensure its, and perhaps his own, posterity by tapping into folkloric interest. Then too, as Dianteill argues, he may have wished to convey a "legitimate image" of the Lucumí religion (2000: 262).

Angarica's books have been more successful than he could have imagined. Unlike Ortiz's books, which have been regularly republished over the years by Cuban state and American university presses, Angarica's books have been reproduced in an underground economy. Indeed, if plagiarism is the highest honor, Angarica would be pleased to know that *botánica* shops from New York to Havana carry photocopies or retyped versions of his books, which may or may not advertise his authorship or even bear his name. Only Lydia Cabrera's often-cribbed *El Monte* (1954) and *Anagó* (1958), a Lucumí glossary, seem to have attained equal honor as religious canon on the streets of Havana and in the notebooks of santeros (see Dianteill 2000: 228–29).

Angarica's books, in their ongoing circulation, trace out the double binds that the two secular stances created for santeros. The continuing metaculture of suspicion toward things Afro-Cuban forced most practitioners to stay underground, whether they were impoverished, ghettoized blacks or wealthy whites sneaking out for a ceremony. The emerging folkloric stance gave Santería a new cultural cachet, but only when mediated by the distancing discourses of historical research or folkloric performance. Folklore sought to reveal what was hidden and explain what was occult, creating a new double bind for santeros, who might have enjoyed the attention but certainly feared the social and spiritual consequences of revealing their secrets.

I have already suggested that the folkloric stance arose and persists because of its relationship to a compelling ideology of national identity based on creolization. The object called "Santería" can be made to fit this ideology, especially if Santería is construed not as Lucumí or even Afro-Cuban but as just plain Cuban (as some Cuban folklorists I spoke with would have it). Within the ideological matrix of a creolized nation, a santero resisting the urge to relegate his "superstitions" to the past and reveal his secrets remains marginalized, cut off from the new commercial possibilities offered by folklore. In the realm of political life, too, republican elites and then later the Revolutionary state mobilized the same national ideology to condemn black Cubans as racist, counterrevolutionary, and unpatriotic if they insisted on addressing racism or

recognizing a separate black culture (de la Fuente 2001: 3–4). This marginalization or appropriation of any explicitly Afro-Cuban stance, whether religious or
political, fits the hegemonic workings of a mestizo national ideology, as scholars have shown for other Latin American contexts (Rahier 2003; Wade 2001;
Williams 1991; Wright 1990). Indeed, one common aspect of a national "myth
of mestizaje" is to sustain contradictory attitudes of both "pride in African-
influenced culture and persistent bias" (R. Moore 1997: 15), an ambivalence we
can now account for as the result of interacting interpretive stances.

Contemporary metacultural double binds

It is hard to avoid slipping into the present tense when discussing how the secular stances of suspicion and folklore pose difficulties for anyone who has adopted a sacred stance toward Santería. The same three stances toward Santería
continue to coexist in early twenty-first-century Cuba, and the tensions among
them continue to give Santería a place of prominence, while generating quan-
daries for santeros.

Let us return to the Museum of the Yoruba Cultural Association where the
chapter began and revisit its bulletin board. The notice calling for good ritual
hygiene to combat the spread of dengue-carrying mosquitos, as benevolent
and reasonable as it may seem, indicates that the suspicious stance toward
Santería has survived, fitting neatly into the Revolution's scientific socialist
framework alongside the folkloric stance that allows a religious association
to open a museum.[20] As it turns out, this notice was part of a larger public
health initiative against dengue that targeted supposedly unsanitary religious
practices like maintaining vessels of sacred water on altars. A santero in Santiago had told me of visits from public health inspectors during an outbreak
of dengue in the mid-1990s when they insisted that santeros throw away the
"unhygienic" water, water santeros regard as holy and potent. These visits were
insulting and traumatic for santeros, not least because they evoked an earlier,
pre-Revolutionary era during which police raided practitioners' homes, de-
stroying or confiscating their sacred objects, also in the name of public health
and hygiene (Angarica n.d.b: 81; de la Fuente 2001: 50–51, 352 n.115; Hagedorn
2001: 107–15).

The public health initiative fits into a larger pattern of ongoing official suspicions about Afro-Cuban religions. In a paper presented at an American Anthropological Association conference in 2001, Cuban researcher Marcos Marin
Llanes discussed public health concerns about santeros, who, the researcher

suggested, were ignorant of health issues because they lack cultural sophistication. Meanwhile, well-intentioned researchers, civil servants, and police perpetuate the harassment of santeros. Many santeros I met had stories about police interfering in Santería rituals, even carting all the participants off to jail because practitioners had failed to obtain licenses to hold the ceremonies as the law requires. Nor are civil servants alone in their nagging suspicions. In Santiago, stories continue to circulate about santeros purportedly arrested for sacrificing children in rituals. Three university professors and a santero separately described to me a recent case (no one could remember the year) in which a child victim had been a disabled relative of one of the alleged perpetrators.

The old suspicion that Santería is linked to crime occasionally gets smuggled into recent scholarship. Take, for example, Argüelles and Hodge Limonta's account of Cuba's syncretic religions (1991), an account that ostensibly adopts the folkloric stance. While they reject the Revolution's initial hard-line position that religious adherence is counterrevolutionary, they nonetheless conclude that believers tend to be found in less educated and less politically active (that is, less revolutionary) sectors of society. They also use their data to support what they describe as a mesticizing of religious practitioners as more poor whites succumb to the attraction of religions like Santería (147). In such claims, we find the covert return of the contagion metaphor, together with the implication that superstitions like Santería will disappear with the education of adherents. In an even clearer continuation of the suspicious stance, Argüelles and Hodge Limonta briefly reprise the criminal link to religion when they point out that unauthorized religious activity has caused problems in prisons (167–70).

Suspicion haunts Argüelles and Hodge Limonta's text even as they assert their folkloric stance most strenuously. In a discussion of the Revolution's impact on religious practices in Cuba, the authors argue that it rescued the Afro-Cuban folk heritage from obscurity by revalorizing it (142–45). Implicit in this claim, of course, is that Santería is something from a darker age. By folkloricizing Santería, by setting it into a historical narrative where it is doomed to die out unless preserved explicitly by folklorists, the authors imply that Santería's role in that narrative is as a remnant of Cuba's past.[21] For the suspicious stance still embedded in Revolutionary notions of scientific progress, the current fluorescence of popular religiosity must be disturbing indeed, since it signals the Revolution's apparent failure to sufficiently educate and raise its populace out of crime and superstition.

The *doble moral* of Santería today

An encounter I had while visiting the Museum of the Yoruba Cultural Association illustrates how religious practitioners themselves navigate the interspace produced by conflicting evaluative stances toward their religion. As I stood reading the bulletin board, a man entered from the street, glanced at the guards, and sidled over to talk with me. He showed me his Association card to "prove" that he was a legitimate babalawo and surreptitiously offered to give me an inexpensive Ifá consultation in his home or lead me to a *paladar*, a private (sometimes illegal) restaurant. By approaching me to offer these services, the babalawo enacted the all-too-common role of what Cubans call a *jinetero* (hustler), one who makes a living by guiding tourists into the mostly underground economy of private dining and lodging, prostitution, and other subversions and co-optings of the state-run tourist economy. In seeking to recruit me as a paying client for his religious services, the babalawo engaged in a behavior that many religious practitioners I know would condemn as "commercializing the religion."

My field consultants in Santiago were quite familiar with the double bind of the babalawo in the museum. He was, we might say, trapped by economic circumstances into taking an opportunity to "commercialize" his religion, even if doing so was questionable both in its legality and its religious implications. In the eyes of some santeros, those who aid in the folkloricization of Santería are also guilty of "commercializing the religion."

Santeros recognized these double binds, even referring to them as inducing a case of "la doble moral" (double morality), a term Cubans use to describe the problematics of taking contradictory public and private stances, namely espousing Revolutionary values while discretely subverting those values in the name of economic or political survival. The ongoing "special period in time of peace," declared in 1990 after the 1989 collapse of the Soviet Union and its support of the Cuban economy, has made such double morality endemic. The government radically changed course to prevent complete economic collapse by rapidly developing a new tourism economy and legalizing the dollar to better channel the flow of remittances from abroad into state enterprises like "dollar stores." This new economy has introduced gross distortions of the classless socialist ideal that still circulates in official calls for citizens to sacrifice in order to save the fatherland. Revolutionary fervor is harder to come by when only a small minority of Cubans directly benefit from official work in tourism and the dollar economy, while everyone else continues to experience severe shortages, stagnant wages, and rising prices.

Desperate economic times have forced all Cubans, not just santeros, to cope with hardships by "inventing" (their word) often morally dubious or illegal private, entrepreneurial activities to generate income in dollars. Those without officially sanctioned jobs in tourism have found ways to unofficially tap into the new tourist-driven dollar economy, often by offering services to tourists: operating private taxis, offering unlicenced rooms for rent, opening speakeasy-style private restaurants, and even engaging in *jineterismo* (hustling and prostitution).[22] Some stalwart supporters of the Revolution lamented the situation that forced them to resort to illegal means to feed their families; for others, these activities were necessary adaptations to circumstances or were everyday acts of private resistance against the constraints of the system.

Caught in a moral conundrum, to salvage the Revolution or to scrape together enough dollars to make ends meet, Cubans joked about living a doble moral in which one publicly supports the Revolution and decries as counterrevolutionary the very activities one privately conducts in order to survive. To dwell on the contradictions of living the doble moral is to court insanity, as filmmaker Fernando Pérez teases out in the 1998 film *La Vida Es Silbar (Life Is to Whistle)*. In the film, a psychologist takes his patient on a tour of downtown Havana to demonstrate to her that she is not alone in having a "complex" that makes her faint when she hears the word "sex." The psychologist demonstrates that people on the street drop like flies when he says "doble moral."

From the 1960s until the late 1980s, some religious Cubans practiced their own brand of the doble moral because the Revolutionary state discouraged religiosity by withholding privileges such as university scholarships, certain jobs, and party membership from those who publicly declared their faith.[23] Many santeros told me that they had practiced in secret while maintaining a publicly atheistic stance, thus living what they described as a doble moral. In one conversation, a santero-folklorist pointedly asked me what I would have done had my chance to attend university hinged on denying my religion. He went on to describe how some practitioners became folklore researchers or performers in order to find an officially sanctioned cover for their religious interests without losing their privileges. When the official climate toward religiosity thawed in the early 1990s, he said, many of his colleagues began to get initiated and to openly wear their religious beads (an observation also recorded in Wedel [2004: 35]).

The contemporary practice of the doble moral may also have deep roots in resistance strategies adopted by enslaved Africans who engaged in various types of subterfuge for their very survival, including disguising the worship of their own deities under the cover of Catholicism. Even today, the doble moral sometimes seems to be a means of covert resistance and is linked to critiques of the Revolution, but it is equally if not better thought of as a pragmatic strategy of coping with political and economic constraints.

I heard many Cubans, including santeros, make circumspect criticisms of the Revolution. People sometimes spoke sadly of their government falling short of Revolutionary goals and ideals they believed in. They lamented that the Revolution's promises for a better quality of life had been betrayed by the hardships of the special period. The santeros who offered critiques in my presence tended to be well educated and sometimes, though not always, occupied the dual positions of being both private religious practitioners and state-salaried researchers. For example, one santero-folklorist I interviewed in 1999 expressed his disillusionment with the Revolution as a reason for having turned to religion some 25 years earlier.

> There was an epoch before my initiation as a santero in which, here in Cuba . . . the cult of men was practiced, because of their ideas and their histories. And I—like all who belong to my generation—joined into this current of believing in men. Until one moment in which I stopped believing in men, and I had the need to find someone in whom to believe. And then I arrived at this religion. I liked it, I began to believe in the gods, and here I am.[24]

This santero's profession as a state-employed folklorist requires him to represent the state's official stance that Santería is part of the nation's folk heritage—a heritage to be studied, represented by museums, enacted in performances, even promoted to foreign tourists, but certainly not to be worshipped. His story, however, reverses the official order by having him arrive at religion as a replacement for faith in the Revolution. I heard similarly subversive narratives from a number of santero-researchers explaining their choice to become religious. Moreover, as professional folklorists they lived the reality of all professionals during the special period: their peso-salaries amounted to perhaps $20 a month in a consumer economy of hard-currency prices, in which hotel maids and taxi drivers earned far more in tips than any professional could match in regular salary. In this economic climate, santeros often took the pragmatic line that the saints help those who help themselves.

Competing moralities

As Cubans themselves explain it, the doble moral is also—perhaps primar-ily—an ever-evolving pragmatic response to the limitations and opportunities of the moment. The state's project of "folkloricizing" Santería has presented new opportunities for private entrepreneurs, including santeros, to explore the commercial potential of *santurismo* or Santería-tourism (Hagedorn 2001: 9, 220–22). *Santurismo*, alongside folkloricization, has contributed to making Santería highly visible in contemporary Cuba. The special period has acceler-ated the state's promotion of a folkloric stance toward Santería, but now with the goal of converting foreign tourists' curiosity about the exotic into dollars: public performances of ceremonies; museums of religious altars; books, CDs, and religious dolls and trinkets for sale; even folklore study-tours and inter-national conferences for the adventurous. In response, santeros worry about the corrosive effect of the state's incursions and the new commercial ethos on sacred values. Many of the santeros I interviewed were quick to point out other santeros' transgressions—including overcharging for religious ceremo-nies; initiating new priests, especially rich foreigners, out of greed rather than divine injunction; and trading religious secrets for dollars—even while they too tended to act pragmatically to "resolve" their own economic difficulties.

Santeros themselves have discovered the commercial potential of religious entrepreneurship, creating a new form of doble moral. Despite a constant cho-rus of concerns about other santeros commercializing the religion, santeros are proud of their own stables of foreign godchildren, and some actively seek out foreigners who will pay in dollars for a ceremony or consultation. The rise of religious practitioners who see the folkloric-*cum*-commercial potential of the sacred has everything to do with the success of the folkloric stance. In later chapters, these dynamics will repeatedly emerge in terms of tensions between communal values and personal interests and in terms of the critiques and con-troversies that help hold the community together. In one instance, described more completely in chapter 7, I witnessed how the religious initiation of a Eu-ropean visitor erupted into a bitter controversy between two groups of practi-tioners in Santiago. The issue was ostensibly over whether the new European santero would be allowed to undergo a second initiation into Ifá. Each group accused the other side of allowing its financial "interest" to trump its sacred duty. In this and countless other situations I witnessed, santeros positioned themselves within a sacred domain and critiqued other santeros by trying to position them outside this domain as financially "interested."[25]

Santeros also worked to preempt criticism by trying to present their own motives as purely religious. Such positioning could get especially tricky when someone regularly crossed between sacred and folkloric stances as a santero and researcher. While I sometimes heard folklorists justify their research to other santeros by referring to the importance of scholarly inquiry, all knew that being a folklore researcher or performer gives access to foreigners and their cash. By virtue of occupation, researchers, and to a lesser extent performers, garnered higher overall social status than those who lived completely in the informal economy carved out by religious activity. Members of both occupations could hope to travel abroad or to work in some capacity with or for foreign tourists. While performers mediated sacred culture for tourist consumption, folklorists, too, could cash in on their middleman status between santeros and foreigners, either directly by serving as specialized informal tour guides or indirectly by writing books or producing recordings. In the hard scrabble to "resolve" financial difficulties, santeros without connections to the state-sponsored folklore institutions sometimes expressed resentment toward those who worked as folklorists or who collaborated with them. Folklorists, then, became especially suspect for commercializing the religion.

My teacher and godfather Emilio occupied such a dual role, as folklorist and as santero. His occupation gave him high visibility in the community, with which came prestige and wealth but also close scrutiny from all sides. Working as he did with foreigners, Emilio took special care of his image among other santeros. On one particularly dramatic occasion, Emilio made a statement before me and an entire assembled family of santeros we were visiting.[26] The occasion was the evening of San Lázaro's Day, and we were hiking around the city, my video camera in tow, to record how people in traditionally Afro-Cuban neighborhoods celebrate this venerated saint. When Emilio made his statement, we were seated with about eight people in a living room, the corner of which had an enormous altar to San Lázaro, complete with an almost life-sized statue of the saint, beautifully dressed in purple robes. The lady of the house had been answering my questions about her religious practice, but as the interview proceeded, she would often defer to Emilio, the *profe* or "Prof" as people addressed him on the street.

Emilio eventually took over the interview, and with my camera trained exclusively on him, continued to explain various points of Santería's history in the city. A *tambor* singer who lived on the street popped his head in the door to greet us, which started Emilio critiquing another well-known singer, Germán, for too blatantly working to get gifts out of saints who possessed their devotees during such ceremonies. He went on: "There are people who sell Santería. They seek in Santería only the commercial part. That should not be done." While critiquing how other santeros commercialize the religion, the irony of having arrived at the house with me and my shiny video recorder must have hit him because he rapidly shifted gears and eloquently began to reprimand me as if I had been pestering him to share religious secrets:

> No matter who you are, however many dollars you have, never will I tell you what is done within the sacred room. For this you have to initiate. There are people who don't follow this.

His demeanor changed from friendly "professor" expounding on what he knows best to stern santero wagging his finger while renouncing the allure of my foreignness, my dollars, and my questions. He attested to the camera and to all present that he would not violate his religious code of silence about the secrets of initiation. Managing his dual role as respected folklorist (with me, his foreign student) and santero (with me, a potential initiate) meant straddling the doble moral of showing respect for religious values while being perceived as pursuing his financial interest in working with me.

While santero-folklorists like Emilio are under special scrutiny by the state and other santeros because of their dual roles, many santeros now find opportunities to come into contact with foreigners. I found that even as they critiqued folklorists for violating the Regla and betraying religious secrets, santeros without official connections were nonetheless quick to play the folklore expert when a situation (such as my appearance at their door) presented itself. Whatever their situation, those assuming both sacred and folkloric stances toward Santería needed to straddle the doble moral of respecting religious values (or Revolutionary values of folklore) while pursuing their own financial interest.

Conclusion

In this chapter I have sought to account for Santería's current prominence and ambivalent position as the quintessential Cuban/Afro-Cuban religion by arguing that it is the consequence of an ongoing, long-term historical pattern of interactions among three distinct metacultural stances toward Santería. These stances toward Santería have offered up competing visions of what Santería is and what value it has for Cuban society. Each stance represents different historical narratives with distinct sensibilities about the role of an African presence in the development of the Cuban nation. A comparison of early contributors to folklore studies illustrates how the three stances toward Santería have inter-acted to produce various double binds for religious practitioners that have fed into the overarching doble moral that has characterized Cuban society during the Revolution, especially since the 1990s. In the case of the well-known doble moral of disguising religiosity as interest in folklore, folkloric promotion of Santería may have actually encouraged participation in Santería, though with the twin dangers of infecting sacred practice with commercial interest or of questioning the Revolution's success by resorting to outdated superstition. The special period of the 1990s has induced santeros to continue to straddle the sacred and the folkloric stances less out of fear than to cash in on Santería's commercial potential. Angarica's passing complaint in the 1950s about santeros using religion for profit suggests that this contemporary double bind, too, has had a long historical trajectory—longer perhaps than contemporary santeros realize.

Having thus set Santería in broader context and raised some of the issues of identity, practice, and belonging that santeros face, in subsequent chapters I examine the interpretation of religious experience and the building of religious community among santeros in Santiago de Cuba. The competing evaluative stances I have sketched in broad historical terms will reappear as positions santeros fluidly align themselves with or against in the course of the localized, face-to-face interactions that make up much of daily life. Rather than seeing these stances as context in which the text of everyday life unfolds, I wish to emphasize the creative role of everyday life and discourse in generating them. That is, each time someone invokes a stance, they add a link to an ongoing speech chain, through which are constituted the cultural and metacultural forms that we experience as tangible, replicable, and historically continuous (or perhaps occasionally novel) culture.

II

Religious Experience

From Skepticism to Faith

Narratives of Religious Experience

*The gods toss all life into confusion . . . that all of us, from our ignorance
and uncertainty may pay them the more worship and reverence.*
—Euripides, Hecuba (l. 956)

Living in Santiago surrounded by santeros, I was immersed in a world of portentous signs. I could not stay on the sidelines and merely observe a ritual or
conduct an interview, because more often than not the deities would direct a
warning or piece of advice to me. "She will have to make the saint," an older
santera once said to Emilio while we were interviewing her, interrupting her
own answer to one of my questions. "Obatalá is her 'angel,' isn't he?"[1] At this,
Emilio laughed loudly and gave me a significant glance. "Yes, indeed!" For
him, the santera's sudden inspiration was a divine communication. She was,
we might say, channeling her own "angel" in that moment. As it happened,
Emilio was already convinced that I am a daughter of the oricha Obatalá and
will eventually have to be initiated.[2] During a special divination ceremony we
had attended several months earlier, the officiating priest had interpreted one
sign from the cowrie shells to mean that someone in the room had to initiate. Since all present but I were already santeros, they quickly surmised that
the message of the cowrie oracle was directed to me. And now, months later,
here was additional proof, una comprobación. Emilio strove to teach me how
to recognize proofs of divine communication, usually by presenting narrative
models in which he or others moved from skepticism to faith. It was as if he
were showing me a map of how to cross over into faith.

Even amid my metaphysical uncertainties, my agnostic skepticism always
struggling with my romantic desire for design in the universe, I marvel at how
the web of divine signs envelops anyone involved in Santería or related popu-

lar religious practices. When I am in Santiago among my religious friends, the universe seems populated with causal forces I was not aware of elsewhere. Every event in life is at least potentially imbued with sacred meaning. And yet I found santeros to be a skeptical bunch who are quick to debunk fakes and exaggerations. They are very concerned with *pruebas* (tests, proof) and comprobación (proof, confirmation). How does the logic of the sacred stance work for them?

In part 2 I delve into the sacred stance that I counterposed to other common stances toward Afro-Cuban religions in the previous chapter. Practitioners and ethnographic observers alike perceive in Santería a durable, shared cosmovision—Geertz's "envisaged cosmic order" (1973: 90).[3] I suggest that this sense of a shared cosmovision emerges out of the repeated actions of practitioners, who consistently deploy a particular sacred interpretive stance to interpret events in their experience as evidence of that cosmic order. There is an almost tautological problem at the heart of the dynamics through which stance shapes experience and experience reinforces stance. That is, the envisaged cosmic order comes to seem presupposed, even as each relevant event entails it anew.

In this chapter I consider how the observer on the threshold—the reluctantly intrigued participant—can learn why any particular experience counts to a particular religious participant as an experience of the sacred, a divine communication, a sign. My first task will be to examine santeros' accounts of religious experiences in order to develop an analytical framework for understanding what religious experiences are and how they are recognized (by religious practitioners or ethnographers). At the end of the chapter, I turn to the question of how rituals contribute to the interpretation of events as religious experiences. I focus in particular on santeros' understanding of rituals as methods of divine communication. Then in chapter 5, I look more closely at the interaction between ritual and reflective discourse about ritual in generating publicly negotiable and intersubjective experiences. Throughout, I straddle and ask the reader to straddle that distinctive interspace between ethnographic analysis and the sacred stance.[4]

Little pinches from Ochún

Ochún, oricha of feminine sensuality and of sweet water, signals her presence when she possesses a devotee by laughing. The possessed devotee, as often male as female, will punctuate her dance and speech with peals of highly stylized, high-pitched laughter: "Ha! Ha! Ha!" But santeros say to beware of Ochún's laughter, because, in a reversal common to possession trance, her laughter often signals her displeasure.

Emilio, whose principal oricha ("angel") is Ochún, often waxed eloquent about her beauty and graciousness. He lovingly danced her gracious, rippling dance, so like a river, and plied her altar with honey, squash, gold cloth, and other offerings she favored. But just as rivers can flood and honeybees can sting, Ochún is volatile and demanding of her devotees. Emilio and other santeros recounted to me the trials Ochún and all orichas would bring down upon their devotees: poor health, financial misfortune. Any sort of problem at all could be a divine message. In one conversation, Emilio referred to these trials as "little pinches from Ochún."

> Within Santería they say "little pinches from Ochún." Those are little pinches because she makes something bad befall you so that you will react. . . . Ochún says it like this when she says, "You are my child. Sooner or later you will have to make the saint". . . . She always gives [her children] trials, trials, trials, until they make the saint.[5]

He explained that an oricha brings trouble to a devotee in order to compel the devotee to pay attention to the oricha's desires. Their most common desire is for their devotee to "make the saint" (be initiated). Indeed, most santeros were firm that initiation into Santería is not something a person chooses. Rather, the orichas do the choosing, and they inform their chosen ones of their selection by causing trouble for them. In Emilio's case, he suffered an unbelievable string of robberies, in which his house was repeatedly emptied out, before he heeded Ochún's call to be initiated as her child. Later in the chapter I will examine one version of his narrative in which he recounts how he came to believe.

Emilio's description of sometimes not-so-little "pinches from Ochún" resonates with Hecuba's lament in the chapter epigraph. Like Job in the Old Testament, santeros interpret their suffering as a divine message, which is to say, as a particular kind of religious experience. The central question I consider in this chapter is how devotees come to recognize certain events that befall them as religious experiences—as divine blessings or punishments. As a corollary question, I ask what we can do with the principal data we have of religious experiences, which consist of first-person reports. I consider what santeros' narratives of religious experiences can tell us more generally about this category of experience. One critically important angle to be examined is the role of narratives in the circulation of shared understandings of the kinds of events—

divine messages, hierophanies, ecstasies, agonies, possession trances, "little pinches"—that trigger or can be interpreted as potentially sacred experiences. But beyond the expectations generated by proper context and performance, it is possible to examine how participants in a ritual, for example, come to interpret or reject (and often opinions vary) any particular instance as a bona fide religious experience.

My approach in the first part of the chapter will be to examine how santeros narrate and narrativize their experiences of divine intervention, which is a necessarily retrospective process. My particular interest is in what I call "narratives of conversion," in which santeros recount the experiences through which they decided to get initiated. Such decisions are particularly suggestive because they so often involve a transformation in a person's orientation toward the religious potential in events, and their accounts make explicit the evaluative process a person recalls using to reach a religious interpretation of their experiences. Moreover, the implications santeros built into their narratives of conversion reach out into the present and future, enveloping me and other interlocutors in a world of religious potentiality and divine potency.

"Look, I didn't believe," began Emilio's elderly godfather, when I asked him when and why he had initiated into Santería.[6] "I was unbelieving, during my youth, I went through it without believing." He then related how his wife's life-threatening illness early in their marriage had driven her first to doctors who could not help her and then in search of religious healing. Religious healers confirmed that medicine could not save her, and that only by initiating into Santería would she survive. Her husband had resisted, although he did accompany her to ceremonies in order to learn about the religion. In the end, to save her life, he joined her in undergoing initiation. There they both were, fifty years later. Everything they had—their health, their house, everything—they owed to their saints. His clear implication was that I, too, would reap blessings from the saints if I stepped from the margins of my inquiry to take the plunge of faith and be initiated into the religion.

Santería is not a proselytizing religion per se, but santeros with whom I had a personal connection often told me their stories in ways that positioned me in their initial stage of doubt. The parallels they set up between their disbelieving younger selves and me implied that I, too, would discover the power of the saints in my own life. As Harding suggests in the case of evangelical Christians (2000: 33–40), learning to replicate the speech conventions of believers marks a successful conversion, as the convert can now inhabit the speaking role of one who has witnessed the sacred power of the saints in his or her life.

Defining religious experience

In order to understand the processes through which santeros recognize religious experiences, it is necessary to explore what ethnographers and religious practitioners mean by "religious experience." As I proposed in chapter 1, we need to consider both the phenomenological and interpretive moments of experiences. That is, experiences have meaning because of the interaction between their immediate, sensory effects on one's organism and the explanatory framework through which one apprehends those effects. We can think of these two qualities of religious experience as the *ineffable* and the *noetic* (Proudfoot 1985). The ineffable is, literally speaking, that aspect of experience which resists expression in words. The noetic, as Proudfoot explains, "is best analyzed as an assumed claim about the proper explanation of the experience," which is to say the juncture between experience and epistemology that we might call understanding (187). It is on the noetic component of experience that I now concentrate, and especially the role of retelling and thus narrativizing events in establishing a religious interpretation of experiences.

As I examine the after-the-fact, interpretive work in which santeros engage in order to arrive at religious understandings of events, I consider a narrative of the most dramatic sort of religious experience: one that impels a religious conversion. My example, Emilio's frequently repeated story of his decision to initiate, illustrates how santeros talk about the processes by which faith overcomes skepticism. In recounting a series of disturbing events, Emilio explained why he converted from the more politically comfortable role of atheistic folklorist to become a devotee of Ochún. His narrative creates a plot line out of a series of robberies that targeted his house over several years, interspersed with visits to a santero who divines the reason for his ill fortune: that the oricha Ochún is "claiming his head" or demanding that he initiate. Here, events that must have seemed puzzling or coincidental at the time become, in retrospect, proof that the deities exist and intervene in human lives. The acts of robbery, strung together in sequence and illuminated by divinations, coalesce into a divine communication and so constitute a religious experience strong enough to trigger a person's religious conversion from Communist atheist to openly devout priest of Ochún. A close look at his narrative illustrates the power of narratives to retrospectively organize events into significant patterns that can thus be recognized as particular types of experiences. Following Stromberg (1993: 3), I suggest that this retrospective narrativization is itself "a central element of the conversion." Moreover, although we cannot assume that narratives represent narrators' actual lived experience as events unfold, such narratives do circulate as models for recognizing future religious experiences. To draw upon terminology from previous chapters, narratives serve a metacultural function by delineating culturally specific categories of experience.

Retelling the telling moment: Narratives of conversion experiences in Santería

Consider this narrative fragment with which Emilio began one telling of his conversion story:

> I didn't believe in anyone. Because, ok, I pretty much developed within the Revolutionary process. And at the beginning of the Revolution, at the beginning of the Revolution here, religion was not well regarded at the beginning, in that environment, because there were problems with religious folks. And as I initiated with the process, little by little, I didn't believe in religion. And I had, I had a religious family tradition, but as I was a new generation, I didn't believe. I was a Communist. I didn't believe.[7]

Autobiographical narratives that begin in this way situate the narrated first person back in time, as a former self who did not believe, or at least who openly abstained from religiosity. The past tense signals an endpoint to the narrated self's lack of belief, marking the narrative as about religious conversion. In certain types of American fundamentalist Christianity, such narratives constitute a semiritual genre of religious speech with the emic label "witnessing" (Harding 2000: 36–37). No such formalized genre exists among Cuban santeros, although frequently enough I encountered stories about coming to believe in the saints. I call these stories "narratives of conversion," although advisedly as no Cuban narrator ever used a term like "conversion." And yet, such narratives form a recognizable type, which boils down to this simple schema: "I didn't believe. I have had tests or proofs. Now I believe."

Such narratives in Santería do indeed recount pivotal, transformative events. They are stories, usually autobiographical, but sometimes passed along secondhand, in which someone experiences problems and as a result begins to try out a sacred stance in order to resolve them. As the person adopts that stance more comfortably he or she typically acknowledges the new religious commitment by being initiated, which means undergoing a tremendously expensive and complicated series of ceremonies. As even a quick read of Emilio's statement suggests, however, the transformation may not be as simple as going direct from nonbelief to belief. There is also the possibility of "closeted" believer going public, of Communist "initiate" moving back into family religious traditions, or of disillusioned Revolutionary seeking pragmatic solutions to pressing economic or health problems and only later (if at all) becoming devout.

This brings me to a second caveat about my use of the label "conversion." It is the label I apply to a process that I have seen unfold only in narrative testimonies, never "live" as it happens. Indeed, I am not convinced that one can pinpoint conversion-as-it-is-happening-to-someone-else, at least not in Santería. What would such an event look like? Santería does not have a genre of performance akin to that represented by the born-again Christian genre of "being saved." It may be that the retellings themselves constitute the conversion process more fundamentally than any events they represent—a focus on the performative, rather than referential, functions of conversion narratives (Stromberg 1993). That is, a series of inner struggles and decisions becomes a nameable and describable event only by being organized into a linear narrative. The performance of a "narrative of conversion" is what marks the speaker as a religious believer, and it does so by establishing a point in time at which this religious orientation came to be true of the person. Let us consider how William James described conversion: [8]

> To be converted, to be regenerated, to receive grace, to experience religion, to gain assurance are so many phrases which denote the process, gradual or sudden, by which a self hitherto divided, and consciously wrong, inferior, or unhappy, becomes unified and consciously right, superior and happy, in consequence of its firmer hold upon religious realities. (1922/1902: 189)

For James, conversion is a retrospective label for a transformation accomplished before naming it, or perhaps consummated by naming it. The perspective embedded in James' words is that of the convert, who describes him- or herself as formerly "wrong" and now "right." Whatever the phenomenological inner experience of conversion may be, conversion is indexed by a person's willingness to publicly mark a discontinuity between former self and current self, where the self has undergone a major shift in perspective toward the sacred. Even when no label such as "conversion" is used, as is the case in Santería, the event is recognizable because it is narrated according to certain conventions. Susan Harding describes conversion in fundamentalist

Christianity as "a process of acquiring a specific religious language or dialect" or of "transferring narrative authority . . . to narrate one's life in Christian terms" (2000: 34).

So what purpose do these narratives serve for those who tell them? Simply put, the retelling reaffirms the narrator's current religious orientation by representing his or her transformation from an earlier, nonreligious identity. The retelling thus also models for listeners how to renarrate their lives in terms of Santería; it conveys the telos of Santería by linking ordinary or extraordinary human events to divine interventions.

A brief comparison of Christianity and Santería may help. Much of Christian doctrine views conversion as an ongoing process: not a single "leap of faith" but a continuing series of reaffirmations of identity and faith—the construction of a "sacred self"—in the face of doubts, temptations, and relapses (Csordas 1994; Harding 2000; K. F. Morrison 1992). To practice Santería, too, is a continuous, even daily, choice the believer makes. As I discussed in part 1, the Cuban context presents multiple religious alternatives, each with its own set of social valences. Moreover, the Revolutionary state has advocated atheism with varying degrees of persuasion over the years, although the current stance is permissive of religious expression. It is possible to imagine someone so secretive in their beliefs and practices that no one else knows, but I am interested here in those whose professions of belief shape their public persona.

My premise is quite simply that the stories we tell ourselves about ourselves shape our sense of self, including our religious or secular orientation toward events. Of course, we tell stories about ourselves to others, too, and in doing so perform who we are at two semiotic levels: the level of the narrated event, in which "I" appear as a character, and the level of the narrating interaction, in which "I" interact with others as I do the telling about myself. Identity-work is accomplished through automatic mapping between these two levels of narrated and interactional texts, represented by the contrast between an unbelieving "I-then" in the narration and a religious "I-now" who tells the story (Silverstein 1985, 1992; Wortham 2001).

When someone recounts their religious conversion to a nonbelieving interlocutor, there is the potential for the retelling to serve as what fundamentalist Christians call "witnessing." Note how Susan Harding describes the effects one powerful episode of witnessing had on her during her fieldwork with evangelical Christians:

> I began to acquire the language that (Reverend) Campbell and other pastors and church people spoke to me. I came to know what it meant to

have a soul, a sin nature, a heart; to say, "God spoke to me" and "Satan is real"; to see God's hand in everyday life and the daily news; to know that there is no such thing as an accident, and that everything, no matter how painful or perplexing, has a purpose. I did not convert, but I was learning their language of faith. . . . For years I stood at the crossroads that Campbell and others fashioned for me, in between being lost and being saved, listening." (2000: xi)

In my work on Cuban Santería, I stand at a similar crossroads, listening to the explanations, stories, and advice of Santería practitioners. These conversations, moreover, have a point: to demonstrate the "little pinches" through which God (in Harding's case) or the orichas (in mine) are manifesting themselves in our lives, in ways our interlocutors suggest we ultimately will have to recognize. The performance in Santería most akin to "being saved" is initiation as a priest. However, the saving grace conferred by initiation occurs much more on a practical than on a spiritual plane. Most priests choose their moment to be initiated because they face an insurmountable problem that the saint has, directly or tacitly, promised to resolve only through initiation. Recall Emilio's "little pinches": the saint chooses the person, then inflicts problems on the person until she gets the point that she must initiate.

At the same time, initiation serves a gatekeeping function between mere believers and those whom the orichas have chosen and who have committed to living under their personal guidance as revealed to them in divinations and under spirit possession. Emilio is one such initiate, a "son of Ochún" who is also a professional folklorist. Our relationship, therefore, has been similarly multifaceted: equally professor-student and godfather-goddaughter. Early on, during my visit in 1998, our work consisted mainly of one-on-one lectures about various aspects of Santería. And it is from this early "getting-to-know-you" period that the narrative I now present is drawn.

During this particular two-hour lecture, Emilio had been listing the four reasons why someone decides to initiate: because of family tradition; because of irresolvable problems; because of serious illness; or purely because of affinity for the religion. He followed a first, general example with that of his own godparents (whose story I summarized earlier). Finally, he described his own case, first explaining that while his family had celebrated certain saints' days in the rural Spiritist tradition of drumming and singing, he was the only one who had ever been initiated into Santería. He then launched into the following narrative, which for the purpose of my subsequent discussion, I divide into sections. In the transcription, bold type indicates heavy emphasis, em dashes indicate phrases that run together, and slashes above specific words indicate Emilio's simultaneous finger-tapping on the table for emphasis.[9]

Section A

But, ah, I confronted a problem that when I began to travel abroad thieves persecuted me **a lot**—They persecuted me **a lot**. And I was **always, always** things were being lost to me—things were being lost to me. They **robbed** me—**robbed** me.

Section B

And the **police . found** the **thieves**, but **could** not prosecute them, nor **do anything**, because (2-second pause during which a woman shouts in the distance). Nothing.

Section C

And **then**, I **began** to **get consultations**. And it was that **Ochún** was **demanding** my **head**. It is said in this way. And that as long as **I** didn't make the saint, they **weren't**, the robbers weren't going to stop.

Section D

And I didn't **believe** it. **I was** like **five** or **six years** in **that**. And they were **robbing me. Robbing me, robbing me, robbing me**.

Section E

Until they gave me a **final test**. That they said to me "If you
$$\quad\ /\qquad\qquad\qquad\qquad\quad /////$$
don't make the **saint,** during the **next** trip that you have, you are
$$\qquad\qquad /$$
going to **lose it all**". . . . **Like this they told** me, "You are
$$\qquad\quad /\quad\ /$$
going to **lose** it **all.**

Section F

And I didn't do it like that. "I am going to make the **saint**. Don't worry godfather." Because **then** I had said it **already** to the **godfather**. No, I am going to make the **saint**. But . ptch (smile and breath intake with smacked lips) .. the **trip** came, and it slipped my mind and I did **nothing**.

Section G

And like **five months** later they corr-, carried away **everything, everything. I lost everything, everything, everything, everything, everything, everything, everything, everything**. [They] **left** me an **empty** house.

Section H

(2-second pause: Emilio looks directly at me, smiling, tapping the table)

// /// // // /// //

And **I had** to make the **saint** because of that **problem**.

Section I

Look, from then on nothing, **nothing more** happened, see? Like that. And everything has gone very **well** for me.

Section A: Summary of intractable problem

In Section A, Emilio introduces his own story as an example of one reason for initiation. This section is characterized by repeated phrases that follow a poetic pattern of AABBCCDD: "they persecuted me a lot, they persecuted me a lot," "always, always," "things were being lost to me, things were being lost to me," and "they robbed me, robbed me." Emilio's rapid-fire utterance of these repeated pairs foregrounds the pattern. Such repetition, which occurs throughout this narrative, works rhetorically to magnify and multiply Emilio's problems in the narrative.

Emilio told me and others this same story on two other occasions over the course of six months and alluded to it several times with me a year later. This story seems to be a stable and important part of his narrative repertoire. In two other tellings I recorded, the repetitive structure is preserved, with identical repetitions of "they robbed me," as we see here, along with a listing of the years that he was robbed—1989, 1990, 1991, and 1993—a list he then repeats. The effect is the same in all the versions: to rhetorically multiply his problems.

Section B: His first attempt at a solution—the police—fails

In Section B, Emilio's first response in the narrative is to go to the police, who are unable to stop the thieves for reasons Emilio does not explain: he leaves "because" hanging after we are momentarily distracted by a woman shouting.

I suggest that the depiction of an initial attempt to find an everyday solution to personal problems is an essential part of Emilio's and others' narratives of conversion, because seeking the aid of police, doctors, or hospitals represents rational problem-solving, not superstitious response. This is the kind of rational action anyone in a similar situation would take. By including this phase in the narrative sequence, the narrator suggests that only when ordinary means fail does one resort to extraordinary means. Emilio and others frequently prefaced their stories of amazing cures and other religious miracles by saying "I am not a fanatic, but," meaning that compelling events speak for themselves and drive the rational person to certain conclusions.

Section C: Second attempt at a solution: the first warning

In Section C, after normal action on the problem fails, the next logical step in the narrative sequence is Emilio's consultation with a santero. This is a signally problematic moment in such narratives, precisely because it suggests that the person already believed, or, being predisposed to believe, became desperate enough to seek religious help. The step of seeking a divination opens up a channel of communication with the orichas, allowing the robberies to become an interpretable divine message. Emilio is told that the robberies mean that an oricha, Ochún, is trying to get his attention by causing them. To link events with a divination in this way, however, is a profoundly religious act.

In this section, Emilio-the-narrator's current religious orientation permeates his account. He attributes his problems to a particular deity, whose warning he paraphrases: "And that as long as I didn't make the saint, they weren't, the robbers weren't going to stop." He acknowledges that the phrase "demanding a head" might be odd to me, explaining "it is said in this way." Doing so marks a crucial difference between his position and mine in the interaction: he is initiated, whereas I am not, and so I may be unfamiliar with this terminology. Tacitly, Emilio-the-narrator aligns me with his past self who, we learn in the very next line, "did not believe it."

Section D: He does not heed first warning; problems continue

Emilio's disbelief costs him dearly, as he explains in Section D. Again, repetitions in the text serve as phrasal icons that represent the unrelenting multiplication of Emilio's problems. By the end of the litany, his problem has swelled beyond any ordinary case of theft: "robbing me, robbing me, robbing me, robbing me."

Section E: Second and final warning

In Section E, the pivotal line, "until they gave me a final test," raises the question of who or what is being tested or proved—an issue I will defer for the moment. (*Prueba*, which I translate as "test," also means "proof" or "trial.") At first glance, the sentence structurally serves to complete the series of repeated "they were robbing me" phrases in section D. It is also one among a series of implied, unspecified third-person plural agents, "they," that appear across the transcript sections. In section E's "until they gave me a final test" and section D's "they were robbing me," the implied "they" of the third-person plural verb conjugation does something to "me" the narrator. This agent-centric series begins in section C with "they weren't, the robbers weren't going to stop"; continues through Emilio's "they said to me" in section E; and culminates in section G with "they left me an empty house."

Are these unspecified third-person plurals all the same "they?" By the ordinary rules of implied pronoun anaphora in Spanish, they should be. The agent of the first utterance in the series is obviously "robbers," but this subject becomes problematic in the following two utterances in the series. Do "robbers" give final tests? Do they go on to give quotable warnings, as Emilio voices their doing in this section? In fact, the stern, warning voices here are the voices of the deities, and he delivers them emphatically, tapping the table to highlight the message's importance.

Section F: He does not heed the second warning

Emilio reports his response to this second, more direct, warning in part as a spoken answer to his godfather: "I am going to make the **saint**. Don't worry godfather." We can understand this chain of communication—from a deity to Emilio and from Emilio to his godfather—by recalling section C where Emilio first describes getting the consultations that reveal that Ochún demands his head. The narrated events of sections E and F return us to the consultatory domain where a priest conducts a divination for his or her godchild, reports the deities' answers and commands, and then discusses with the godchild a plan of action. In Emilio's case, because a deity has already claimed his head and continues to bring him trouble, the plan is to initiate him. But Emilio does not follow through, and this is the source of his chagrined smile and implosive bilabial "ptch" in "but . ptch .. the trip came."

Section G: Problem reaches climax

The result of Emilio's inaction is devastating, as the crescendo of "everythings" palpably illustrates. "They" (unspecified) leave him nothing but an empty house. Thieves may do the dirty work, but higher powers are allowing the thieves to get away with it. The implied agency of "I lost everything" even suggests that the narrator blames himself.

Let us now return to the question of who or what was being tested or proved in section E. Concern with proof is a common trope in Cuban religious participants' talk about consultations. The deities, in essence, must prove that they are the authors of what the divining priest conveys either by revealing details of past events or current problems known only to the client or by making predictions that come to pass. If Emilio doubted their predictions before, he now has his conclusive proof: they predicted the theft of all he owned five months before it happened. Or to cleave to Emilio's account, where his nonbelief creates a self-fulfilling prophecy, the deities drive this terrible misfortune because he refuses to believe. If we now understand the logic of Emilio's decision to believe and to be initiated as a priest, what happens next is the key to this narrative's interactional effect.

Section H: He invites the listener to join him in heeding the deities

Section H consists of a space and a two-second silence in which Emilio looks straight at me, again tapping the table emphatically. Implicitly he asks, "What would you do?" His tapping, harkening back to section E where the deities warn him of the danger of inaction, helps convey the meaning of the significant pause: "Look what happened. What conclusion would you draw as a reasonable person?" Finally, almost anticlimactically, Emilio continues "And I had to make the saint because of that problem."

Section I: The problems disappear

Section I is Emilio's testament to the correctness of his decision to initiate. Once compelled to believe by the force of the deities' interventions in his life, he follows their wishes and sees his problems disappear. Emilio's "look" and "see?" invite his audience to witness his success, while the temporal shift of the narrative from past to present introduces his speaking self as the endpoint of the self-transformation he has narrated. We might read the two-second pause that precedes "And I had to make the saint" in section H as a discontinuity between Emilio-past and Emilio-present—that is, as the moment of conversion.

To conclude, we see that the focus of this narrative is not on the eventual solution of Emilio's problems, but on the process by which he came to believe. The narrative is structured by Emilio's religious logic, where repeated robberies drive the sequence of responses: first police; then, in desperation, consultations; initial skepticism; and finally acceptance of a religious interpretation of events, marked by religious initiation and the disappearance of the problem. What interactional effect does this narrative have? It positions me, ethnographer and audience, in parallel with Emilio-past: a dabbler in Santería who might get a consultation, but has made no religious commitment and professed no belief. In the temporal logic of the narrative, Emilio ferries me across the terrain of crisis and rational response he once traversed to emerge as a believer, ready to initiate. He shows me a map from here to there, from skeptical interest to belief and initiation. His narrative does not, at the moment of telling, convert me or anyone else in his audience, but rather lays out how the world looks from a religious orientation, how events of ordinary life can be retold as experiences of the sacred, stories with the power to make a person believe.[10]

This, then, is why I defend my label of Emilio's story as a narrative of conversion. Conversion is not recounted as an instantaneous event or a sudden realization so much as a realization reached over time in rational response to compelling events. Its mark, if you will, is a person's readiness to retell the events in their lives as a story of divine interventions. If initiation serves as the critical public marker of religious commitment in Santería, the ongoing work of being a religious person finds one form of expression in retelling the telling moments of one's life.

Two facets of religious experience: Phenomenological and interpretive

Emilio's narrative of conversion exemplifies the "after-the-fact" meaning-making that is essential to religious experience. But our everyday sense of experience as a moment-to-moment phenomenon of consciousness and subjectivity may make us wonder whether the long-term events strung together in such retellings are really part and parcel of experience itself. Are after-the-fact interpretations of events like robberies really religious experiences in the same sense as the "raw" visions and sensations of the numinous that William James so vividly described?

Religious experience, as a subspecies of experience in general, consists of an interpretive as well as a phenomenological modality. This is not a novel claim.[11] Even Friedrich Schleiermacher (1963/1821) and William James (1922/1902), in now-classic definitions of religious experience, hint at both modalities.[12] Schleiermacher defines religious experience as a "feeling of absolute dependence," coupled with an intuition of God or "God-consciousness." Rudolph Otto (1958/1950), the early-twentieth-century German theologian who developed Schleiermacher's views, called this the "experience of the numinous," a concept also taken up by Mircea Eliade in *The Sacred and the Profane* (1959).[13] For his part, James defines religious experience in terms of the two criteria I mentioned earlier: ineffability and a noetic quality (Proudfoot 1985).

Lining up these two definitions shows that Schleiermacher's sense of absolute dependence includes both the phenomenological experience of ineffability, of sensing oneself a part of something much more powerful than oneself (shades of Durkheim), and also an epistemic moment of attributing causality to an entity more powerful than oneself.

What are the implications of these modes for knowing what counts as a religious experience? In a common framing of this question, Watts and Williams (1988: 23) ask "exactly how religious people move from the raw experience itself to a religious articulation of that experience." While their inquiry is compelling, its assumptions deserve examination. First, the idea of "raw experience" focuses on private and subjective sensations. We need to pay equal attention to intersubjective constructions of experience, like Emilio's narrative and the events it recounts. Second, the question assumes that experience is in its nature something initially "raw" and unorganized that we individually and collectively structure. We need at least to acknowledge an alternate philosophical view that experience is organized from the start and has some sort of inherent structure.[14]

For example, consider how neurobiologists and cognitive scientists study what Watts and Williams call "raw" religious experience by combining physiological studies, brain imaging, and more complex models of consciousness.[15] These researchers are heavily influenced by William James and so tend to define religious experience more narrowly than I do as an altered state of consciousness. This is too limited a view of religious experience. Their very techniques limit them to studying brain activity during the sorts of religious experiences they have been able to capture in subjects willing to sit quietly in labs for brain scans during and after their experiences—namely yogic, zen, and Christian prayer meditation (Azari et al. 2001; Newberg et al. 2001). Based on this and related work, Newberg and his coauthors postulate a neural scenario for the cognitive and emotional effects of slow, contemplative rituals such as prayers in realizing the mind's "mystical potential" to produce certain kinds of "transcendent states" (27–32).[16] These transcendent states constitute temporary but extraordinary transformations that those experiencing them may attribute to sacred power. In fact, the conditions of intense physical or mental activity that provoke such states include many found in religious rituals: focused meditation, rhythmic motor activity, chanting, and rapid dancing, for example. But none is the exclusive provenance of religious experience. Running, for example, can also provoke the transcendent state they call flow state. While their physiological studies allow them to identify transcendent states in the lab, Newberg and his colleagues note that religious experience cannot be externally verified; only the subject can report on what his or her experience in a given moment means. In other words, intention and interpretation matter deeply.

The mind's mystical potential, we can conclude, turns out to be inextricably bound to a person's frame of reference—what I have called their interpretive stance. That stance delineates both the social practices that appropriately provoke those states and the interpretation of the experience of being in those states. Religious practitioners locate themselves within the sacred stance both explicitly, through self-identification *as* religious practitioners, and implicitly, in responding to events and situations, including those identified as religious experiences. Stance is tied to selfhood and self-presentation, insofar as who we are is at least in part determined by how we position ourselves in interactions. This positioning over time and across many situations produces a durable noetic orientation, or, more abstractly, an episteme, a way of knowing that includes beliefs, analogies, principles of causality, and standards of proof.

But where does a religious episteme come from? Let me be clear that I do not locate epistemes inside the head as a private affair, although some epistemic elements may in fact be cognitive. Epistemes are intersubjective, as indeed is cognition itself as psychologists are beginning to regard it. Consisting of some subset of publicly circulating interpretants, epistemes may be highly stable or quite labile. Because they are most usefully thought of as social phenomena, rather than internal mental models, I focus on their enactment as religious stances. Doing so avoids the intractable problem of how to access other people's internal thoughts and projects religiosity outward as a positioning in response to provocations, which may be events or other positionings (Kirsch 2004).

It seems plausible that episteme shapes experience, not in deterministic ways, but by delineating the realm of the possible and the fallback principles of relation and causality. Believing something to be true of the world allows one to experience certain instances of it. If one believes that the saints directly intervene in people's lives, it becomes possible to experience the curing of an illness or the cessation of robberies as divine intervention, evidence that a saint has heard one's pleas and chosen to give protection. This sort of religious experience is quite different from what James or Schleiermacher had in mind, but it broadens rather than contradicts their definitions of religious experience.

Hood and coauthors argue that "almost any experience humans can have can be interpreted as an experience of God" (1996: 184). I am inclined to agree in the sense that someone with a religious episteme may read signs of divine intervention everywhere. The transcendent states of consciousness described above are only one type of religious experience. David Hay (1982), identified nine categories of religious experience in the survey responses he gathered as part of an interview study (cited in Watts and Williams 1988: 20–22). A perusal of his list shows that not all categories involve the same kinds of mental states or events. He cites, for example, experience of God's presence, of an unnamed presence, of the presence of the dead, of the presence of evil, of the presence of divinity in nature—all of which are mystical experiences that could correspond to transcendent mind-states of the sort that might be detectable in scans of brain activity patterns. Hay also lists premonitions and conversions, which might qualify as similar sorts of numinous experiences, although these seem to require some degree of hindsight in order to be recognized as specifically religious experiences. A premonition usually has to be fulfilled to count as a divine message, and a conversion requires some sort of retrospective glance back at an earlier, unconverted self. The two other categories on his list, answered prayer and meaningful patterning of events, are purely retrospective interpretations of events. It is hard to imagine either of these last two producing the same sorts of neural and other physiological correlates that accompany more immediate mystical states.

To come full circle to the dual phenomenological and interpretive aspects of religious experience, it seems plausible that different types of self-identified religious experiences fall along a spectrum that extends from a phenomenological pole to an interpretive one. Watts and Williams suggest that prayer, for example, "can be understood, at least in part, as an exercise in making sense, from a religious standpoint, of events in the world in the life of the religious person" (1988: 7). Making sense, seeing patterns, or striving for control are as fully subjective events as feeling oceanic bliss or falling into trance, although each may have very different proximate triggers in any particular religious practice. In all cases, we can recognize religious experiences in others only by relying upon how a person acts upon or reports his or her experience. Someone who consistently takes a religious stance will probably have a variety of such experiences or at least be open to the possibility that they and others can have them. They may be able to describe what counts as a religious experience even in the absence of having had that particular experience.

Ritual models of religious experiences

My account of religious experience and how participants and observers identify such experiences retrospectively has focused on how individual interpretations of experience are shaped by a religious episteme. The next question to consider is how such epistemes circulate so that santeros find them compelling and repeatedly adopt them to a sacred stance. One key site of circulation is ritual. Ritual activity—the divinations Emilio received, for example—clearly mediates at least some sorts of religious experiences, although it does so in tandem with the discourses about ritual that surround it, such as the narratives in which Emilio recounted his divinations. Rituals in Santería help mediate religious experiences by demonstrating causal links between ritual acts and transformations that are attributed to the manipulation or intervention of sacred power. Another way of saying this is that rituals develop plotlines that can then be taken up as implicit models for action or even as explicit narratives of action.[17] For example, consider how a divination ritual producing messages—warnings, demands—from an oricha might contribute to someone's notion that the oricha is sending him "little pinches." That is, rituals serve as metacultural vehicles for communicating a sacred stance toward events that transpire during them and also, by extension, to other nonritual events as well. Their power as replicators of religious culture is linked to their performative character: they are most effective when they convey implicit messages and models of action through the ways in which they shape participation.[18]

Divine communication as religious experience

Practitioners of Santería almost always couch their descriptions of religious experience in terms of communications with the orichas and other spirits. Santeros understand rituals to be fundamentally about channeling divine communication in order to access sacred power. Sacred power, called "aché," manifests itself by causing transformations, including temporary but dramatic transcendent states (possession trance, for example) or long-lasting patterns of intervention in people's lives (cures, changes in circumstance, solutions to intractable problems). Such transformations, indicators of aché and therefore of religious experience, can only occur when there is communication between the sacred and the human realm. Rituals in Santería, whatever other purposes they may serve, always focus on opening two-way communication with the deities, ultimately in order to ensure their blessings and protection. Santeros refer to the cowries or coconut pieces that comprise the oracle generically as "the saint," even when no single, specific saint is being invoked.[19]

I now wish to consider how the analogies between different types of rituals of divine communication allow participants to transfer the logic of one ritual to the interpretation of other, related types of rituals. Rituals can produce religious experiences either as a direct result of their performance (as in possession trance when an oricha manifests "in person") or by pointing to other events that replicate their logic, thereby setting up other sorts of events to be religious experiences (as in divinations that suggest portentous patterns in life events).[20] This second mode, in which a ritual serves as a model for a particular configuration of causal relations, occurs through the transfer of interactional tropes from the ritual setting to other settings. Such interchanges can also occur between different types of rituals, so that one reinforces a sacred interpretation of another. One example is the array of rituals that mediate divine communication in Santería.

Rituals of divine communication in Santería and related religious practices fall into four basic categories: prayer, divination, mediumship, and possession trance. Of these, all but mediumship are practiced within the bounds of Santería. Mediumship is central to Spiritist practices, in which it replaces divination and full possession trance. In any case, anyone participating in religious activities in Cuba is likely to have experienced multiple types of each, because devotees of any given tradition in the popular religious complex tend to sample other practices or even be mandated from within their particular tradition to participate in rituals of another tradition. For this reason, I consider mediumship, which is most characteristic of Spiritism and Muertería, within the spectrum of experiences of divine communication in Santería.

Despite variations in each across different religious practices, the four basic categories can be arrayed along a spectrum based upon whether they enable one- or two-way communications with the divine and the degree to which the divine has an embodied presence during communications. Consider figure 4.1. Prayers are human appeals to the divine, but no immediate answer in kind is expected. The three technologies or types of divination in Santería—using four coconut pieces, sixteen cowrie shells, or an Ifá chain—have in common that they establish a two-way channel of communication between human beings and the orichas. Santeros often refer to the cowries, for example, as *la lengua* (the tongue) of the orichas, because when santeros pose questions and make requests while using the cowries, the saints respond with answers, permissions given or denied, and additional demands or advice in the form of signs. The santero interpolates the signs formed by patterns of coconut pieces or cowries into words and sentences. That is to say that the santero relays a message understood to be authored by the divination oracle.

Prayer	Divination	Mediumship	Possession trance
One way	Two way	One or two way	Two way
Human → Divine	Human ↔ Divine	Spirit → Human	Human ↔ Divine
		Human ↔ Spirit	

Figure 4.1. Diagram of possibilities for divine communication in Afro-Cuban religions.

Unlike the technologies of divination, mediumship uses the human mind as what one Cuban practitioner I interviewed called a radio transmitter of spirit messages. Spiritist-influenced mediumship may involve spontaneous transmissions, in which the spirits inspire a medium to give unsolicited advice and warnings to someone. This type of mediumship, which can even happen on the street among passersby, is one-way communication from the spirit world to humans, who have no immediate way to respond, except to seek out a diviner or medium to continue the conversation later. The fully ritual mediumship during Spiritist ceremonies allows two-way communication among mediums channeling spirits and other participants. However, the mediums seldom act out the spirit that speaks through them to the extent that someone in possession trance will. Only in spirit possession do the deities and humans come face to face in full two-way communication. Humans initiate the conversation by attracting the saints with songs. Once fully present, and if the possessed santero has received the proper ceremony, the saint not only inhabits the santero's body but also speaks through the santero's voice. In this way, the saint fully interacts with those present, dispensing advice and other imperatives.

If perfect two-way communication between human beings and the divine is the ideal, that ideal is most closely approached when the orichas descend in possession trance, although orichas and santeros are not completely fluent in one another's languages. The orichas speak a nonstandard, error-ridden, and heavily accented Spanish, and the santeros struggle within their limited knowledge of Lucumí, the language of the orichas. Despite these communicative limitations, we can still read across the chart in figure 4.1 from prayer toward possession trance as a progression toward ideal, fully intelligible two-way communication.

Such a progression works both ways, however. Divinations and possession trance rituals in Santería in many ways follow the same structural template and share the same participation framework. In both cases, a communicative triad arises, in which a santero serves as translator between cryptic divine speech and ordinary human speech. Mediumship generally does not have this triadic structure, and this may be one reason it remains at the margins of Santería, despite its broader popularity in Cuba's popular religious complex.[21]

But what of prayer? Prayer in itself is one-way communication, but it can become part of a broader cycle of two-way communication when one's prayers are answered. Prayers are answered not so much in words as in events, patterns, or changes in circumstances. These life events must come to be imbued with sacred significance. One prays to one's saint for help, and sometime later an intractable problem disappears. A religious interpretation must link the two events as a cycle of human request–divine response—in other words, a religious experience of divine communication. I suggest that experiencing the pattern of human request–divine response during the short time span of a divination or possession trance ritual aids recognizing such patterns over longer time spans in the course of living life. Moreover, these cycles of ritual communication intersect and overlap in larger-scale cycles that build relationships between particular humans and particular deities, as in Emilio's relationship with Ochún. What an oracle says in divination may only come to pass over several months as a pattern of life events that reveals divine intervention, as with the house burglaries Emilio suffered over several years. Or what a divination oracle says may explain such a pattern after the fact. In Emilio's narrative, the oracle not only gives a supernatural explanation for past robberies, but it predicts another theft if he fails to get initiated, a prediction that comes to pass.

These cycles of human-divine communication are prominent in Santería rituals, and it is no accident that they are defining features of religious experiences in Santería. The central concept of divine communication, in effect, provides a framework for interpreting transformations in ritual or life as religious experiences by attributing them to divine intervention. In practice, reaching consensus on what counts as a true religious experience can be problematic for santeros, as we will see in the following chapters.

Conclusion

In this chapter I analyzed a narrative of a type of religious experience best described as a "meaningful patterning of events" (following Hay 1982), which therefore challenges the assumption that religious experiences can be located "in the moment." In Emilio's account, the series of robberies he suffered in life slowly gains religious significance as a divine communication, a "little pinch from Ochún" telling him to initiate. Whatever other reasons he may have had for becoming a santero, his retelling the story of the robberies is what currently has significance for him. Indeed, he frequently referred to this story in my and others' presence and, in retelling it, continually reaffirmed his religious stance and encouraged his interlocutors to seek similarly meaningful patterns in our experiences.

I have argued that one commonality among disparate sorts of religious experiences, whether they occur in ritual or everyday life contexts, is the acknowledgment of an encounter with some form of sacred power, whether anthropomorphized (sensing a divine presence) or abstract (sensing the sacred force, aché). In Santería, sacred power is wielded by fully anthropomorphic orichas who seek to communicate with humans (recall once more Ochún's "little pinches").

In his narrative, Emilio comes to recognize Ochún's little pinches because he seeks advice through a divination. The warning he receives reveals a new, divine level of agency behind the robberies and provides a prueba (test) of it in the form of a prediction that later comes to pass. The divination ritual, then, in Emilio's life and in his subsequent narrative, serves as an interpretive model for nonritual events that precede and follow it and pulls those events into a compelling plotline, one he continues to replicate every time he repeats his story. Emilio's narrative thus illustrates how rituals can contribute to the framing of certain events as religious experiences.

I have also argued that rituals are crucially important as conduits of Santería's sacred stance and of the need for practitioners to maintain open communication channels with the divine. Rituals, however, are not the only important site, since the reflective discourses they provoke also play a central role in generating the sacred stance. Such reflective discourses, we will see, may have characteristics and employ interpretive frames quite different from the rituals they discuss. Emilio's narrative is an example of one type of reflective discourse that simply takes up and retells a ritual event, inserting it into a longer plotline without any hint of doubt or controversy. Indeed, his narrative makes a divination ritual its pivot point as the moment he is given proof that the orichas are responsible for his troubles.

In the next chapter I examine how santeros actually evaluate religious experiences in rituals, a process that turns out to be much more problematic and contested than Emilio's thoroughly digested narrative suggests. Santeros' skeptical attitudes turn out to be key features of their religiosity as it is expressed in reflective discourses in which they test possible interpretations of events for their religious implications. Finally, in part 3, I consider the repercussions of these meaning-making processes for the emergence of a local religious community of santeros.

5

Skepticism in Faith

Evaluating Religious Experiences in Rituals

El santero tiene que comprobar si es verdad que hay un santo o no.
(The santero must confirm whether or not there truly is a saint present.)
—Emilio, March 25, 2000, Santiago de Cuba

Emilio's statement in the epigraph encapsulates a common skeptical attitude among santeros that rituals and other putatively religious events must
be probed and tested for veracity. When someone falls into possession trance
during a ceremony, santeros carefully attend to their behavior, including their
responses to various "tests" and myriad other potential clues about whether
the oricha is truly present.

Religious faith is an interpretive process, one that focuses santeros' attention
on rituals both as events providing potentially religious experiences (like communicating with deities) and as metacultural models for interpreting other
sorts of events as we saw in chapter 4. In this chapter I examine how santeros
evaluate the potentially religious experiences offered up by rituals by drawing upon both the interpretive frames of rituals themselves and other sorts
of framing discourses. One such discourse is evident in an exchange between
Emilio and a ritual singer in which they discuss the importance of skepticism
in their religious practice.

With this discussion in the foreground, I go on to analyze a particularly
vivid ritual performance in which a santero was possessed by his oricha, who
engaged in a rich exchange of insults with a ritual singer that culminated when
the oricha dressed down the singer by ordering him to undergo a purification
ceremony. Fascinating in itself as an illustration of how rituals frame themselves by invoking interactional tropes that cue participants in to what is going
on, this ritual performance became even more intriguing to me when I played

back a video recording of it for two santeros who had agreed to help me transcribe it. Their struggles to make sense of what was being said and sung took on special significance as they developed plotlines for what was going on and began to evaluate the performances of key actors such as the ritual singer and the possessed santero.

The conclusions they each independently reached, as tentative as they were, startled me: there was something fishy about the ceremony. And yet they were not prepared to completely discount the sacred power of the events that transpired. One of the transcribers had even accompanied me to the ceremony, and at the time he and I, along with everyone else present, seemed caught up in the power of the ceremony. His later critical appraisal, then, revealed to me that Santería rituals (and perhaps other kinds of rituals as well) are riddled with indeterminacies that simultaneously allow consensus to develop among participants and allow ruptures of that consensus. One major source of such indeterminacies is the largely unintelligible register of ritual speech called Lucumí, which calls out for interpretation, especially when an oricha delivers messages in Lucumí.[1] Santeros bring attitudes of skepticism within faith to their interpretations of such ritual performances.

"Religion is a competition"

Religious Cubans often discuss ritual events in terms of "tests" and "proofs." Consider the following excerpts from a conversation involving Emilio, a young ritual singer I'll call Desi, and me. I was taping an interview with Desi, whom I had often seen leading the singing at ceremonies. In the passage below, Desi and Emilio discuss santeros' concern with testing one another's ritual knowledge. Desi had been explaining the importance and difficulty of singing Lucumí ritual songs correctly. The special rhythms with which the batá drums opened each new song were especially tricky to learn, Desi explained,

> Because there are times the drummers come out with a rhythm, and they are testing you. They are testing you to see if you are knowledgeable. They come at you with kum-kum-ba! Tun-ba, bi-bi Tun ba, bi-bi! And you'd better know that that is the prayer to Eleggua, that they are playing you the opening so that you will sing to Eleggua. I can go right now to Havana, and if they want to test me there, some of the drummers . . ."

At this, Emilio cut in to confirm that this is exactly what happens, and we all laughed knowingly. Desi went on:

Yes, yes. In the religion, really everything is a competition. The religion is a competition of, and in reality a good competition. Because it is a help to me if I discover that there are so many songs there that I don't know. That in playing me something that I don't know, I then concern myself with that, and I learn, and I must learn that thing.[2]

In a religion of "muchos poquitos" (many details) as santeros often said, any small mistake could ruin a ritual's effectiveness by offending the saints. The competitive spirit with which santeros test one another is productive because it keeps everyone on their toes and points out room for improvement. It also serves a crucial role in the interpretive process through which ritual events take on religious significance. Santeros' competitive mutual evaluation extends to situations in which the orichas are said to be physically present: the santero who falls into possession trance is him- or herself subject to intense scrutiny, as Desi and Emilio discussed a moment later in the same conversation. I had commented that singers closely focus their attention on anyone showing the onset of possession trance. They begin to direct their songs to that person, who may begin to react to the song. Desi responded by describing the singer's objectives in singing to the person possessed by a saint: [3]

The work of the singer is to make known to the saint what, to ask the saint for what you want, and through your knowledge try to discover whether the saint is really there or not. Because it could be a saint, but some arrive [in trance] and the saint is not present. That also happens in the religion.

Emilio added that the "santero has to test what it says; he must confirm whether or not there truly is a saint present," which he does by using *tratados* or "treatments." Treatments are Lucumí song lyrics that the lead singer wields to achieve particular effects on the saints. Although the lyrics are unintelligible to the vast majority of santeros, the orichas understand Lucumí, and so a possessed santero should respond appropriately. Desi gave an example of how a treatment would work. (I leave Lucumí words untranslated, allowing Desi to provide their glosses.)[4]

Because, ok, the saint can have a plate of honey, and to say to the saint, iyalode, which means great lady, iyalode, great lady, wole die mi, please listen to me. Emi ni eyeumo ni, I am asking that you listen to me as the singer, and that I want to eat honey, or drink honey. And if he doesn't give me that honey, the saint is not present.

Note that Desi addresses his Lucumí words to a female saint, "great lady," but describes the respondent as "he," meaning that the possessed priest is male. His pronoun choice is telling, because it implies that Desi is testing the possessed santero, not the saint, for an appropriate reaction to his Lucumí words.

Desi and Emilio went on to explain that knowledgeable but unscrupulous singers could abuse *tratados* (treatments) to get saints who had possessed someone to deliver them everything on the altar: not just honey, but rum, cake, candies, money, and so forth. "And who," asked Emilio, "is most guilty of that?" Desi named another well-known local singer, Germán, whom Emilio had told me was notorious for manipulating the saints. Germán is the singer in the ritual I analyze below. His reputation played a role in events, allowing the santeros who watched my recording to cast aspersions on the proceedings and to relish how Germán got his comeuppance from the descended saint. My analysis will show the principles of testing and competition that Emilio and Desi described in action, as well as their consequences for santeros' interpretations of putatively sacred events.

What should already be clear is that the skepticism that santeros evince toward one another complicates their interpretation of religious experiences. But all is not skepticism: we have already seen that santeros also manifest tremendous faith. I suggest that a certain skeptical attitude is intrinsic to how the santeros I knew practiced their faith. This is especially evident in how they evaluate candidate religious experiences, especially during rituals.

How santeros evaluate a possession trance

The case study presented here centers on a possession trance during a tambor, or festive ceremony, held in honor of the orichas. I examine several key moments during the two hours in which events unfolded to illustrate how santeros evaluate ritual performances through expectation and retrospection. I also consider how two other santeros viewing the video recording later interpreted events. The example demonstrates that religious experience is multifaceted and its authenticity very much in the eye of each beholder; different participants may report very different interpretations of events, based on their evaluations of the details of how a ritual unfolded. In my analysis I seek to understand how participants reach those interpretations.

Possession trances occur within the bounds of particular rituals and loosely follow a similar sequence. The one possessed signals his or her transformation according to particular conventions, and convention also shapes how other participants respond. In this case, a young santero had been hired to "dance his Yemayá," meaning that the sponsor of the ceremony had paid the santero to come and be possessed by his oricha, Yemayá, who is the female deity of the ocean and maternal love. The santero agreed, and the ceremony proceeded normally, with the visiting Yemayá doing all the things that saints do when they "descend" to join a ceremony. Other participants treated Yemayá respectfully, with the possible exception of the lead singer, who engaged in a banter of ritual insults with the deity.

Although this banter conformed to the ceremony's conventions, it had an interesting effect on two santeros who later watched the video of the event with me. I had asked each of them separately to help me transcribe the songs and speech, much of which incorporated Lucumí and was difficult to hear over the general hubbub of the tambor ceremony. As they watched the video, the santeros grew more and more skeptical of the performance of this Yemayá, eventually concluding the possession did not seem to be a real and full one. Either the Yemayá was faking it or perhaps, as one of them more charitably suggested, it was not an oricha but a muerto, a spirit of the dead, who had taken possession of the young santero. In itself this was a serious charge that cast doubt on all the proceedings of the ceremony, because in a properly run Santería ceremony the spirits of the dead are not able to possess anyone. They found corroboration of their skepticism in the exchanges between the lead singer and Yemayá. The lead singer was also skeptical, they suggested, which was why he dared retort when the supposed Yemayá criticized him. But they, like the audience of participants at the time, took seriously Yemayá's mandate that the lead singer undergo a purification ceremony. Each constructed a story line out of the interchange between singer and saint that began with insults and ended with Yemayá besting the singer by publicly commanding him to undergo a ceremony.

Arrival at this analysis required much concentrated effort to decode the Lucumí speech of Yemayá, some of which remains tentative in the transcription. In a few places, the transcripts produced by the two santeros differed, as each constructed a different plotline for the encounter and worked back and forth between transcribing lines and deducing a plotline to make sense of the event. These layers of interpretation and suggestion reveal the indeterminacy of deciding whether an event constitutes a religious experience. The first question is how to know who might be having a religious experience. After all, ceremony participants might simply go through the ritual motions, reacting as if the saint were truly present even where a possession is suspect. If the entranced santero is indeed having a religious experience—not faking or mistaking his possession or simply getting caught up in the moment—what does it mean that other religious specialists remain unconvinced or become unsure? If as visceral and dramatic an event as a possession trance can be fraught with such indeterminacy, such possibilities for multiple readings of events, what of more subtle encounters with the sacred? Again, we must investigate how rituals contribute to framing certain experiences as specifically religious experiences.

Possession trances in Santería

By possession trance I mean what psychologists call a dissociative state achieved in certain festive ceremonies in which a person's body is said to be temporarily inhabited by a deity or spirit. I borrow this term from Cuban scholars of religion, because it is more general about the agency doing the possessing than "spirit possession" (Cutie Bressler 2001). Within Santería rituals, orichas possess their devotees, not the spirits. It is considered an aberration for someone to be possessed by a spirit, which would signal that the spirits of the dead (the muertos or eggún) were seriously displeased. Possession by spirits or the channeling of their voices during trance is normal within Spiritist and muertero ceremonies and consultations, which some santeros also engage in, but separately from Santería rituals. We will see in the ceremony analyzed below that one of the doubts cast upon one priest's possession trance is that he acts as if possessed by a muerto and not by a saint.

Santeros understand possession trance to be a state in which a person's body is "mounted" by an outside presence. Depending upon the skill, level of initiation, and willingness of the "horse" to be mounted, the possessing saint may only briefly seize control or may "descend" for several hours. The saint may resort to gesture and pantomime to communicate or may speak freely, again depending upon whether the "horse" has received the ceremony to "open his tongue" (abrir la lengua) to the saint. Although possession trance is part of a highly improvisatory ritual, its proceedings follow a definite schema and the boundaries governing what can happen within it are well established.

About the ceremony

Possession trances in Santería occur within the bounds of festive ceremonies that are generally known as *bembés*. Bembés are not exclusive to Santería, so santeros often distinguish their distinctive bembés as *tambores*, meaning "drums," or as *wemileres* (or *güemileres*), a Lucumí word for a *tambor* in which consecrated batá drums are used.[5] I opt to use the Santería-specific term tambor, which is the word I most commonly heard santeros in Santiago use, especially because *wemilere* is a subtype of tambor.

A tambor is a festive ceremony held in honor of the saints. Music, dance, and merrymaking are essential characteristics, and yet, as much like parties as they might seem, tambores are serious ceremonies in which protocol is carefully monitored. A santero will host a tambor in his or her private home by hiring one of the half dozen consecrated sets of batá drums in Santiago or one of any number of unconsecrated batá sets as well as a singer. There are always three and only three batá drums played, and the singer is always male. These prescriptions distinguish Santería's tambores from the more free-form and variable bembés other religious folk in Santiago hold for their saints or spirits. In addition, if the tambor host wants to ensure that a particular oricha will descend to offer advice and bless the proceedings, the host may opt to hire a santero known to be skilled in receiving their oricha in possession trance. This doesn't mean that others can't also go into trance, and this element of surprise adds drama to all bembés: you never know who will show up.

Although the host of a tambor may specifically invite family and fellow santeros, word spreads once someone has hired the drums, and many neighbors and other religious or simply curious onlookers may also come. It is quite usual to count 50 or 60 people crowded into a modest-sized living room during a tambor. When the room gets too full, or as participants overheat or tire, they spill out into the yard and street, drawing more passersby into the festivities. Participants in a tambor drink rum, talk, join in the call-and-response singing, and in addition rhythmically clap, dance, and call out. The festive energy bordering on chaos is essential to heating up the event enough to attract the saints. Once the tambor gets their attention, the goal is to incite them to descend and mount their devotees to join in the fun. Indeed, the drum rhythms, clapping, and dancing, together with the intense sensoria of rum, sweat, heat, and bodies pressed close together certainly ripen physiological conditions for transcendent states in participants. I am not liable to fall into trance myself, but I have certainly felt transported by the experience of a tambor, as if the rhythms, and not I, had control of my body.

There is a definite tension between the ritual need to build energy and the dictates of ritual structure. Many times I have heard santeros in charge of a tambor admonish the crowd to drink and chat less in order to sing and dance more. Sometimes a senior santero or the singer will silence the drums and demand that all *aleyos*, or noninitiates, clear out of the room to make space for santeros to dance and sing appropriately. Many santeros have commented to me, usually shaking their heads knowingly, that Santiagueros don't know how to behave themselves in *wemileres* because they are accustomed to the wildness of regular bembés where, santeros claim, anything goes. In the tambor I will soon examine, the singer stopped the drums at one point early on to complain, "así no se puede guaranchar" (it is not possible to party like this), after which a senior santera who had helped organize the tambor exhorted the crowd to sing.

At this, despite the continuing din of people talking and laughing, the drums started up and the singer resumed singing. The singer hired to lead the songs of a tambor bears an enormous responsibility for the tambor's success. He (and in Santiago it is always a man) must know dozens, if not hundreds, of songs in Lucumí and which orichas each song can be used for. He must also have mastered the proper order of songs for the start of the tambor and know how to handle the delicate situation of guiding a possession trance to fruition by carefully choosing songs and "treatments"—specific lines he interjects in the call-and-response—to alternately pique and assuage the temperamental oricha. A singer's skill is judged by his repertoire, his ability to generate excitement and participation in the crowd, and his adeptness in guiding an oricha down in possession trance.

Singer and setting

Germán was the singer in the tambor we investigate here. He is much in demand and makes his living through religious work in the informal economy. Most santeros in Santiago regard him as one of the best lead singers in the city, although a few quietly complained that he would have better mastery of Lucumí if he applied himself. He has a reputation for being something of a rascal. Germán is renowned for his skill in bringing down the saint and infamous for his ability to sing gifts out of the saint once it has taken possession. That is, he knows how to alternate praise and insult so that the oricha will give him offerings from the altar: cakes, bottles of export-quality rum, dollar bills. "Sometimes the host (of the tambor) will despair, because that Germán will empty his altar and carry it home," laughed one santero. In the tambor examined here, Germán gets his comeuppance from the oricha.

Tambores begin formally and gradually become more improvisatory. During the afternoon before the tambor proper begins, the drummers arrive and play the *Orun seco*, or "dry" song cycle for the spirits of the dead. No singing accompanies the drums through their set program of rhythms for each oricha in its proper turn. Then a senior santero and the host do a divination with coconut-shell pieces to ensure that everything is auspicious. Later, the drums start again through the proper progression of oricha songs, this time with the singer leading the small group already present in song. This opens the main part of the tambor, which some santeros call the "Orun de Ayé Aranlá," or "Song of Ayé Aranlá."[6] Next, singer and drums play songs for the orichas of all santeros present, who identify themselves by stepping forward to dance a greeting to their principal oricha and greet and make an offering to the drums. As evening falls and the place fills up, the singer may choose any song he wishes, switching to songs in honor of the principal oricha of any newly arriving santeros, who are supposed to come forward to dance when they hear their oricha's songs.

It is during this longest, free-form section of the tambor that saints may descend to possess those present. A person can only be possessed by his or her principal saint, although not all priests are capable of possession trance. Sometimes someone falls into trance for the first time or only part way, running out of the room to avoid being fully possessed. In the course of the tambor described here, about six people fell into trance to varying degrees, but only two of them fully descended to talk as their orichas. One had been hired as a *subidor*, literally a "riser"—one who "rises" into possession trance reliably. Once fully possessed, he was taken into the back to be dressed in his oricha's regalia, then emerged to dance and speak to the crowd in the main room for about two hours. The other descended spontaneously, and once arrived, settled himself in the altar room to dispense advice to several participants for maybe a half hour.

Layers of interpretation of the tambor

With the permission of the tambor's host, I was able to videotape most of the tambor, including sequences in which participants fell into possession trance and in which the just-described activities of the two descended saints occurred. I will now discuss some transcribed segments of the video in order to illustrate what makes a possession trance a potential religious experience. I have already discussed how not all participants necessarily share a religious experience in the same moment. In the case of a possession, there is the experience of the person falling into trance, accessible only through his or her intersubjective performance (which incorporates reactions of other participants) and (at least potentially) through retrospective accounts from the possessed person, who invariably says that he or she remembers nothing. There are also the perspectives of witnesses to the possession trance, who themselves perform various crucial roles as the audience in whether and how they ratify the oricha's presence. Triangulating among these perspectives and performances clarifies the ways in which the ritual frames events as particular *kinds* of events, while allowing room for multiple interpretations of what the events mean.

The recording of the event permits an additional layer of interpretation, which was provided by two santeros who separately viewed the videotape later to offer their transcriptions and comments. Because recordings of tambores are noisy, transcribing individual voices is difficult. When those voices are speaking in an esoteric register, the ambiguities multiply. Where transcriptions differ, I have chosen to retain both, because the differing interpretations accompanying such divergences are telling. Beyond the transcriptions they provided, my transcribers' efforts to make sense of events as they unfolded on the video provide a particularly revealing view of the interpretive efforts santeros seem to go through when participating in ceremonies—a process of critical observation of which I saw evidence many times but which the video playback let me probe to a degree seldom possible during the rituals themselves. I have divided my analysis of the tambor into five consecutive segments based on the principal activity occurring at the time.

My goal in examining these transcriptions in such detail is to address the chapter's central question of how santeros evaluate the religious experiences that rituals directly provoke. Each time someone falls into trance, ritual participants must decide whether or not they are face-to-face with a deity who has possessed one of their friends or neighbors. To do so, I argue, they attend to the finest-grained details of the possessed person's behavior, including their speech. I will first identify several interactional tropes that mark possession trance and shape how people and deities interact. These tropes constitute patterns of speech and other behavior that first convey cues about where in the transformation between human and divine registers the entranced person is located at any moment and second distinguish the fully possessed person as a special divine participant to be treated in specific ways. I will also consider the two santeros' after-the-fact reactions to the video playback. Their interpretations of events provide a close look at religious practitioners' sensitivity to doubts and problems when they reflect upon whether an event constitutes a religious experience.

Segment 1: Falling into possession trance

The first segment covers a stretch of 17 minutes during which Mario, the subidor hired to dance his oricha Yemayá, fell into possession trance. During this time, the singer, Germán, led participants in about ten songs of which all but

Figure 5.1. Ritual participants dance the *aro de Yemayá* around the santero hired to be possessed by her.

two were songs for Yemayá. As he began the first one, several of the senior santeros in charge of proceedings organized all the santeros present into a circle around Mario and the host of the tambor, a young man named Ramón. Mario quietly rocked in place, his body facing the drums and his head down. Ramón danced at his side, glancing at him from time to time. Meanwhile, about a dozen santeros, men and women, danced in a slow, counterclockwise circle around the pair. Germán stood just outside the circle, leading their singing, and looking between Mario and the drums (see figure 5.1).

This circular configuration and the songs that accompany it are called the "*aro* of Yemayá," a Lucumí name that, as santeros explained it to me, refers to Yemayá's character as the oricha of the ocean. The aro dance represents a swirling whirlpool, which is one facet of Yemayá's personality as the ocean.

As the circle danced, they sang enthusiastically and many clapped rhythmically. One santera shouted out: "¡habla!" meaning "talk!" While it is not clear whether this command is directed to the participants or to the orichas, it serves to encourage both the singing and the onset of possession trance. For eight minutes, through three songs, this activity continued.

Already the participants' expectations were clear: everyone present knew that the pensive Mario in the center of the circle was waiting to fall into trance

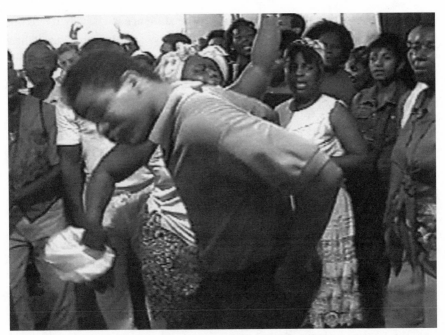

Figure 5.2. The santero falls into trance as Yemayá takes possession of his body.

and that the activity around him was to encourage that moment. As Germán began a new song, Mario suddenly convulsed, his limbs flying. He threw his head back, his face contorted, and then hid his face in his hands. As he seemed to lose control, Germán stepped forward to sing loudly at him, and the circle of dancers watched closely, reaching out to steady him or restrain a flying arm or bracing themselves as he stumbled against them. Mario's eyes were squeezed shut. At first, he stood for a moment as if frozen. Then suddenly his entire body convulsed violently. This alternating pattern of paralysis and convulsion continued for about three minutes, often in seeming response to Germán's lines in the call-and-response songs (see figure 5.2).

Santeros use the Spanish verb *arullarse* to describe the hectic bodily movements at the onset of trance. When Mario began to tremble and flail, both santero-transcribers told me he was "arullando" (losing bodily control).

Tropes of trance and signs of doubt

In order for the oricha Yemayá to manifest her presence, Mario must temporarily disappear, so that a different self animates his body. As Corin describes it, possession trance involves the self's "permeability to some kind of Otherness" (1998: 88). It is not surprising that the transition between Mario and Yemayá is heavily marked by interactional tropes. The audience itself helped cue the transition by encircling Mario in a dance for Yemayá and singing songs to her. Mario's fall into trance then performed the estrangement of his mind from his body. The tremors and convulsions, which are usually involuntary bodily movements, signaled his loss of control over his body. He began to rub his head, the seat of one's spirit in Santería, drawing attention to a struggle within it. His eyes closed, marking a loss of consciousness.

Once Mario was absent, a new presence exerted itself over his body. Amid the convulsions, Mario began to dance again. Over six minutes, Mario-Yemayá opened his eyes and began to dance in a grandiose, powerful way, all sweeping arms and huge steps. The culmination of the process was his performance of the swirling aro dance, in which he spun dramatically and cleared a wide area where earlier the santeros had crowded in and encircled him in a much more sedate version of the aro. Santeros explained to me that Yemayá dances the aro to signal her presence and her power to remove sicknesses.

Meanwhile, Germán had responded immediately to the first signs of Mario's trance by moving in toward him and singing the songs directly to him (figure 5.3). This change in focus created an equivalence between Yemayá, as the addressee invoked by the song lyrics, and Mario, as the addressee marked by the gaze and gestures of the singer. Yemayá was "in" Mario's body, ready to receive

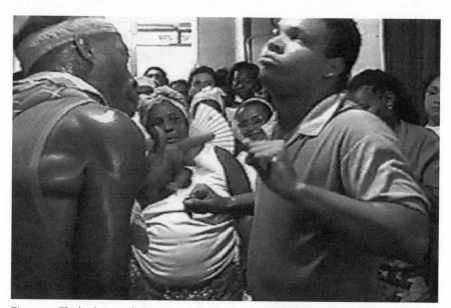

Figure 5.3. The lead singer directs his song to the man falling into trance.

her songs of praise. When Mario turned away or held his face in his hands, Germán would pursue him, shouting his song at his head. More often than not, Mario would sink into convulsions again.

The song that triggered the onset of trance is a familiar one at tambores and is obviously directed to Yemayá. Surprisingly, however, the words are partly in Spanish, suggesting that the song is not part of the true Lucumí canon of Santería, but borrowed from the more heavily adulterated corpus of bembé songs, many of which substitute Spanish phrases for unintelligible Lucumí (see ch. 3 n.8).

Lead (Germán): <u>Wini wini Yemayá</u>, yo estoy solito, que le vamos a hacer
Chorus: <u>Wini wini Yemayá</u>, yo estoy solito[7]

Germán continued with several other songs, each addressed to a different camino or "path" of Yemayá. The crowd enthusiastically sang the chorus, and as Yemayá emerged dancing out of Mario's earlier stillness and trembling, Germán sang his lines less stridently and more conversationally toward Yemayá. As he began to sing the "aro of Yemayá," Yemayá promptly began to dance the aro, her special dance.

In this and in other possessions I observed, two interactional tropes inform the sequence of falling into possession trance: (1) the body's estrangement from its owner's control and its possession by another controlling force and (2) the possessing entity's responsiveness to the situation. By responding appropriately to the songs, the entering deity proves its identity. Moreover, the deity establishes a basis for two-way communication with participants.

But one of the santeros who examined the video had already detected an error: Mario-as-Yemayá had opened his eyes of his own accord, whereas his eyes should have remained closed until another santero touched the lids. He explained that the person being possessed would not have the volition to open his own eyes and that the saint would not be fully in possession until the eyes were opened. Therefore, this minute "error" suggested that Mario, not Yemayá, was present. The critiquing santero then spread the blame to the other participants, pointing out that the initial song triggering the trance had not been a proper Lucumí song, but an adulterated song borrowed from bembés.

Segments 2 and 3: Greeting the arrived oricha

At the time of the tambor, however, nothing seemed amiss. In the second segment, lasting only a brief two minutes, Yemayá was fully in control of Mario's body and fully responsive to the situation. She began greeting people, then was taken into a back room to be dressed in her clothes. From this point, I refer to Mario in his trance state as the feminine Yemayá. Having finished her aro dance, Yemayá greeted each drum by lying before and resting her head on it. Next, she stood and hugged each drummer (figure 5.4) and then, in a higher-than-normal pitch of Mario's voice, began to speak:

1   Yemayá: ¡Ah! (greets Germán by prostrating herself)
2   ¡Ah! <u>Bobo ku e yuma</u>
3   Many voices: <u>O-oo</u> (Germán now kneels before her)
4   Yemayá: <u>Bobo ku e yuma</u>
5   Many voices: <u>O-oo</u>
6   Yemayá: ¡Ah! <u>Baba a Yemayá enso boboyu</u> ¡Ah!

Though they could not decipher its exact meaning, the santero-transcribers recognized Yemayá's utterances here as a formulaic greeting. One santero said that all arriving saints make this greeting, whereas the other claimed it was a greeting special to Yemayá. The ready Lucumí response of the other participants in lines 3 and 5 suggests that the greeting is a common one, although this was the only time I heard it used during a tambor. After the exchange, Yemayá began to hug individual participants and to say a few words to each as

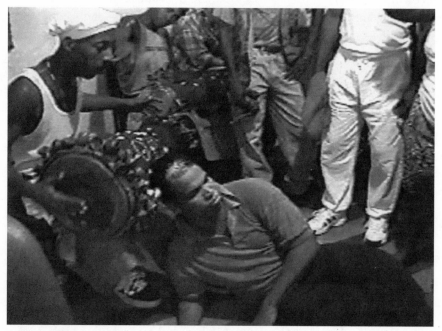

Figure 5.4. Yemayá greets the drums.

Figure 5.5. Yemayá speaks with one of the other ritual participants. The money tucked in her cap is an offering to her that she can dispense to others as she wishes.

she made her way toward the back altar room (see figure 5.5). The drums and singing resumed.

Two additional interactive tropes emerged in this segment of Yemayá's greetings: the saints' responsiveness to and Otherness from their human children. The saints are known to demonstrate affection for and intimacy with their human children. In ceremonial settings, a saint typically greets all the santeros but lavishes special attention on those for whom he or she is the principal saint. As an example of this, Yemayá sometimes followed her greeting and hug with an act of blessing or purification, such as rubbing someone's stomach or wiping sweat from her own onto another person's face. In addition to showing affection, Yemayá's purifying act specifically illustrated the Otherness of all possessing entities, who freely transgress ordinary social mores and whose sweat, even, has aché. Many typical behaviors of possession trance invoke this trope of Otherness. Perhaps most striking in this regard is the oricha's speech, which incorporates many Lucumí words and phrases. In addition, the speech of possessing saints is heavily accented and riddled with errors, as if the speaker had only a rudimentary grasp of Spanish. We will see examples of this as we go on.

As the singing and drumming continued during the next 25 minutes, Yemayá finally reemerged from the back room. There, Mario's t-shirt and pants had been replaced by a bright blue blouse and puffy breeches, all with white trim and sequins. Yemayá's colors are blue and white, and while female devotees wear a dress in these colors, males wear breeches. Yemayá also wore a blue sequined cap, under which had been tucked a number of dollar bills that flapped down over Mario's eyes.

Yemayá moved through the crowd toward the drums, again stopping to greet several people and telling one man, "Emi lenu ba umbo aro (arawo?) que binu ara que elese. ¡Abo!" The man smiled and nodded. Although Yemayá's words were not completely intelligible to either of the santero-transcribers, one suggested that the first part of the phrase, "Emi lenu ba umbo," means "I will speak to you," while the second part, "ara que elese," refers to good fortune due to the influence of the orichas. In other words, Yemayá's words can be interpreted as a blessing. For those receiving a blessing or a bit of saintly advice, such moments may be particularly vivid religious experiences, although I do not know what the man felt as he smiled and nodded or whether his feeling changed over time as he reflected on Yemayá's words.[8] In the next segment of the tambor, the singer Germán was in a similar situation of receiving a message from Yemayá and did give some clues about how he interpreted Yemayá's words.

Segment 4: Saint and singer clash

During the first part of the next 13-minute segment, Yemayá again danced and listened to Germán's singing. As he had done earlier, while Mario was falling into trance, Germán again directed his lines to Yemayá. Now, however, the songs were addressed not just to Yemayá but to other orichas or to both Yemayá and another oricha. Opposite the chorus, santeros interject treatments into a song. While singers tend to have a stock of preexisting treatments to draw from, their combination in particular songs can be improvisatory. In this way, the lead singer uses the medium of song to communicate with a saint and try to elicit a particular response. For example, lead singers may use a line that refers to a particular legendary escapade of an oricha to praise or even provoke that oricha. Santeros and singers agree that singers have to use caution in singing inflammatory lyrics so as not to seriously anger an oricha. Germán, like other singers, sometimes deploys provocative treatments to elicit offerings and gifts of money from the orichas.

In Germán's song series, the two santero-transcribers cataloged his treatments as one "for Yemayá with Ochún and with Changó"; one for Yemayá alone; one for Changó alone; and another for Obatalá. After six minutes of these, Yemayá, who had stopped dancing and was staring hard at Germán, pulled a dollar bill from under her hat to give him. Germán, smiling broadly, pocketed the dollar and turned up the heat. He continued with the same song for Obatalá, a bembé song with lines in Spanish that one santero explained could be used as a treatment for any oricha:

Germán: <u>Bobo isale</u>
Chorus: <u>Bobo isale</u>
Germán: Para que me llame
      So that you will call me
Chorus: <u>Bobo isale</u>

Yemayá then shook off her hat and backed away toward the altar room, still staring hard at Germán. Germán followed, still singing. Thus far, the sequence followed a pattern familiar to santeros, one invoking the trope of the orichas' responsiveness to human interests. Yemayá's stares indicated that she felt provoked by songs praising other orichas and could be moved to prove her own greater generosity by giving the singer gifts. Having given Germán money, she now headed toward the back altar room to get another gift from her altar.

But instead, Yemayá abruptly turned back into the main room. The drums fell silent as she drew near. What follows is a transcript of her conversation with Germán, as many of the other participants looked on curiously. Unproblematic Spanish utterances are translated into English. Where my transcribers offered glosses of Lucumí phrases, I include them in quotation marks. Where they could not translate a Lucumí word, I retain it in the translation to give a sense of its unintelligibility. Where a Lucumí word is well known to santeros, even if unglossed by my transcribers, I bracket it in my translation. Orichas also sprinkle their utterances with markers of bozal Spanish, a sociolect derived from the nonstandard Spanish spoken by Africans who learned Spanish only imperfectly (Isabel Castellanos 1990; Schwegler 2006). Characterized by peculiar pronunciation and faulty grammar, bozalisms create intelligibility problems where the line between Spanish and Lucumí may be ambiguous (Schwegler 2006; Wirtz 2005). Where a phrase contains ambiguous words that my transcribers nonetheless interpreted as Spanish or where a phrase contains bozalisms, I mark the original line with an asterisk and, where possible, give a literal rendering in English of the nonstandard usage.

8   Yemayá: <u>Emi o ago</u> (chanted)
      "Ask my permission!"

9   Germán: <u>Nago</u> (kneels)

10   Yemayá: <u>Ei omode</u>, ¡Sabo!*
     "You are a child, do you understand?"

11   Germán: Sí señor
     Yes siree

12   Yemayá: Dicha fuera aque son mucho que amor en amure, si tú son
     mi amor*
     "Remember as much as people may talk, if you are my child"

13   Germán: Sí
     Yes

14   Yemayá: <u>Emi ni</u> son la ma're de la mundo*
     "I am" the mother of the world

15   Germán: Sí señor
     Yes siree

16   Yemayá: ¡Sabo!*
     Do you understand?

17   Germán: Sí señor
     Yes siree

Yemayá admonishes Germán to respect her as the oricha who is "mother of
the world" (line 14). His place is as a child, the parent-child relationship being
a common metaphor to describe the relation between orichas and their human devotees. In fact, Germán's principal oricha is not Yemayá but Eleggua.
Germán responds, perhaps a bit impertinently, with the informal, "yes siree,"
in lines 11, 15, and 17, which is denotatively marked as addressing a male, "sir,"
but is pragmatically gender neutral, conveying playfully vigorous agreement.

Yemayá, for her part, is speaking seriously, but in the barely intelligible style
that marks orichas' speech during trance possession. Instead of asking, "¿en-
tiendes?" (do you understand), she chooses the incorrect verb for "to know"
and then does not conjugate it correctly: instead of "¿sabes?," she says, "¡sabo!"
(See for example lines 10 and 16.) Yemayá's speech is littered with faulty agreement between nouns and verbs and between articles and nouns. Such errors
are stereotypical bozalisms, and they mark Yemayá's lack of fluency in Spanish.
Moreover, Yemayá mixes codes, combining the Lucumí first-person pronoun,
"emi ni" (in an emphatic form a Yoruba speaker would recognize) with the
Spanish "are the mother of the world" (using an incorrect third-person plural
conjugation of "to be") in line 14. In other words, Yemayá, like other orichas,
speaks in much the way enslaved Africans likely once did as they struggled to
learn Spanish in Cuba.[9]

Yemayá then sang a Lucumí song unfamiliar to my transcribers, although another santera identified it as a bembé song introduced into Santería tambores. The onlookers enthusiastically picked up the chorus, as Yemayá sang each of her lines several times through, and the drums, too, joined in:

18   Yemayá (sings): <u>Rumbe sarawe yaranyara, rumbe sarawe yaraña</u>
19   Many participants: <u>Rumbe sarawe yaraña</u>
20   Yemayá: Ofuncito son hombre <u>yaraña</u>*
       (proper name) are man <u>yaraña</u>
21   Many participants: <u>Rumbe sarawe yaraña</u>
22   Yemayá: Yo tiene pantalon <u>yaranyara</u>*
       I has pant <u>yaranyara</u>
23   Many participants: <u>Rumbe sarawe yaraña</u>

Germán then stepped up to the drums to take up the lead. Each transcriber heard a different line.

24a   Germán (sings): Yo soy hijo de Eleggua <u>yaranyara</u>
        I am a child of Eleggua <u>yaranyara</u>

or

24b   Germán (sings): Los hijos de Eleggua <u>wara wara</u>
        The children of Eleggua "look for mischief"

At this, the drums fell silent, and Yemayá interrupted Germán's singing. Before examining her retort, consider what is unfolding through Yemayá's song and Germán's rejoinder. In lines 8–16, Yemayá admonished Germán to show her more respect. Her song in lines 18–23 may continue in this vein. One santero-transcriber pointed out that Yemayá's "rumbe sarawe" in line 18 sounds like the folk name of a plant, *rompe zaragüey*, an herb Spiritists use in purifications (see D. H. Brown 2003: 309, n.1). He suggested that her song is an insult—what Cubans call a *pulla*—directed at Germán (see Isabel Castellanos 1976: 155–58). In this case, Yemayá may have been hinting that Germán needed to undergo a purification because he had been disrespectful to her. If so, it is not surprising that Germán broke in to retort that he is the child of Eleggua (line 24a)—an indirect counterchallenge, perhaps, that Yemayá will have to take on Germán's protector, Eleggua, if she plans to bother him.

The other transcriber's version (line 24b) also permits the interpretation that Yemayá and Germán are trading insults. In saying that "the children of Eleggua look for mischief," Germán may have been reminding Yemayá about his principal oricha's characteristic penchant for trouble. In either case, Yemayá quickly silences Germán. If we follow the santero's narrative thread, after another round of *pullas* in the next section, Yemayá pulls rank on Germán, prescribing a special purification he must undergo and, in essence, reminding him that she is the deity and he a mere human. What had Germán done to merit Yemayá's anger? As events unfolded on the video, the first santero-transcriber recalled and reinterpreted the earlier songs Germán had been singing in his attempt to win gifts. Germán had perhaps gone too far in praising too many other orichas at Yemayá's expense and thus irritating her.

Let us briefly consider an alternate interpretation proposed by the second santero-transcriber. He viewed the lines alluding to masculinity (20 and 22) in Yemayá's song as problematic. Was she saying perhaps that she embodied a masculine *camino* or "path" of Yemayá? And who was Ofuncito? Repeating his earlier doubts about how real Mario's trance was, he tentatively suggested that Mario was as likely to have been possessed by a muerto, a spirit of the dead, as by the oricha Yemayá. He reminded me that Germán had made an error in singing a bembé song to bring down Mario's trance and that Mario's eyes had opened without the proper touch by another santero. Now Mario-Yemayá was singing in the style of a true *bembé de sau* (old-fashioned, rural bembé) in which a muerto might announce his presence by singing his own name (Ofuncito?) or by dropping hints about his male identity: "yo tiene pantalon yaranyara" (line 22). Germán had then continued in the bembé vein by singing another bembé song line: "The children of Eleggua look for mischief."

I hasten to point out that the santero-transcriber was very tentative in offering this interpretation. For him, a clear narrative had not yet coalesced to make sense of the exchanges between Germán and Yemayá. However, his uncertainties reinforced his growing doubts about Mario's Yemayá. As the video continued, both santeros became convinced that something was wrong about this Yemayá and that Mario was not fully possessed by a saint, but by what santeros euphemistically call a *santico* (little saint). In other words, he was faking. This interpretation would account for Germán's disrespect of Yemayá, suggesting that he, too, had doubts about the authenticity of her presence and so was willing to play games and trade insults with a false deity and to push the limits for his own gain. Mario's "Yemayá"—here in scare quotes to signal the counterfeit oricha—was desperately trying to be convincing. "Her" subsequent critique of Germán and demand that he undergo purification was an attempt to play the divine role by invoking the proper tropes of oricha behavior, including prescribing a ritual to remove an offense.

The two santero's vacillating interpretations highlight the problem religious participants themselves have in deciding whether an event constitutes a religious experience. Participants' interpretations of given events may change over time with new information, just as both santeros became less willing to regard Mario's trance as a truly sacred possession as the video continued.

As the encounter between singer and saint continued, Yemayá responded to Germán's interruption by reminding him of her status as an oricha and cautioning him against insulting her, perhaps because Eleggua would not protect someone guilty of offending another oricha. The exact wording of line 26 is uncertain.

25   Yemayá: Sabo mi amor, <u>ochanbera</u>* (head to Germán's chest)
        Do you understand my dear, <u>ochanbera</u>

26a   Aquí toda la ocha cuando son <u>piguera</u> son de la misma tierra
        Here all the orichas when they are <u>piguera</u> are from the same land

26b   Recuerda mi <u>omo</u> que toda la ocha cuando son <u>siguere</u> lo mismi tiene*
        Remember my "child" that all the orichas [even] when they are "crazy" have the same thing

27   Germán: Sí, sí
        Yes yes

28   Yemayá: Sabo, mi amor*
        Do you understand, my dear

29   Germán: Yo sí entiendo
        I do understand

30   Yemayá: La cosa
        The thing

31   Germán: No te preocupe, yo sí entiendo, yo sí entiendo
        Don't worry, I do understand, I do understand

32   Yemayá: <u>Emi ni</u> quiere que en este hogá sea*
        (I) want it to be in this home

33   (sings) <u>E okana e okana</u>

34   Germán: Nunca va a llegar eso
        That will never happen

35   Yemayá: (sings) <u>Okanani okanani wa, okanani okanani wa abure la ocha</u>

36   Germán: Nunca va a llegar eso
        That will never happen

Yemayá improvises a second song, in lines 33 and 35, in order to critique German. One santero-transcriber glossed its meaning as a reference to the heart (*okan*) and to how all are brothers (*abure*) in the saint. In other words, Yemayá's song censured Germán's penchant for creating trouble and discord. In his duplicate interjections in lines 34 and 36, Germán replies that brotherly harmony will never exist. Yemayá, nevertheless, "wins" this round by drawing the audience into the call-and-response that follows in lines 37–42, effectively silencing Germán with group song.

37 Yemayá: <u>Okananiwa abure kanani</u>

38 Many participants: <u>Okananiwa</u>

39 Yemayá: <u>Abure karane</u>

40 Many participants: <u>Okananiwa</u>

41 Yemayá: <u>Abure karane</u>

42 Many participants: <u>Okananiwa</u>

At the song's conclusion, Yemayá announced the ritual Germán had to perform to appease her and remove the offense of being so disagreeable. By making this announcement public, Yemayá ensured witnesses as to whether Germán carried through on his purification or not. The unspoken coda of such ritual prescriptions is always that if one ignores the oricha's mandate, one dares the oricha to cause the very problem the ritual is supposed to prevent.

43 Yemayá: ¡Sabo! Entonce <u>emi ni</u> quiere que ponga afinidad*
    Understand? So (I) want you to behave agreeably

44 Como són, y ponga amor, ¡sabo!*
    How is it? And act with love, understand?

45 Cuando llegue el <u>edún</u>, el último <u>dún</u>, de este año, ?no?
    When the end of the (year), the last (year) of this year, no?

46 ¿Cómo son? ¿El último <u>dún</u>?
    How is it said? The final (year)?

47 A few voices: El fin del año
    The end of the year

48 Yemayá: Al <u>ejilá</u>, ¿cómo son?
    At (twelve), how is it?

49 Two women: (unclear)

50 Yemayá: Al <u>ejilá</u>
    At (twelve)

51 Female: Oiga, mira
    Listen, look

52 Male: El, el diciembre de este año
The, the December of this year

53 Yemayá: ¿Cómo son el día?*
How are the day?

54 Woman: El día doce de diciembre
The twelfth day of December

55 Yemayá: A la doce lodá,¡sabo!*
At twelve (at night), understand?

56 Many voices: A las doce de la noche
At twelve o'clock midnight

57 Yemayá: Dice, me lo va a buscar un carbón, sabo*
It says, you will go find me a charcoal burner, understand

58 Male voice: El carbón
The charcoal burner

59 Yemayá: Me le va a la ina a ese carbón*
You will to the (fire) to that charcoal burner for me [that is, "you will light it"]

60a Yemayá: Sabo, cuando de la sonsa me lo va a prendé'*

60b Sabo, cuando de la sonsa le va a dar ina*
Understand, when at eleven you will light it (for me)

61 Cuando llega la dosa vamo' a apagar ese carbón*
When twelve arrives let us extinguish that charcoal burner

62 Female: A las once
At eleven o'clock

Yemayá's performance continued to hold at least some of the audience's attention. Her apparently limited competence in Spanish, oblique statements, and questions like "¿cómo son?" (how is it said?) drew participants into a sort of guessing game in which they deciphered her message to Germán as he (somewhat impatiently) listened. In a call-and-response not unlike the songs themselves, she inserted Lucumí words into Spanish sentences, allowing someone from the audience to translate the unfamiliar word and reveal her message: *Dún* is year, but here it is also used to mean the last day of the year; *ejilá* is "twelve," meaning 12 o'clock, although someone first guessed it to mean the 12th day of the 12th month. She kept the audience's attention through this guessing game until the ritual instructions were clear: at 11 p.m. on New Year's Eve, light a charcoal burner, then at midnight extinguish it. She went on in a similarly oblique and only partly intelligible manner to explain that Germán should douse the charcoal brazier with "omi tuto" (cool water). She makes the prescribed ritual a metaphor for his problem: like the charcoal burner, he gets overheated and so must have his fire or anger cooled with water.

While Germán's temperament is well known in the religious community, it seems that he triggered Yemayá's censure on this particular occasion by offending her. Perhaps she was piqued that he sang songs to other orichas or acted overly greedy in manipulating her into giving him so many gifts. His willingness to keep provoking her by invoking the protection of his own oricha, Eleggua, may also have annoyed her. Indeed, she gets in one final insult by suggesting that the ominous signs for the coming year are Eleggua's fault.

63   Yemayá: Porque el <u>edún</u> que viene ningún <u>edún</u> son buena*
       Because the (year) that comes, none of the (year's signs) are good
64   Germán: No, ninguno, ninguno, sí, sí
       No, none, none, yes, yes
65   Yemayá: Porque son de Eleggua
       Because they are Eleggua's
66   Germán: Sí, sí
       Yes, yes
67   Yemayá: Pero que viene <u>modá</u>
       But when (tomorrow) comes
68   Several voices: Es peor
       It is worse
69   Yemayá: <u>Modupwe</u>, en este sentido
       (Thank you), in this sense

Throughout this interchange, Germán seems humble, almost obsequious, in agreeing with her.

Segment 5: The singer offers excuses

Publicly chastened, Germán begins to sing again, this time choosing songs for Yemayá and not other orichas. The subtleties of Yemayá's and Germán's interaction, so apparent to my transcribers, were probably missed by most participants at the time, primarily because Yemayá's speech uses enough Lucumí and nonstandard Spanish to be very oblique. Such obliqueness of meaning is typical of orichas' speech when they become present during possession trance. Yemayá's insults have more weight because they are embedded within tropes of trance possession, especially speaking and singing in Lucumí and giving advice and ritual mandates.

Germán interrupted his singing and stopped the drums twice during the next few minutes to complain that people were not singing properly. The second time he framed his complaint as an apology to Yemayá.

> Yemayá, I am religious, but the singing cannot continue like this because people have to help me out. The singing cannot continue [like this]. We are with the consecrated drums.[10]

Germán first explains that stopping the drums is not a sign of disrespect by declaring that as a religious person, he is appalled that other participants are not singing. Given that Yemayá has only just finished berating him for not being religious enough, his choice of words comes across as a more general protestation that he *does* act responsibly as a devout santero. As to his complaint, many people in fact were singing, although others were chatting, sometimes shouting, over the music. His final comment is a reminder to those present that the ceremony is no ordinary bembé, but a *wemilere*, a Santería ceremony with consecrated batá drums. If we recall his earlier disrespect in too obviously trying to get Yemayá to give him gifts, this sudden holiness seems ironic. He may indeed feel chastened by Yemayá. It is also possible to view his current show of religiosity as annoyance at being publicly called to task for his behavior. Spreading the blame around to others is one way of recovering face.

In response to his pious complaint, Yemayá supported Germán by putting her hand on his shoulder and calling out to the crowd, "<u>fun mi aña</u>" (give me consecrated drums), a way of asking for proper participation. The din of many voices continued, and someone in their midst tried to shush them. One man can be heard commenting on Germán's complaint: "It won't be singing for him, but for Yemayá." This remark suggests that some participants regarded the entranced man before them as the embodiment of Yemayá, and that Yemayá had at least some of the audience's support in demanding more respect from Germán.

The tambor continued for over another hour, with Yemayá present throughout, until she closed the ceremony by again dancing the aro, this time with a bucket of water to remove impurities and cast them out into the street. Both of the santero-transcribers continued to be skeptical of her authenticity until the video recording's end, finding the trance unconvincing. This conclusion strengthened their interpretations of earlier events between Yemayá and Germán.

Conclusion

This extended case study illustrates the complexities of identifying and understanding religious experiences in real-time events, as well as their intersubjective construction. The entire ritual event is governed by participation frameworks that conventionalize this sort of ceremony, which I have described as performable tropes of interaction that signal what is afoot. These are suggestive, never deterministic, which is why the unexpected can transpire in a tambor and why some might even dispute or find problematic any particular event, even when it is framed as a religious experience. Indeed, I have suggested that such rituals have built-in ambiguities, often generated by the unintelligibility of Lucumí songs and orichas' speech.

At the same time, the ceremony does have a coercive effect, or perhaps better said, various mechanisms of emplotment (including those produced by unintelligibility, such as the need for decipherment), so that everyone present continues to conform to expected participant structures, even when joining in the chorus of a song whose words they do not understand, or trading insults, or admonishing other participants. By continuing to act as if a deity were present, whatever their private doubts, other participants give the deity a chance to be present and to deliver a religious experience, at least to some (including, I suspect, the one possessed). The ritual itself conveys the sense that a consensus emerges about whether to treat any particular possession trance as authentic, but this emergent consensus does not prevent anyone present from forming a separate opinion about what has transpired, as did the santeros who later viewed the video recording. In doubting the presence of an oricha, the santeros demonstrate the importance of a skeptical eye for ritual details when one is evaluating a ritual performance. Santeros present at tambors may privately conduct running critiques of events and their details in order to decipher the experience. Certainly, we will see in later chapters that they extensively discuss rituals after the fact.

Given the rich, even overwhelming, sensorium of a tambor, we might be tempted to focus on the phenomenology of this ritual to the exclusion of the interpretive side of experience. Both are present, however, and both are shaped by the expectations generated by the ritual form itself. The overriding trope of tambores, and indeed of most rituals in Santería, is that humans and deities must enter into two-way communication in order for humans to achieve their desired ends. Such communication is difficult to accomplish, and even when achieved, humans must struggle to interpret what the saints say in their cryptic manner of speaking.

The very difficulties involved in making sense of rituals and their outcomes encourage santeros to continue to ruminate over them, whether privately or together. While my video playbacks generated a unique opportunity to evaluate the tambor ceremony, the two santeros' readiness to engage in critique reminds us that their general attitude is one of skepticism, of seeking proof in events. The next chapter explores some of the reasons for santeros' skepticism. They focus their doubts not on the orichas, but on one another. Chapter 7 then explores the consequences of santeros' skeptical discourses for their sense of religious community.

III

Religious Community

6

Respecting the Religion, Advancing in the Religion

El perro tiene cuatro patas, pero coge un solo camino.
(The dog has four paws but takes just one path.)
—Proverb used by santeros

The proverb above, one frequently cited in divination results, could be a metaphor for Santería: everyone seems to be going in their own, individual direction, but somehow, through all of the critiques, skepticism, and personal agendas, one gets a strong sense of a unitary religious endeavor. My central question throughout has been how the interpretive ferment surrounding rituals produces Santería as a religion and moral community. In part 2 I examined religious experience as a focus of ritual practices and reflection and a product of their interaction, considering in particular how individual participants construct (and deconstruct) intersubjective religious meanings in their experiences. Those chapters also hinted at the prevalence of critical and skeptical stances in santeros' reflective discourse. In part 3, I examine how these ritual and interpretive practices generate moral community. I save for chapter 7 a discussion of how critical discourse (of the sort we saw abundantly in chapter 5) can promote skepticism and individualized interpretations of ritual experiences without the entire enterprise dissolving in doubt. But first I examine how rituals within Santería encourage both collective ideals and individual strategizing among religious participants and how santeros adapt ritual forms to both normative and their own sometimes subversive uses.

The tension between these two pulls, the communal and the individual, is captured in two common phrases santeros use. On the one hand, santeros often admonish each other to "respect the religion," meaning to adhere to the Regla, defer to those higher in the ritual hierarchy, and put religious values ahead of personal gain. On the other hand, santeros talk of "advancing in the religion," by which they ostensibly mean gaining deeper religious knowledge. But advancing in the religion also carries connotations of gaining higher ritual status and materially benefitting from one's religious practice. These possibilities are inherent in Santería (and across the popular religious complex), which is pragmatically focused on improving life in the here and now.

Why, then, is there tension between these two tendencies? Santeros' brand of religious skepticism, we have seen, takes the form of vigilance about their fellow practitioners' motives, which santeros explain as an important safeguard against those who would abuse their access to sacred power. Santeros perceive a slippery slope between properly advancing in the religion and using the religion exclusively for one's own ends. They label the extreme case "witchcraft," but they are suspicious of a wide range of less grievous "violations," from cutting corners in ritual procedures to disrespecting the hierarchy to blatantly using rituals to advance a secular agenda (making money, gaining status). Even tiny details like the ritual singer Germán's choice of songs or the possessed santero's open eyes in chapter 5 can raise suspicions about ritual impropriety. In discourse about rituals, santeros balance their own interest in advancement with critiques and skepticism about others' motives. As my analysis of the tambor ceremony in chapter 5 illustrates, santeros' skepticism fuels divergent individual interpretations of communal events.

What keeps everything from flying apart or degenerating into recriminations? To address this question I explore how rituals maintain a dynamic balance between communal goals and individual agendas. For example, in the divination ritual I analyze later in this chapter, the santero adheres to canonical ritual forms of performing a divination: he invokes the entire community of spirits and santeros; he voices the oracle's response in Lucumí; and he interprets the results first through proverbs. In these and myriad other ways, ritual practices in Santería promote collective ideals and shared meanings. But at the same time and just as typically, the santero also shapes his interpretation of the divination results to suit his interest in gaining a new godchild and what he perceives to be his client's interest in "advancing in the religion." That is, ritual practices in Santería also promote individual agendas and personalized interpretations that may contradict collective ideals and shared meanings.

The engines connecting the communal and individual impulses of religious practice are to be found in both ritual forms and reflective discourse such as gossip. The very divisiveness of gossip and other discourses of critique paradoxically works together with ritual forms to anchor shared meanings. In chapter 5, I focused upon santeros' evaluations of each others' ritual conduct, and this chapter and chapter 7 are likewise full of gossip, critique, and controversy. In this chapter, I present an analysis of a divination I received in order to examine how ritual forms used in divinations metapragmatically reinforce communal values and meanings at the same time that santeros doing the divination find ways to use those same ritual forms to advance their and their client's personal agendas. There was no irony in the marriage of these two aspects, the individual agendas embedded within shared ritual forms. Something similar is at work within another highly entextualized form of speech: the proverb. On the one hand proverbs, such as those sprinkled throughout this chapter, by virtue of being recognized as proverbs, have a certain traditionalizing and normative moral force. They seem to convey "common sense." But as Winick (1998) points out, proverbs' meanings only appear to be fixed, when in fact they are highly contextualized and frequently employed creatively, revealing quite elastic meanings. As with ritual forms, like divination, the staying power of proverb lies in just this capacity to invoke timeless tradition and consensual meaning, while being endlessly adaptable to novel situations and purposes.

Morality tales and divine sanctions

> *Las orejas no pueden pasar la cabeza.*
> *(The ears cannot surpass the head.)*

So said Emilio to me, my husband, and two new initiates we were visiting during their initiation. Emilio's friend, a senior santero, had invited us to pay our respects to his two latest godchildren to initiate. One afternoon of the week-long initiation ceremony is set aside for this "presentation" of the new initiate. The two new initiates, called "iyawós," were sitting on the mats that delineated the boundaries of their altars, dressed in their special initiation outfits, surrounded by the ceramic vessels containing their newly "born" saints. They had been yawning and restless throughout our visit, bored at being confined to their altars for several days already. After saluting them by prostrating ourselves and placing some money in the baskets at their feet, we sat in the room with them for a polite amount of time chatting among ourselves, since they seemed uninterested in conversation. Then Emilio stood up, turned to them, and offered his advice. He told them to always respect their elders in the religion, then gave the proverb above, "the ears cannot surpass the head." He repeated the pithy phrase with satisfaction, then explained it to them: new initiates will always be junior to those who initiated before them and so must always respect their godparents and other ritual elders, who are the source of their religious status.

The proverb rang in my ears, especially because we had just been discussing

Emilio's distrust of babalawos. Babalawos, the special male-only sect of priests who specialize in the Ifá system of divination, are a group apart from regular santeros. Ifá is simultaneously a part of Santería and a parallel to and distinct religious practice from Santería (see D. H. Brown 2003: 146–57). Many babalawos were first initiated as santeros before undergoing initiation as babalawos, although it is also possible to be directly initiated into Ifá. Once a babalawo, a man cannot later be initiated as a santero. Babalawos are considered the most elite and senior of priests in Santería. In Santiago, as I will describe in chapter 7, there was a fair amount of friction between santeros and babalawos, of which there were no more than 15 in the entire city in 2000. As Emilio had been saying, the santeros resented having to show respect to young upstart babalawos, young men who had not stopped to be initiated as santeros before becoming babalawos. In an often-repeated refrain, santeros like Emilio would complain, "Why should I, a santero initiated X years, bow down to some new, young babalawo who doesn't even know the 'secret' of initiation or much of anything else in the religion?" Emilio had explained to me that young, ambitious men took this quick route out of greed, to quickly move to the most prestigious role, thereby subverting religious initiation for selfish, even pecuniary motives. As babalawos, they could charge exorbitantly for consultations and earn a good living. Their godfathers in Ifá were just as guilty, he said, because they agreed to initiate the upstarts in order to make money charging for the initiation. Worst of all, the babalawos were perceived to be arrogant, like ears trying to surpass the head.

If a key aspect of Santería's sacred stance is recognizing divine interventions in the course of life events, a closely related one is understanding that the saints, sooner or later, punish those who disobey or abuse them. Divine and human sanctions serve to reinforce collective religious aims by policing those who would adapt the religion to their own ends. The community's first line of sanctions is gossip and other evaluative talk about specific rituals and particular individuals. Santeros frequently discuss ritual "violations" they have witnessed or heard about. Violations include neglecting details or steps of rituals, disrespecting one's ritual elders, using the saints to do witchcraft—in other words, a whole range of mistakes, omissions, and willfully wrong acts. A santera friend, on a different occasion, and completely independently of Emilio, made much the same complaints about young babalawos, but she went so far as to angrily call skipping over initiation to go directly to Ifá a "violation."[1]

Gossip is one important discourse that reinforces the Regla. While santeros might bicker over the details and applications, they all agree on basic tenets

such as respect for one's elders and for the religion. Disagreements over interpretation and accusations of violations fuel the gossip mill and circulate the
basic tenets—the exceptions reinforce the Rule. Occasionally, a consensus will
emerge condemning someone for some infraction, but more commonly, rivals
or rival lineages cast aspersions on one another behind each others' backs.

Santeros thus use gossip in ways that both further their own individual
interests (compare Paine 1967) and that serve as an informal mechanism for
maintaining social cohesion and normative values (compare Gluckman 1963).[2]
This seeming contradiction is possible because gossip is highly context-sensi-
tive, taking different forms in different settings, and because, as Brenneis (1984)
demonstrates, gossip may affect different relationships in different ways, so
that the gossiper reinforces his solidarity with his audience while advancing
competitive status claims against those he gossips about.

According to the trail of gossip among santeros about ritual violations, the
orichas have their own, more direct ways of policing compliance. As Emilio's
narrative of conversion in chapter 4 illustrated, the orichas punish in the same
way they confer blessings: by intervening directly in one's life. By his own account, Emilio's problems with recurring robberies stemmed from his delay in
accepting his oricha's call to initiate. On many occasions, Emilio shared with
me dozens of juicy tidbits of gossip, some of it years old, about santeras who
refused to obey food restrictions imposed by their orichas and then choked to
death on the very forbidden food they consumed; about santeros who killed,
with or without magical help, and who ended up jailed for life, despite their en-
treaties to their saints to rescue them. Such narratives, and the critical, watchful attention to detail they promote among santeros, are strong mechanisms to
remind people why they should adhere to the Regla. And yet, for all the talk,
santeros can be remarkably footloose in cutting corners or advancing obvious
personal agendas through religion. Usually these shortcuts and other strategic
acts work out, but the ideology transmitted through gossip says that such behavior always courts catastrophe in the form of divine sanctions.

However powerful the admonitions to conform to the Regla, however popular the "morality tales" of gossip, practitioners nonetheless do all manner of
things in the name of the religion. They seek shortcuts, they compete for prestige, and they work for personal advancement, all individually oriented aims
that sometimes conflict with the shared vision encoded in the Regla. This is not
to say that the Regla promotes a selfless, otherworldly ethic. Santería is far too
pragmatic for that. Rather, the Regla overtly promotes values of cooperation
and mutual assistance among practitioners and between people and orichas

at the same time that it promotes obedience and respect for its hierarchy of authority. But practitioners make room within these strictures to pursue their own agendas. I now consider how the tensions between collective aims and individual strategies play out within rituals.

Conflicting interpretations of a possession trance

Flecha entre hermanos.
(An arrow between brothers.)

For a good example of the tension between collective and individual interpretations of ritual, consider the chapter 5 analysis of the interactions between the singer and the santero possessed by Yemayá during a tambor ceremony. The singer and the descended saint, Yemayá, traded insults through ritual songs, until Yemayá bested the singer and put him back in his place by enacting the familiar trope of the saint giving pointed advice to the wayward devotee. The players conformed to the collective aims and roles of the tambor—its script, if you will—while pursuing their individual strategies to best each other.

My examination of two santeros' later reactions to the video recording of the tambor illustrated a parallel tension between shared meanings and individual interpretations. To the extent that the ritual participants adhered to their ritual roles, the tambor invoked shared meanings about what is accomplished in rituals of its type. For example, formally speaking, the tambor succeeded in luring an oricha, Yemayá, to make an appearance to show her satisfaction with the proceedings. At the same time, individual interpretations of the tambor differed: the two watching santeros had their doubts about whether the Yemayá performance they saw constituted the real thing. When they assigned blame, they did so by comparing the particular event to an ideal type, point by point. What songs were sung? Who opened the possessed person's eyes? How did the Yemayá speak? Discrepancies between type and exemplar suggested where to place blame. For example, one santero faulted the singer for using improper songs that did not belong to the canon of Lucumí songs. He also pointed out that the Yemayá opened his eyes without anyone touching them. The other santero found Yemayá's admonishment of the singer compelling and appropriate to a saint. Their ideas about a proper tambor ceremony drew upon their experiences at other tambores and knowledge gained from circulating meta-discourses about tambores in general and in particular.

The tambor example demonstrates that ritual structures are persuasive but not deterministic. They encourage participants to conform to expectations in how they act and react. But at the same time, there is ample room for multiple interpretations, although interpretations differing from full acceptance of the proceedings may only be shared privately and after the fact. The example also illustrates how canonical forms of ritual may simultaneously serve both collective and individual purposes. In the competition between the singer and the Yemayá, both used songs appropriate to the ritual occasion. At the same time, the singer chose songs within the canon that allowed him to wring as many gifts out of the descended saint as he could. The Yemayá invoked first the form of ritual songs, then the form of giving divine advice, to bring the audience into the *pullas*, insults, with which she goaded the singer.

These examples raise questions about how rituals, as events that both impose collective ideals and advance individual interest, generate a common sacred stance. In what ways do rituals exacerbate or resolve the tensions between collective aims and individual strategies? Between shared meanings and individual interpretations? How do these crosscutting purposes nonetheless promote the circulation of a cohesive sacred stance?

Two conflicting tendencies: "Respecting the Regla" versus "advancing within the religion"

> *Él que sabe no muere como él que no sabe.*
> *(He who knows does not die like he who does not know.)*

Santeros explain this somewhat cryptic proverb to mean that the orichas hold initiated santeros to a higher moral standard than other people, because they are supposed to know better. In evaluative discourses about religious ethics, santeros frequently refer to "doing what is correct," "obeying the Law," and "respecting the religion." The most frequent critique they level against each other is failure to do these things. Although santeros' overt emphasis on acting correctly suggests that respect and obedience are prized markers of religiosity, it also suggests that on many occasions santeros are not acting correctly, whether because of intent, neglect, ignorance, or other priorities (such as cost cutting or saving time). In other words, it is a matter of communal concern that practitioners pursue individual agendas at the expense of shared ritual aims and procedures.

Nonetheless, there are ways in which the individual agendas that cause santeros so much concern actually advance collective aims and shared meanings. First of all, they provoke discourses of critique and concern, which serve to circulate shared meanings and even create a religious community through discourse networks of shared stories and commentary. Such discourses may serve a normative function, alerting participants to the criteria for correct ritual procedure. Second of all, individual agendas themselves derive from participants' sense of what is ritually possible, and this sense of the possible derives from and reinforces a common religious episteme. For example, ritual participants work to establish divine communication because they hope the saints will tell them how to improve their lives and advance themselves. They may wish to advance spiritually, as well as materially, but the major marker of spiritual advancement remains moving up the ritual hierarchy, which is as political as it is spiritual. As another example, santeros often actively recruit godchildren, because a larger ritual lineage of godchildren increases the godparent's standing. If any of the godchildren are foreigners, paying hundreds or even thousands of dollars for rituals, the godparent may materially benefit as well. Again, a religious necessity—building ritual lineages through initiation—opens space for individuals to strategically pursue their own aims. As individual santeros recruit new godchildren to their fold, and as some of these godchildren initiate and move fully into the ritual hierarchy, the entire religious community expands.

The consultation: How individual agendas get advanced in a divination ritual

> Es la cabeza que lleva al cuerpo.
> (It is the head that carries the body.)

As an example of how such individual aims can be advanced legitimately through ritual, and how they interact with communal religious aims, I will examine segments of a consultation. I begin with a normative account of a consultation's structure and purpose in order to lay out the communal religious aims it expresses. The ritualized forms repeated in all divinations create a substrate of shared meanings out of which each divination is improvised. In order to "read" the oracle and deliver its message, the diviner must apply a standardized set of divination signs and interpretations to each client's particular situation. Reciting time-honored ritual forms gives authority to the divination proceedings, but divinations must also be highly contextualized and contextualizing, giving particular aspects or events of the client's life heightened salience by linking them to the occult or the divine as embodied in the highly entextualized signs of the oracle. After all, the point of a divination is to allow the orichas to speak and give advice on one's earthly problems. To see how this miracle of divine communication occurs, and how, in the slippage between traditional ritual forms and personalized message, individual agendas can creep in, I do a close reading of a consultation I received.

Background on divination

In Santería there are three divination systems that can be used for a consultation: the most basic coconut shell divination, which offers simple yes-no answers; the more common cowrie shell divination, which uses sixteen cowries to permit more complex and subtle answers; and the most complex Ifá system of divination, which is the special purview of babalawos. All three systems of divination elaborate, to differing degrees, on the same basic participation framework: the santero mediates between the client and the sacred plane by conveying the client's questions and concerns to the oracle, by using the oracle to produce divine responses and, finally, by interpreting those responses for the client.

Most noninitiates who come into contact with Santería do so by attending tambores or seeking out consultations. A tambor, by virtue of its public nature and festive atmosphere, attracts the attention of neighbors and passersby, some of whom may come in for a look around or a chance to enjoy the party. Consultations, on the other hand, are private encounters between a santero and a client. A person may seek out a consultation for any number of reasons, but most typically, the person is in some sort of physical, economic, or spiritual distress or is otherwise facing an intractable problem for which they want a solution or cure. Whether or not they have much faith in the results, all clients, even first-timers, enter into a consultation with expectations. Clients' expectations may be shaped by experiences with other types of consultations or by circulating ideas about religious consultations in general.

Indeed, the three divination systems of Santería are but a few of the possibilities for religious consultations, since Spiritist mediums, Paleros (practitioners of Palo), and others also practice various types of divination and mediumship. In this context of multiple offerings, some clients will visit a santero for a consultation simply by word of mouth, because they are desperate for relief and somewhere they heard that this person does good consultations. As Kirsch (2004) argues for a different setting of religious pluralism, people's beliefs— their faith in what is possible—are flexible, tied to ritual action, and changeable based on post hoc evaluations of a ritual's effectiveness. Once drawn into Santería, even before initiating, the newcomer will experience ever-growing pressure to stop shopping around and instead be loyal to one particular santero chosen as a godparent. Various ceremonies, culminating in initiation, cement the bond between neophyte and godparent. Indeed, initiation sanctifies the godparent-godchild bond as the cornerstone of ritual kinship and hierarchy and the organizing principle of religious community.

Opposing the pressure toward obedience and fealty is a tendency in Santería toward skepticism. We have already seen how skeptical and critical santeros can be of one another's ritual performances. A different manifestation of religious skepticism is shopping around to get different kinds of consultations from different religious practitioners, in search of comprobación (proof). Uninitiated religious practitioners who have already chosen a godparent must balance their search for comprobación with their loyalty in order to maintain propriety. Given the intense competition among santeros and with other religious practitioners, godparents worry that their wandering godchildren may receive bad, or even malicious, advice or may be stolen from them. In the following section I describe and analyze part of a consultation I received from a santero I met at a tambor. I examine how his interpretation of divination results plays into the competitive dynamic through which santeros critique one other's practice and steal one anothers' godchildren.

My consultation with Alberto

As sometimes happened when I met with a new acquaintance, I arrived at Alberto's house for what I thought was to be an informal interview, only to discover that he thought I had wanted a consultation. As I entered his house, a few family members and a goddaughter were sitting downstairs and asked me to wait with them. When Alberto called for me to come upstairs, he and his wife, Maura, were seated at a table that was obviously prepared for divination. Seizing the moment, I asked whether I could record the consultation, and he agreed with delight. Below, I excerpt the section of our consultation in which he divined my sign and interpreted the results to me. I aim to show how the step between reading the divination sign and interpreting its meaning for the client allows santeros to pursue their own and their clients' individual agendas in ways apparently given divine sanction by the formal aspects of the ritual that reinforce its character as divine communication.

After initial prayers and invocations, Alberto gently cast the sixteen cowries onto the table, where he, Maura, and I leaned over them to count how many had landed with their "face side" up. After silently counting six cowrie shells face up, Alberto declared, "Obbara," which is the sign for six. Maura momentarily disagreed, having counted only five face-up cowries, which would be the sign Oche. But a quick recount settled that there were six. Alberto then said "Obbara ibate matate," scooped up the cowries, and shook them again, beginning anew the call-and-response sequence in Lucumí, with Maura responding, that had preceded his previous throw.

1.   Alberto: Padre Eleggua (2 seconds) Eleggua <u>idé mepwé</u>
2.   Maura: <u>Aku ellí</u>[3]
3.   A: Eleggua <u>idé mepwé</u>
4.   M: <u>Aku ellí</u>
5.   A: <u>Aku elle omo, aku barikú . babagua. ¡Ochareo</u>!
6.   M: <u>Agaché</u>
7.   A: <u>Ochareo</u>
8.   M: <u>Agaché</u>

The only words above recognizable to someone outside of Santería would be in line 1, "Padre Eleggua" or Father Eleggua, which mark this sequence as a plea directed to the oricha Eleggua, who mediates all communications between the human and the divine. This time, they counted eight cowries face up, and Alberto declared the sign to be "Unle, Obbara Unle."[4] Maura wrote the complete numerical sign "6–8" in a notebook, just below where she had already written my name. Then Alberto began the process of elaborating additional information about this sign.

The process of constructing a divination result in Santería is, as we already begin to see, very mechanical: shells are cast and counted; a result is tabulated. The steps of elaboration, while more complex, also contribute to the overall sense that divinations produce clear, verifiable results. In cowrie divination, this elaboration is done by giving the client two of five objects to hold hidden in their hands before each additional throw of the cowries. Then, the result of each throw or pair of throws determines which hand the santero will call for, right or left.[5] The client then opens that hand, revealing one of the two objects. Each of the objects signifies something about "who" is talking and what sort of luck the client has. The five objects, called *ibo* in Lucumí, include a piece of chalky ground eggshell paste (called *cascarilla*), a dark pebble, a large round snail shell, a *guacalote* seed pod, and a piece of bone or a porcelain doll's head. When the client holds the *cascarilla* and the pebble, the oracle will determine whether the sign comes with *iré* or *osogbo*, good or bad fortune. The choice between the bone and the pebble determines whether it is the spirits of the dead or the orichas who are talking to the client. When a yes or no question is posed, the snail shell means "yes" and the pebble means "no." The system gets more esoteric from there, with many degrees and types of good or bad fortune and many possible consequences of receiving a message from a particular source, whether spirit or saint.

Santeros must memorize a great deal of information in order to properly do a cowrie divination. Santeros learn from working with their more experienced godparents and, if they have access and inclination, from private or published notebooks on divination. There are 16 cowries and so 256 possible signs, most of which can bring iré or osogbo and each of which can signify that the saints or the dead are speaking. Already, there are almost a thousand basic possibilities, each of which then gets further refined.[6]

Ideally, and in santeros' descriptions of how cowrie divination works, the system is completely self-evident and the meanings of choices are predetermined. Anyone knowledgeable who watched could verify the results simply by recounting the shells. For that matter, the act of writing the results in a notebook reinforces this notion of verifiability, of being able to reconstruct how a santero arrived at a particular sign and elaborated it. Each initial sign (6–8 in my case) cues an entire corpus of associations, from the list of orichas who speak through that sign, to proverbs, legends and parables involving the orichas and other beings, required sacrifices, and so on. After the initial sign, additional signs demand the left hand; others demand the right hand.

In my divination, Alberto cast the cowries seven more times, getting four results: first 4, then the pairs 7–6, 11–7, and 5–6. For each of these four results, he called for me to reveal the object I held in one or the other hand. The first cast decided whether my sign, 6–8, brought iré, "blessings," or osogbo, "ill fortune." The result was four cowries face up: Iroso. Iroso is one of the "senior" signs that does not require a second throw. Alberto called for my left hand, in which I held the white, chalky cascarilla. "Iré," he declared, then handed me two objects again and prepared the cowries for the second throw, calling for arikú, which is the strongest type of iré. The next cast was seven cowries face up, or Oddí, which as a "junior" sign required a second throw. Next was six, Obara, forming the pair Oddí Obara, which required the object in my left hand again. "Arikú," declared Alberto. As he repeated "arikú with Oddí Obara," Maura wrote down the new signs and results. Two more cycles of this process produced the additional pairs 11–7, or Ojuani Oddí, then 5–6, or Oché Obara. The objects in first my right, then my left hand produced the full result: my sign was Obara Unle, with "Iré arikú yale," meaning 6–8, "with blessings from the dead of the strongest kind." Maura wrote in her book approximately the following:

Kristina Wirtz

6–8

Obara Unle

4, 7–6, 11–7, 5–6

con Iré arikú yale

This written representation encodes what the oracle "said" in its purest form, prior to any interpretation. I have presented the almost mechanical process by which this "letter" emerged, throw by throw and result by result, in order to illustrate how ritual forms surround and create this magical step of divination in which the orichas "speak." Kuipers (1993) suggests that more formalized registers of ritual speech allow speakers to displace responsibility from themselves onto a distant past, so that the words carry the authority of "tradition." Highly extextualized speech does this, he suggests elsewhere, because it exactly replicates and therefore iconizes previous speech, thus literally resembling the "speech of the ancestors" (Kuipers 1990). Du Bois (1992) argues that the highly entextualized signs and messages from oracles are a special case of displacement of responsibility, such that there may seem to be no author, which he describes as meaning without intention. In Santería's divinations, authorship sometimes seems to reside with a generic "santo" and sometimes with specific orichas who "speak" through the shells, as in this case. Santeros are being quite literal when they characterize divinations as divine communications. "The cowries are the mouth of the saint," they say. Of course, what first emerges is cryptic to the point of being unintelligible to the client. What do all these numbers and Lucumí words mean? What are the orichas saying? In answer, the santero must now interpret the cryptic "letter" as advice that speaks to the client's situation. In Parkin's more poetic turn of phrase (1991: 175, 183), the diviner "straightens the paths from wilderness" by moving from the esoteric manipulations of the shells toward greater and greater articulateness and intelligibility (also see Peek 1991: 134).

Alberto marked the start of his interpretation of my results by saying: "Ok, let's talk." After a few seconds' pause, he first asked whether I had received previous divinations. Yes, I had. "Obbara Unle," he said, "is where Eleggua comes speaking through Obbara Unle." As he continued, he switched between referring to me with the polite *Usted* (Ud.) and the informal *tú*, both translating as "you." He went on:

9   Where Eleggua says, "<u>Iré, arikú, moyale</u>."

10   Eleggua says that (he) brings <u>iré</u> with <u>Iroso</u>, and

11   <u>arikú</u> he brings with <u>Oddí Obara</u>, and <u>moyare</u>
12   <u>Ojuani Oddí</u>. Eleggua says that you (Ud.) were
13   born to be the head. That you (Ud.) were born to
14   be an intellectual, an intelligent person, a
15   person capable of deepening whatever knowledge,
16   or desires for knowledge, isn't it true? Your
17   (tú) own interest, isn't it, in how to arrive at
18   the thing so that afterward you (Ud.) will know all the
      steps that
19   you (Ud.) want to make, now it won't have any doubt,
20   true? Because once learned, and once you (Ud.)
21   have a set path, so that that future day that you
22   (Ud.) accept the saint, already you (tú) will
23   know all the manipulations, not the secret, but
24   you (Ud.) will know already from which position to
25   defend yourself, for that future day.[7]

Alberto begins by repeating the Lucumí results twice in lines 9–12. Both times, he frames the Lucumí words with "Eleggua says." The divination results, he means, come from Eleggua. The third time, too, he begins with "Eleggua says," but now he explains in Spanish the meaning of the signs. He tells me that I am born "to be the head," an expression usually referring to leadership or religious privilege. Alberto expands upon it to say that I am a thinker, someone inquisitive and intellectual. As he continues, his characterization of me begins to take on a religious significance: I am studying and preparing before I initiate into Santería, so that I will know how to protect myself as soon as I am initiated. The "secret" he refers to in line 23 is the initiation mystery, special knowledge about something that happens during initiation that is known only to initiates. In other words, Alberto is praising me for getting a head start in learning about Santería before initiating, while reminding me that there are limits to what I can learn until I initiate. In his interpretation of my divination sign, he has already assigned me very pragmatic motives for wanting a divination: to learn more about the religion so that I can advance quickly once I initiate.

Maura then suggests a proverb that she and Alberto then repeat: "La cabeza es la que lleva el cuerpo," meaning "it is the head that carries the body." Such proverbs accompany each of the divination results. Some santeros record proverbs in Lucumí in their private religious notebooks, together with their translations, but the proverbs are now most often given in Spanish, and indeed, many are not unique to santeros or divination contexts. Alberto's initial statement that "you were born to be the head" has some of the punchy, aphoristic flavor of a proverb. Maura's interjected "it is the head that carries the body" is even more proverbial, in being indirect and metaphorical and cleverly relying upon natural order (or an inversion of it) to make its point. Both point to the spiritual importance of the head in Santería, which is where a person's principal oricha is "seated" during initiation and which controls a person's destiny.

Proverbs carry the weight of tradition in much the way Lucumí divination signs do: both are formulaic and conventional, and both hearken back across time to ancient, collective wisdom. Just as the system of Lucumí divination signs is authoritative in part because it channels the speech of the orichas, proverbs channel the speech of our ancestors, who were presumably wiser and pithier with words than we are. Some of the authority and wisdom that inheres in these word forms presumably carries over to each successive speaker who animates the ancestrally authored words. Not surprisingly, particular proverbs accompany particular divination signs and are often recited as a first pass at interpreting the sign for the client's situation. The fluidity of proverbs' meanings is evident in Alberto's adaptation of "born to be the head" to refer to my research rather than to leadership or privilege. Once uttered, the proverbs, like the divination signs that cue them, are "superabundant" in meaning and therefore ambiguous, requiring further interpretation to render them applicable to someone's particular situation (Peek 1991: 134; Werbner 1973).

Alberto proceeds to interpret the proverb Maura offered, much as he had interpreted the Lucumí signs and initial "you were born to be the head":

26   Here is where, here is where blessed Saint
27   Barbara, Changó place your head. For what? The
28   head is so that you (Ud.) may think, the head is so you
29   may analyze and observe. Or be very observant
30   within everything that has to do with you (tú) within
31   spiritual and Santería matters, which faith is
32   the one that can [give] you (tú) (1 second) ah ..
33   <u>iré</u> (blessings). I am referring, for example, you (tú) have
34   your elders, you (tú) have your godparents, right?
35   And up to now, have they done anything for you so
36   that you (tú) have gotten results?[8]

Alberto begins his interpretation of the proverb "it is the head that carries the body" much as he did his initial interpretation of my sign: he invokes the saint who is speaking. Just as he introduced the interpretation of my sign by directly quoting Eleggua: "Eleggua says . . ." (line 12), here in lines 26–27 he indirectly attributes his words to Santa Barbara and Changó. In other words, Saint Barbara and Changó are the ones giving me my potential to think my way through a situation. His advice succinctly captures Santería's pragmatic philosophy that the gods help those who help themselves. Seldom do the saints directly heal or solve anything during a divination. Rather, they mostly dispense advice and suggestions upon which the client must act in order to solve the problem.

Saint Barbara is the Catholic saint who corresponds to the oricha Changó. Santeros often use the names interchangeably. Here, Alberto uses them in the plural, then distinguishes between the two religious perspectives they imply in line 31, calling one "spiritual matters" and the other "Santería matters." He thereby suggests that I may need to consider both religious practices, Spiritism and Santería, to find what I need, although by using the Lucumí word "iré" to stand for what I seek (line 33), he suggests a tacit preference for Santería. His invocation of Saint Barbara/Changó is likely motivated by my divination sign, which is Obbara, the letter associated with Changó. Another factor may be that Alberto is a son of Changó. In any case, he quickly gets to the point by asking whether my godparents have gotten results for me in lines 34–36. By asking the question in this way, the diviner introduces doubts, implying that the divination results suggest that my godparents have not been looking out for me. Upon reflection, it is difficult to see what in my very positive divination sign motivates Alberto's apparent concern. It is more likely that he is injecting his own agenda—gaining a foreign godchild—into the proceedings.

Most of the rest of our consultation revolves around Alberto and Maura's repeated attempts to discredit Emilio (and my uncomfortable attempts to shift topic), not because they personally know him, but because some combination of the divination results and my presence there suggested that I might be amenable to switching my loyalties to them. Their interpretation of the divination results has moved from the weighty generalities signaled by Lucumí divination signs and proverbs to the particulars of my situation, in which the divination results speak to both my and their interests.

They proceed from their question about whether my godparents have given me tangible results to the repeated suggestion that I need to initiate. They flatter me repeatedly. At one point, Alberto praises me for seeking a consultation by pointing out that "there are very few people who go along verifying," a reference to the skeptical stance that motivates some religious clients to seek out what we might call "second opinion" consultations in search of "proof" that their results are correct. He goes on to say that seeking verification links to "where Eleggua says Oddi Obbara, where there is speech, Oddí is the mother, Oddí is travel, Obbara is advancement, prosperity, and in Ojuani Oddí . . . Ojuani is 'prendición.'" While his point is not entirely coherent, Alberto does list a range of rich, attractive associations of my divination signs. The final one, "prendición," is a Spanish word that santeros use to mean that an oricha is claiming someone who will need to be initiated. They go on to more explicitly link my initiation with my future prosperity. Maura says:

37 The motive, why? Yes you (tú) have to make a step,
38 but why? That this step will bring you life, it
39 will bring you prosperity, no? But here Eleggua
40 says that you (Ud.) were born to be king, you
41 were born to seek money, you were born to seek
42 advancement and more than advancement.[9]

A moment later, Alberto expands upon how being a santera might directly improve my economic possibilities:

43 A: But Changó says that by your own hand, with
44 your initiation, you (Ud.) can resolve many
45 things in life.
46 Maura: And you have knowledge
47 A: And you have knowledge, why? Because you (tú)
48 are able to bring people from there to here and
49 you can increase your investment of money. It is
50 not that you (tú) are going to go into business, it's
51 that Changó is going to put this development in
52 your hands.[10]

Here, Alberto and Maura stay within the form of a consultation even as they push their individual agenda and encourage me to pursue mine through religious initiation. They evoke an entire scenario in which I will make money by banking my religious knowledge to arrange tours from my home country to Cuba. Making the saint will bring me opportunities to prosper, not because I will cross that gray line into commercializing the religion, but because the saints say I should prosper. Alberto and Maura frame each piece of advice they give to quote an oricha: "Eleggua says; Changó says." Religious adherence brings rewards, and so if the saints want me to initiate, they will improve my life tangibly once I do.

Individual agendas advanced through ritual

Was this encounter exceptional? I do not believe so. The orichas do in fact work on behalf of their devotees to help them achieve exactly these sorts of material improvements in their lives. Alberto and Maura may have been particularly unsubtle, but their own motives and those they attributed to me are widely recognized and frequently expressed dynamics of religious participation in Santería. First of all, as a foreigner interested in the religion, I fit into an established category of desirable godchildren. Seldom did I meet a santero who did not boast of at least one foreign godchild. Second of all, on a half dozen other occasions I received or witnessed consultations in which secular aims were similarly prominent. At the same time, I observed other consultations with Cuban clients in which the santero focused on upbraiding the client for being too "interested" (in personal advancement) and for showing insufficient "respect for the religion." Cuban practitioners and clients nonetheless would openly explain to me that they sought material advancement through religious advancement. They claimed to desire only modest improvements in their economic situations, often saying that they "didn't want to become a millionaire," just be more financially secure, healthier, and happier than now. It was reasonable for Alberto and Maura to expect that I, too, sought economic betterment through the religion.

As to Alberto and Maura's strategies to encourage me to become a regular customer, or perhaps even a godchild, a fair number of santeros make their living exclusively by offering consultations and participating in ceremonies, and most santeros regard such complete dedication to religious vocation as necessary if one wishes to "advance in the religion." A santero masters the ritual knowledge by doing, santeros explain. And if one exclusively lives by religion, one must earn a living by religion. At the same time, many of the same santeros who seemed determined to push an agenda during a consultation would decry the commercialization of the religion in interviews or casual conversation. There is a fine, if ever-shifting, balance between adhering to the dictates of the Regla and using the religion as it is intended, to improve one's life. Rituals such as the consultation I described are an important site for articulating individual desires with shared religious ideals. But what is it about the ritual performance that allows individual and collective interests to simultaneously be advanced?

The distinctive feature of rituals is their adherence to densely patterned, often overdetermined forms of speech, action, and other sensory stimuli. A consultation, for example, places santero and client in a distinctive participant structure in which the santero mediates between the client and an intangible third voice, that of the saints. Even the small excerpts above re-create the flow of a consultation: first, the santero speaks to the saints; next the cowries clink as they land on the table or mat; then the santero represents their pattern as an unfamiliar word, like Obbara, and a numeral, like 6, and both are written down. The attentive client might thus learn that Obbara is equated with the six face-up cowries. Only when he has finished throwing the cowries several times does the santero begin to report what "the saint says" and offer his interpretation.

Note that the santero marks each step of the communicative process with distinctive language. In particular, code changes and markers of quoted speech differentiate the santero's voice from the voice of the saints. The tacit but widely accepted understanding of these code changes is that the santero translates between human language and divine speech, but the saints author the message. The santero's authority lies in his mastery of the process: he knows the Lucumí necessary to mediate the encounter. At the same time, the santero is positioned to ride the line of authorship and responsibility, moving between translating words authored by the saints and claiming the right of interpretation. Figure 6.1 illustrates this model.

My analysis of Alberto's consultation has thus far illustrated the second half of the communication process, labeled "divine responses" in figure 6.1. I traced out how the santero converted cowrie shell patterns into Lucumí labels, then interpreted them into advice, proverbs, and even commands in Spanish—all attributed to the saints. In doing so, he injected his own desires and what he

Figure 6.1. Diagram of human questions and divine responses.

understood to be mine into his interpretation. And yet, the consultation adhered to proper ritual protocols; Alberto even framed some of his interpretations as quoted speech of the orichas: "Eleggua says; Changó says." We begin to see, then, how ritual forms—in particular the necessary gradations of authorship between divination signs and diviner's interpretation—permit santeros to work between shared and individual meanings and thus to ritually advance individual agendas by adapting conventional signs to particular situations. In addition, the religious collective is called into service for individual strategies in the as-yet-unexamined first half of the communication process diagrammed in figure 6.1.

Invoking the collective to aid the individual

Si agua no llueve maíz no crece.
(If rain doesn't fall, corn won't grow.)

Santeros often explain this proverb to mean that one must attend to the orichas in order to reap the benefits of their help. Rituals that offer up the proper prayers, songs, and offerings are the rain that allows one's corn to grow. If one wants the orichas to speak truly in a divination, one must ritually prepare by invoking the entire human and divine community's support. Having seen the outcome of a consultation, let us now examine the setup, in which the santero opens communications with the divine through Lucumí invocations. Earlier, I presented one short example of the way a santero requests the oracle to speak—how he converts the human "questions, pleas" link of figure 6.1 into Lucumí that will invoke the saint's help. Recall that before the second throw of the cowries, Alberto began a sequence of Lucumí speech with an invocation to "Padre Eleggua" (lines 1–8). I will now examine an excerpt from the very first part of my consultation with Alberto and Maura in order to show how formulaic uses of Lucumí frame a divination by differentiating divine and human voices and by assigning authorship to the divine voices. In doing so, the possibility of divine voices authorizing human agendas is set up.

Indeed, a good deal of ritual preparation precedes the moment in which the santero offers the client advice. From an outside perspective, we would say that the preparations create the triadic participant structure and inject into it divine authority and presence. As Briggs (1994) argues in his Foucauldian analysis of a shamanic cure, we must focus on relations of power rather than relations of meaning to understand what is happening in these preparatory ritual steps. From an emic perspective, santeros would explain that they are opening communications with the divine. Doing so imbues the advice offered in a consultation with divine authority, authority it would not otherwise have.

As I already pointed out, Alberto and Maura were delighted to let me record my consultation with them. I was surprised at how readily they agreed, because santeros usually frown upon recording such rituals. When we had finished I understood why: Alberto and Maura wanted to hear the entire recording. We went downstairs to play it on the stereo, and others in the house also listened in. Alberto and Maura most wanted to hear the opening incantatory prayers, which we listened to twice. On other occasions, too, even when they had been initially reluctant to allow me to record a ritual, I found that santeros and babalawos wanted very much to listen to how they had prayed their opening prayers and songs. They seemed to take a special aesthetic pleasure in a good performance. Their special interest in these prayers alerted me to the prayers' importance.

As I mentioned in chapter 2, santeros call these opening incantations the moyubá or *moyubación*. The word itself comes from one of the sections of the incantations, so the label is metonymic. When asked what the word "moyubá" means, most santeros come close to its derivational meaning from Yoruba: "I pay homage."[11] The moyubá must open any ritual activity in Santería, because it invokes the web of spirits, ancestors, and ritual kin whose cooperation is necessary to open a communication channel to the orichas. For this reason, although the moyubá follows a particular and relatively set form, each santero must personalize it to include his particular ancestors and ritual kin, as well as those of any other santero present. The moyubá recitation is a magical act, because the utterance of a moyubá is sufficient to create the state of affairs it invokes: after saying the moyubá, santeros can safely assume that they in fact have the cooperation of all those invoked.

The converse case proves the rule: if a santero forgets to moyubar, or leaves someone out, the ritual will not proceed properly. I saw this happen in one of the first ceremonies I attended in Cuba. The gathered santeros were already well into preparations for a purification of someone's head. Before calling the client in, they did the mandatory divination with coconut shells to make sure that the saints were pleased and would bless the proceedings. The coconut shell came up with Okana Sodde, three of four shells landing face down. The sign means "No" and forecasts misfortune. The santeros were taken aback and sat for a moment conferring about what could have caused this bad sign to emerge. Finally, they asked whether there was something that had not been done. The coconut shells now landed two up and two down, a firm "Yes." Again, they conferred, reviewing each step they had completed, until one of them remembered that when he said the moyubá, he had not included the deceased kin of his client. They asked the coconut shells whether this was the problem, and the answer came back, "Yes." The santeros laughed with relief, finished up the divination, then the lead santero repeated the moyubá, calling through the curtain separating them from the client for the client to recite the names of the deceased in her family at each pause in the recitation.

Although this story demonstrates the importance santeros place on the moyubá, its ubiquitous performance does not in itself draw attention. Perhaps because it must be said so many times, even repeated during the course of a single ritual, santeros usually recite it very rapidly and quietly, often practically under their breath. On the occasions I was permitted to record, my tape recorder often had difficulty picking up the moyubá, especially in a noisy room. Nonetheless, it is crucially important. With the moyubá, the santero invokes the entire community of santeros, spirits, and orichas to cooperate with his ritual and thus to support his intentions.

While its performance may not have the allure of more dramatic genres such as songs and possession trance speech, the moyubá does get a lot of attention when santeros discuss their religious practices. When I interviewed older santeros about ritual speech, they were sometimes resistant about giving me examples, fearing that I intended to steal ritual secrets. I began to follow the lead of my santero-researcher companions in suggesting the moyubá as an example. Most santeros were happy to discuss the importance of the moyubá and some even recited theirs for me. As with most longer Lucumí texts, they could give me the gist of what they were saying but not an exact translation of specific phrases. These uncertainties are reflected in my own attempts at translation, below.

Alberto's moyubá is typical of the hundreds I heard and the ten or so I recorded. He begins by invoking "Father Eleggua" with "omi tuto" or cool water, because Eleggua is the oricha of divination. The omi tuto section wishes coolness, "tuto," on the proceedings, and as he speaks, Alberto sprinkles water from a coconut shell cup.[12] Santeros explain that Eleggua "opens and closes the way"; he is the messenger who therefore determines whether the message will get through to the other saints. Since divination is an exercise in opening two-way communication with the deities, santeros must first ensure Eleggua's cooperation. The passage is addressed to Eleggua and much of it is in Lucumí (marked with underlining).

53   Padre Elegba . aquí tiene Ud <u>Omi tuto</u>, <u>ana tuto</u>, <u>tuto laroyá</u>, <u>tuto</u>
      <u>ile, tuto la forolá, tuto iyé kofo</u>.
      Father Eleggua . here you have <u>cool water, a cool path, tuto laroyá,</u>
      <u>cool house, tuto la forolá, tuto iyé kofo</u>.

Having put down the coconut shell of water, Alberto continues, now introducing my presence and announcing his ritual intention to do a divination for
me. Before starting, Alberto had carefully written down and practiced saying
my hard-to-pronounce name, so that the orichas would be sure to recognize
who I was.

54   ¡Elegba! Que se va a registrar Kristina . Wirtz . para salud, estabili-
      dad, y su elemente, Elegba.
      Eleggua! That we are going to "register" Kristina Wirtz . for health,
      stability, and your element, Eleggua.

55   Para que todo sea <u>iré owó, iré omo, Iré barikú babagua</u>, para que
      Ud. la libre de <u>ikú</u>, de <u>aró</u>, de <u>ofo</u>, de <u>iña arayé</u>, <u>atikú</u>, <u>akokan</u>, . <u>tilla</u>
      <u>tilla, elene onoyú</u>
      So that all will be <u>blessings of money</u>, <u>blessings of child</u>, <u>blessings</u>
      <u>of barikú babagua</u>, so that you will free her of <u>death</u>, of <u>sickness</u>, of
      <u>suffering</u>, of <u>strife</u> <u>arayé, atikú, akokan</u>, . argument, <u>elene onoyú</u>

56   de todos los <u>osogbo</u> y toda las perturbaciones Elegba, que Ud la ponga
      a ella en (vez/pues?) tu salvación, para que todo sea .. <u>mai godó mai</u>
      <u>godá</u>.
      of all the <u>ill fortunes</u> and all the disturbances, Eleggua, that you give
      her (instead) your salvation, so that all will be .. <u>mai godó mai godá.</u>

The English translations here capture one aspect of the original performance: the interplay between intelligibility and unintelligibility. I translated
all Spanish phrases and all Lucumí words that most santeros would be able
to recognize and translate, but left unanalyzed and unglossed those Lucumí
words and phrases for which most santeros cannot give more than a vague,
general meaning. In choosing this santero's-eye perspective for my translations, I obscure how much less intelligible the invocation would be for many
clients. The client would follow the gist of the santero's words, because Spanish,
not Lucumí, provides the syntactic framework, and there is a high proportion
of Spanish to Lucumí words. Even the uninitiated client would gather, from
context, that Alberto is calling upon Eleggua to bless and protect them. Indeed,
some phrases seem Spiritist or Catholic, as in the line asking for "your salva-
tion." Others, though full of unintelligible words, would have contextual mean-

ing. For example, one gleans from context that the series "Iré owó, iré omo, Iré barikú babagua" is desirable, whereas the following series, "de ikú, de aró, de ofo, de iña arayé, atikú, akokan, . tilla tilla, elene onoyú" consists of bad things to be avoided. Even with such guesswork, the uninitiated client listening to the stream of invocatory prayer would find the Lucumí sections as mysterious in their unintelligibility as were the uninterpreted divination signs that later followed. The santero's fluid recital demonstrates his authoritative knowledge, his fluency in this liturgical language.

The santero, although he can fluidly recite the invocations, may himself know some passages only by rote memorization. He would have the benefit of knowing the meaning of key Lucumí words, such as "iré" and "osogbo," "blessings" and "ill fortune." Other words in the series of blessings and ills are well known among santeros: *ikú* is "death" and *aro* is "illness." However, some words and phrases would only be familiar to santeros from the moyubá, since they are not otherwise widely used. For example, many santeros are not sure what *tilla tilla* represents exactly, but they guess it means something bad, such as struggle, upheaval, or fighting.[13]

In the next section, Alberto once again calls upon Eleggua, but then proceeds to invoke the dead, whose cooperation is also necessary for any ritual to succeed.

57 Padre Eleggua . Ibayé,
   Father Eleggua . Ibayé

58 Ibayé ibayen tonú to' esa ciencia oculta que está embelese Olodu-mare
   Rest in peace all those occult sciences which are at the foot of the Creator

59 Ibayé ibayen tonú to' iyalocha, omolocha
   Rest in peace all santeras, santeros

60 Ibayé ibayen tonú to' eggún que vive en este ilé[14]
   Rest in peace all deceased who live in this house

61 Ibayé ibayen tonú to' eggún que vive en esta ará
   Rest in peace all deceased who live in this land

62 Ibayé ibayen tonú to' eggún que vive fuera de esta ará
   Rest in peace all deceased who live outside this land

63 Ibayé ibayen tonú to' eggún que acompaña a Kristina . Wirtz
   Rest in peace all deceased who accompany Kristina Wirtz

64 Ibayé ibayen tonú to' eggún que acompaña a todo iguoro que coggua ilé

<u>Rest in peace</u> all <u>deceased</u> who accompany all the santeros who <u>live in</u> this <u>house</u>

65   Ibayé ibayen tonú to' <u>eggún</u> que acompaña el <u>Iye miye Balefún</u>
<u>Rest in peace</u> all <u>deceased</u> who accompany the (<u>proper name</u>)

66   <u>Ibayé ibaye tonú</u> to' <u>eggún</u> que acompaña . a <u>Ochún iguá</u>—
<u>Rest in peace</u> all <u>deceased</u> who accompany (<u>proper name</u>)

67   <u>Ibayé ibayen tonú</u> to' <u>eggún</u> que acompaña a mi madrina
<u>Rest in peace</u> all <u>deceased</u> who accompany my godmother

68   <u>Ibayé ibayen tonú</u> to' <u>eggún</u> que acompaña a mi padrino <u>Mellukó</u>
<u>Rest in peace</u> all <u>deceased</u> who accompany my godfather (<u>proper name</u>)

69   <u>Ibayé ibayen tonú</u> to' esa ciencia oculta
<u>Rest in peace</u> all that occult science

Alberto continues with five more lines following the same formula of "ibayé ibayen tonú" plus the names of the dead, then repeats line 69. Most santeros gloss "ibayé ibayen tonú" as "rest in peace."[15] Many santeros would insert a far greater number of proper names than did Alberto, who began with general, blanket categories covering all the dead and only then proceeded to list specific people. He uses Lucumí "names in saint" for those who initiated as santeros and regular Spanish names for uninitiated, deceased family members. While santeros say that it is preferable to use Lucumí names, in practice many combine or substitute ordinary nicknames for the deceased santeros in their lineage.

Alberto's use of the Spiritism-derived "occult science" in line 69 requires explanation. Spiritism provides a much more elaborate system for dealing with the spirits of the dead than does Santería. Most santeros also participate in Spiritist ceremonies, which combine Christian, scientific, and other influences into a theology of mutual assistance between suffering humans and spirits seeking transcendence. Most of the moyubás I heard during my research included a line invoking the "science" or "sciences" to mean all the spirits of the deceased who help the living.

In the sections presented thus far, Alberto's moyubá has invoked the support of the spirits of the dead for his ritual. The preponderance of Lucumí in even the highly repetitive sections indexes the expertise of the santero and the difficulty of communicating with divine beings, who speak a different language.

Upon finishing the *ibayé* section, Alberto continues with the *kinkamaché* section, which invokes the support of living santeros. The invocation "kinkamaché" foregrounds yet another ubiquitous and universally used Lucumí word with an uncertain translation. Most santeros gloss it to mean "health" in the sense of wishing someone "good health."[16] But this denotation is deceptively simple, because the performative effect entailed by the kinkamaché section is to ensure the cooperation of all the santeros who are in one's lineage or present during the ceremony.

70   Kinkamaché el erí de mi madrina Omí Oñí
       Health to the head of my godmother (proper name)
71   Kinkamaché . el de mi Ayugbón Nike Ogún
       Health to that of my assisting godfather (proper name)
72   Kinkamaché Omí Niké, Kinkamaché Ogún Niwé, Kinkamaché Omi-
       ni Omí yalé, Kinkamaché eh. Ochún Cholí, Kinkamaché Ocha Inle,
       Kinkamaché Obbá Kotó, Kinkamaché . . . (seven more proper names)
       followed the sequence)
       Health to (series of proper names)
73   Kinkamaché to' 'yalocha omolocha, to' y 'tan hecho Elegguá.
       Health to all the santeras children of the oricha, all and who have initi-
       ated with Eleggua.

Alberto starts by invoking his godparents, following standard form. From there he invokes living santeros in his ritual lineage by their "names in the saint." He closes with the obligatory catchall "health to all santeros" to protect himself in case he has forgotten someone. With this, Alberto has called upon the support of the entire religious community, including spirit and human members. The very act of ritual invocation ensures the religious community's support. Alberto must now ritually invoke the orichas who enable the divina-tion. At the same time, he introduces me as the beneficiary or client of the divination. He thus sets up a communicative triad between client and oricha, with himself as the mediator of communications, just as the entire religious community, through the performative logic of the invocations, mediates be-tween him and the oracle.

Having completed the initial moyubá, Alberto prepares the divination. First, he asks me to hold my payment for the divination over the cowries and to pray silently for what I desire. Then I am to kiss my fist of money and place the money onto the pile of cowries. Next, Alberto again calls on Eleggua, ad-dressing him directly with formulaic pleas to banish ill fortune and permit only good fortune for the client who has made the offering. Again, Eleggua's divine role as gatekeeper is invoked, because he has the power to open the door to good and close the door on evil.

74   Eleggua, <u>achiri oguó, achiri omo, achiri barikú babagua</u>, para que todo sea <u>kosikú, kosi(agua)ofo</u>, y <u>kosiano</u>.

      Eleggua, <u>achiri oguó, achiri omo, achiri barikú babagua</u> so that all may be <u>no death, no (agua)ofo</u>, and <u>no illness</u>

(5 seconds)

(Alberto picks up rattle and shakes it throughout the following section)

75   Padre Eleggua (3 seconds), Eleggua (1 second) Aquí está su <u>omo Otá Lekún</u> que va a registrar a Kristina Brit, Wirtz, Father Eleggua (3 seconds) Eleggua (1 second) Here is your <u>child (proper name)</u> who is going to register Kristina Wirtz

76   Paz, salud, estabilidad, firmeza Elegguá, para su salvación a ella y to' sus seres queridos

      Peace, health, stability, strength, Eleggua for her salvation for her and all her loved ones

77   Para que la libre de <u>ikú</u>, de <u>ano</u>, de <u>ofo</u>, de <u>iña, . aro, tillatilla ti terí osobbo</u>, to' los malos <u>okú</u>

      So that you free her of <u>death</u>, of <u>sickness</u>, of <u>suffering</u>, of <u>strife</u>, <u>illness</u>, <u>argument, ti terí bad signs</u>, all the bad things <u>okú</u>

78   Para que todo sea . <u>iré owó, iré omo, iré bariku babagua</u>, Elegguá.

      So that all may be <u>good fortune of money, good fortune of child</u>, good fortune of <u>bariku our father,</u> Eleggua.

The rattle Alberto shakes throughout this and the next section helps attract the attention of the oricha. Alberto repeats the "ibayé ibayen tonú" section, much as he did earlier, in lines 58–69. Before repeating the kinkamaché section, he first inserts the following invocation:

79   La bendición de to' lo' muerto' que me acompaña

      The blessing of all the deceased who accompany me

80   La bendición de Changó mi pa're,

      The blessing of Changó my father

81   Dame la bendición de mi mamá, la bendición de mi papá,

      Give me the blessing of my mother, the blessing of my father,

82   La bendición de mi madrina,

      The blessing of my godmother

83   La bendición de mi <u>ayugbona Nike Ogún</u> (words not clear)

      The blessing of my <u>assisting godparent, (proper name)</u>

84   La bendición de todos los que (me ayudan?) en santo

      The blessing of all those who (help me?) in the saint

This section, almost entirely in Spanish, sometimes appears in santeros' moyubás but seems to be optional. A couple of santeros explained to me that they use longer and shorter forms of the moyubá depending upon how elaborate an invocation a particular ritual seems to require. This section, like those preceding and following, serves to marshal spiritual support.

In the structural logic of the ritual, Alberto's moyubás opened the channel of divine communication and introduced me as a participant. After the first round of moyubá, I was asked to pray directly on my own behalf, keeping the communication channel open by accompanying my silent words with an offering of money. In order to receive a response, I needed Alberto to mediate, to orchestrate the divination. He in turn needed the cowries to mediate, to serve, as santeros say, as the "tongue of the orichas." And the cowries would only speak truly if the entire chain of santeros, living and dead, and orichas, particularly Eleggua, permitted them to. Figure 6.2 illustrates the chain of mediated communication.

I passed an offering of money up the chain to the santero by placing it on the cowries. He accepted the money on behalf of the orichas and then prepared the cowries to "speak," in part by imploring Eleggua to convey the message (and imploring the spirits and other santeros to cooperate). Doing this would allow my silent prayers and his questions to the oracle to be transmitted to the orichas and an answer to come back down the chain, via the cowries.

In the following section, Alberto replaces the rattle he has been holding with the cowries. After some final prayers entirely in Lucumí, he addresses "Father Eleggua," and he and Maura begin a call-and-response exchange almost identical to the one transcribed in lines 1–8. After Alberto says "Ochareo" and Maura answers "Agaché" twice, Alberto at last throws the cowries.

The sequence *ochareo, agaché* (most santeros I recorded say "adaché") pre-

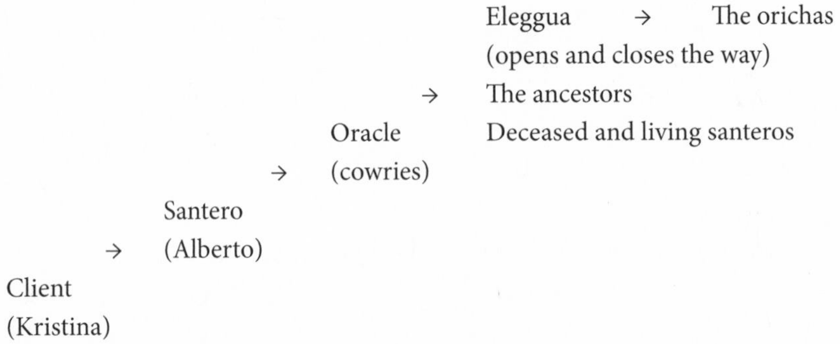

Eleggua   →   The orichas
(opens and closes the way)

→   The ancestors

Oracle   Deceased and living santeros

→   (cowries)

Santero

→   (Alberto)

Client
(Kristina)

Figure 6.2. Diagram of the chain of mediated communication in a divination.

cedes each throw of the cowries. Various santeros explained to me that the call and response implores the cowries to speak truly and to bring blessings. One translation offered that "ochareo" means "the oricha will speak" and that "adaché" or "agaché" means "may it be for aché (sacred power)."[17] The sequence immediately precedes, and thus cues, each cast of the cowries. It expresses and marshals the santero's (and client's) expectations in the moment before the "saint speaks." By so doing, the sequence serves as a tool of emplotment (Mattingly 1998), with each Ochareo eliciting an answering Agaché, so that the entire sequence triggers the orichas' speech through the falling cowries.

This entire, impressively mysterious recitation leads to the section described earlier in the chapter where Alberto constructed my sign out of multiple throws of the cowries and gave me advice. Throughout the long prayers, the client sits expectantly, awaiting the very last step when the santero will begin speaking Spanish and making sense of the divination results. The santero may incorporate his knowledge (or guesses) about the client's situation into his interpretation, but the very forms of the ritual indicate that his interpretation is constrained by the divination results. The divination results, within the ritual frame, are in turn voiced as the speech of the saints.

My analysis of the moyubá demonstrates the central role Lucumí ritual speech has in structuring rituals and rendering them recognizable. In this sense, canonical Lucumí usage promotes the collective forms and meanings of Santería. But the moyubá genre, especially, promotes the collective in a more direct, denotative way, as well. The moyubá expressly invokes the santero's ritual elders, his lineage, and the community of santeros in general. In this sense, a santero's moyubá creates and structures his religious community every time he utters it. The shared norms for a moyubá dictate that the santero must at a minimum name his godparents, his deceased genealogical and ritual kin, and his living ritual kin. If other santeros are present at the same ritual, the santero who offers the moyubá must include them and, sometimes, their ritual lineages in his recitation. The moyubá, thus, is a performed diagram of ritual kinship. Ritual kinship generates a hierarchy that links the living, the dead, and the divine. A santero's particular moyubá invokes these links as they pertain to that santero, as I diagram in figures 1.1 and 1.2.

In true Durkheimian fashion, the moyubá acknowledges the community as the heart of the religion. It would be simply unthinkable to engage in ritual action without first invoking the consent of the community. In a sense, then, the act of *moyubación* acknowledges the community's power to impose collective ritual aims and forms and to judge its members' competence and compliance with those aims and forms. But still the moyubá is an individual, sometimes even private, act of performative magic. While phrased as invocation, its results are, in essence, guaranteed. To recite one's complete moyubá is to receive the spiritual community's support for one's ritual act. This example of ritual speech, as much as the earlier examples of divination and consultation, invokes collective aims and forms to empower individuals to access the sacred for their own various purposes.

Early in this chapter, I explored the range of individual purposes and strategies in Alberto's interpretation of my divination results. In contrast, the moyubá might seem too formulaic to allow much tinkering to adapt it to individual strategy. But in fact, santeros alter their moyubás to fit context and even embellish them to claim illustrious ritual ancestors. Two brief examples will illustrate the potential for santeros to use their *moyubaciones* to make alliances and advance their standing. First of all, a santero praying a moyubá in front of another santero of a different lineage might include his or her godparent or a well-known ritual ancestor of that lineage. Doing so automatically, rather than stopping to let the second santero fill in the blanks, suggests that the santero regards the added people as his own ritual elders as well. If the two santeros share ritual elders, then they are ritual kin themselves. Similarly, santeros may include the names of deceased santeros who were particularly important in establishing Santería in Santiago during the 1920s–1940s. Emilio, for example, often names Reynerio Pérez and Rosa Torres in his moyubá, even though he comes from a completely separate lineage from either of them. Nonetheless, all santeros in Santiago regard Reynerio especially as being the founder of Santería in Santiago, the one who established its presence in the city. Reynerio and Rosa both initiated dozens of godchildren and participated in the initiations of dozens, if not hundreds, more. By naming them in his moyubá, Emilio shows his respect for them but also makes a bid to pull them into his lineup of ritual ancestors, those whose beneficence empowers his rituals to be efficacious.

Conclusion

> Ikú lobí ocha. (Lucumí)
> El muerto pare al santo. (Spanish)
> The dead give birth to the oricha.

This proverb is perhaps the one santeros most frequently quote. It can be interpreted as an acknowledgment that permission must be gained from the spirits of the dead before one can communicate with the orichas. This is precisely what the moyubá does. At another level, santeros say the proverb reminds them that they are linked to the orichas via the ancestors in a continuous chain connecting individual santeros to a religious collective governed by the Regla. Indeed, the living, the dead, and the deified comprise categories through which individuals move, although in santeros' understanding only a few exceptional ancestors, like the Yoruba king of Oyo, Changó, undergo apotheosis to become orichas.

In this chapter, I have taken up the problem of tension between individual and collective religious goals. I have discussed how ritual discourse serves to promote both individual and collective aims and to express both normative and alternative interpretations of ritual events. On balance, the collective side of the equation explicitly promotes obedience to tradition, to the Regla, to one's ritual elders, and to the orichas. The collective need for group cohesion, agreement as to norms, and shared interpretations of events are modeled in canonical ritual forms, expected participant structures of rituals, attention to ritual detail, and, let us not forget, gossip's power to develop consensus, circulate warnings, and even censure those who stray from these precepts. Rituals, it seems, have some power to compel religious participants to conform to a shared sense of purpose or at least to stay in character during performance.

The individual side of the balance promotes participation in religious ritual as a way to get ahead, to advance socially and materially. But in order to achieve individual goals, ritual participants' strategies must draw upon the very tropes and forms of ritual that the religious community collectively agrees upon. At the same time, individuals must be wary of others' intentions and so keep a skeptical attitude, much as I have modeled in my analysis of the consultation I received. But this very skepticism, interestingly, is itself framed by shared ideas of what is correct and what is a violation, what is respectful and what is not, what counts as proof and what as contradiction.

The intersection between individual and collective interests, on balance, actually advances Santería's distinctive sacred stance. The reason is that religious activity and the commentary and reflection it inspires continue to rely upon the same recognizable ritual forms, the same tropic uses of ritual speech. Participants invoke the same patterns of signification, the same frames and imagery, whatever agenda they are individually or collectively pursuing. The net effect is that the more participants' interest is aroused, the more they circulate the ritual forms. They do so both by replicating rituals—seeking out another consultation or sponsoring another ceremony—and by replicating significant bits of rituals as they discuss them after the fact. What they deem significant depends upon their aims—to critique an incorrect ritual step, to recount a divination result. But even as ritual speech is replicated, quoted, paraphrased, and everything else, its ongoing circulation both delineates the religious community and promotes its shared religious orientation.

Chapter 7 takes up another aspect of the question explored in this chapter. Rituals like divination serve to balance both collective ideals and individual strategies, and forms of reflective discourse such as gossip and critique can also promote shared meanings even while enacting more divisive and skeptical attitudes toward santeros' motives. Chapter 7 builds upon these ideas to examine how a moral community of Santería emerges out of participation in rituals and the controversies they engender.

Building a Moral Community out of Critique and Controversy

When I visited Santiago in April 2002, a new acquaintance took me to meet his godfather's family, which is prominent among santeros. Two of his godfather's brothers and his mother were home when we arrived. All are santeros, and one brother has also been initiated as a babalawo, the special caste of priests dedicated to Ifá divination. They were not especially pleased that their uninitiated godchild had decided to bring a foreigner around, and to most of my friend's and my attempts to start conversation, one or another would cut things off by insisting that a topic was secret or that noninitiates were not permitted to attend certain rituals. They eventually started listing ceremonies a noninitiate like me could attend and decided that I could accompany them to a *tambor de fundamento*, or ceremony with consecrated drums, later that week.

Just then, some young men passed the door carrying batá drums. One brother went outside to chat with them, then returned a few minutes later to say that they were on their way to do a regular bembé, not a *tambor de fundamento*. The mother archly commented that I could go see that if I wanted, but that it would probably be carelessly done, because it was just any old bembé. Her comment precipitated a family discussion in which they emphasized that most santeros don't do things correctly. Most are out to make easy money, they claimed. In contrast, their family always does things correctly, lives by the Regla, and has no patience with those lacking respect for or commercializing the religion. They proudly explained that their family is recognized to be preeminent, really a *casa-templo* or "temple-house," a word used to refer to families with prominent ritual lineages whose homes were always filled with "family in the saint" and ritual activity.

As they warmed to the topic, I quietly entered the conversation by asking how long their family had been involved in Santería. They had at least six decades of experience among them. The mother added that her aunt had been one of the first santeras of the city, during the era of the famous Reynerio Pérez, whom most Santiago santeros regard as the founder of Santería in Santiago.[1] Reynerio is deceased, but his large family still maintains a house that most santeros in the city agree is a *casa-templo*, a place guaranteed to hold a *tambor de fundamento* on important saints' days. Knowing this, I asked whether the family had maintained connections with Reynerio's family's *casa-templo*. The mother quickly and firmly said no, absolutely not. Reynerio's family has gone downhill since his death. They recounted a story about an initiation done in the house of a descendent of Reynerio. It was a travesty: why, they even permitted a film crew from a cultural research center to come in and film everything, even secret rituals reserved for santeros only! They were so shocked at the ritual violations that they have since turned down invitations to witness or participate in other ceremonies there.

Later in the conversation, they jointly told another story, in which a babalawo who had for years committed blatant ritual violations fell sick. Not one santero visited him in the hospital, nor did anyone step forward when he passed away to conduct the necessary funerary rites (*ituto*) for santeros and babalawos. Cut ritual corners, disrespect the religion, and die a sorry death, they grimly concluded.

Our conversation mingled gossip, evaluations of ceremonies and santeros, and critiques of everyone outside of this family. Such sessions were quite typical among santeros sitting together while visiting, planning a future ceremony, or waiting for a current ceremony to begin or end. They often began with the equivalent of someone bemoaning how the religion was going to hell in a handbag and they often concluded with participants agreeing that they were among the few santeros left who really respected the religion. Since many sessions of critique, like the one recounted above, took place among members of a particular ritual lineage, their other most common conclusion was that their lineage did things correctly and was therefore deserving of its prominence.

While such conversations might seem quite distant from formal ritual speech practices examined in the previous chapters, they are in fact often quite closely linked. Indeed, ritual performances like Alberto's consultation for me in chapter 6 or Yemayá's appearance at the tambor in chapter 5 often provoke reflective discourses in the form of retellings, critiques, and so forth. A ritual is like the pebble landing in water that produces a ripple of commentary, a transfer of its sacred episteme and message into nonritual discourse on nonritual occasions. Among Santiago's santeros, reflective discourses on rituals may simply report on what happened, but more often recountings come with a point. Santeros frequently critique rituals in which they have participated. Often these critiques merge into ongoing disagreements or even provoke controversies. On such occasions, the ripples of initial commentary may produce additional ripples, as discussions continue, referring back to what has already been said, as well as to the original ritual itself. Of course, the ripple metaphor assumes that a ritual is in itself an isolated, originary event. It would be more accurate to think of rituals as occurring in a matrix of overlapping discourses (the pond surface in a rainstorm), some of which promote cohesion and some of which fuel tensions and controversies among individuals and subgroups within the community. In short, controversy, as much as consensus, may make the religious community tangible.

In this chapter, I zero in on how ritual events provoke critique and controversy, as well as consensus, and how critique and controversy serve as engines of religious community. How can it be that everything does not simply fly apart, given that religious participants may pursue individual agendas and at the same time be suspicious of other participants' agendas? First of all, some aspects of rituals and other religious activities function to bring participants together, whether to forge consensus or reinforce hierarchy and respect for the Regla. In addition, controversies about religious activities themselves require some basis of agreement about what, exactly, is in dispute. That is to say that religious community emerges as that (ever-changing) group of people who participate not only in the same rituals, but also in the same reflective discourses—the same disputes—about those rituals. For our purposes, controversies suggest the outlines, or at least give a sense of the center of, particular communities, even while pointing out fissures within a community. The "center" or "core" of the community, as such, consists of those who are most enmeshed in rituals and the reflective discourses they provoke.

Two examples developed in the chapter, one quite typical and one extraordinary, reveal how after-the-fact commentaries draw upon, even echo, ritual speech, and how, in referring back to what was said and done in rituals, critiques actually advance both a sense of community and a degree of consensus about what it means to be a member of the religious community of Santería. In previous chapters I have described how santeros approach rituals with an odd combination of high expectation that the orichas will communicate clearly and powerfully and with skepticism about most other santeros' motives and ritual abilities. These two somewhat conflicting tendencies come together in santeros' close attention to ritual detail.

Santeros' attention to and concern with "proof" are formally recognized in a ritual participant role called "witnessing." In major rituals such as initiation ceremonies, those responsible for planning must formally invite a number of santeros to serve as witnesses. The semiritual invitation is called *levantando*, or "raising" a santero, and requires that the host or hostess pay a small fee called the *derecho* to the santero's principal oricha. Santeros explain that the role of "raised" santeros is as much to witness events as to help with preparations. Indeed, those who do help with various preparatory steps and other ritual activities receive additional *derecho* payments for some of these. By witnessing ritual events, santeros can ostensibly later confirm that everything was done correctly and that particular divination results, for example, were received. Of course, witnessing also gives santeros fodder for the gossip mill and food for the critique of ritual events.

As the examples below detail, ritual participants, as witnesses, may reveal multiple motives for critiquing a ritual. Most immediately, they express concerns about following the Regla, showing respect for the religion, and attending to ritual detail. A santero who feels that these tenets have been violated may be motivated to speak up during the ritual itself or later. But deeper analysis of critiques suggests that these concerns often serve as triggers for santeros to position themselves with regard to other sorts of agendas and tensions, which, not surprisingly, principally concern social relationships. Many types of social relationships are mobilized in critiques: positionings on the ritual hierarchy of priests, relations of ritual kinship, friendships and enmities. These relationships play out in whom one critiques, whom one chooses as audience for the critique, and how others respond to the critique. In the first section of the chapter I revisit the structures of ritual kinship and hierarchy that santeros enact in creating a moral community.

The two sections that follow present two extended examples of critiques arising out of rituals. In both I explore the interactional alignments that emerge as a result of the critiques. These positionings have implications for the processes of creating new links of ritual lineage, advancing claims for ritual authority, and differentiating one's own from other lineages—in other words, for structuring religious community. The first example examines how a santero critiqued his friend's initiation ceremony after the fact, with me and others in his ritual lineage as audience, and with what effects. The second example examines a larger-scale situation in which evaluations of ritual events were embedded in later rituals, which in turn provoked a major controversy among the two castes of priests, santeros and babalawos, in Santiago.

Ritual kinship and authority in Santería

Godparents and gods-as-parents

Any discussion of religious community in Santería must begin and end with how religious participants structure ritual relationships. Indeed, the two cases I examine later in the chapter make sense only in light of the nature of ritual kinship in Santería.

Ritual kinship ties are formalized through initiation. While anyone can seek out a consultation with a santero or find a tambor ceremony to attend, other types of religious participation require initiation into Santería or what santeros call "making the saint." When someone decides to be initiated, they do so under the supervision of a santero they choose to be their godparent. While many santeros have uninitiated godchildren, initiating is understood to render the relationship permanent and, theoretically, inviolable.[2] In parallel with this human connection, someone undergoing initiation also cements a bond with a particular oricha who is that person's principal oricha or "Guardian Angel." Santeros I spoke with often linked these two bonds, one human and one divine, by pointing out that in the idiom of initiation ritual, the godparent's principal oricha "gives birth to" the godchild's principal oricha (although they are likely to be different orichas).

Initiation rituals produce additional ritual ties. First of all, by joining the godparent's ritual lineage, the new initiate gains an entire "family in the saint." The godparent of one's godparent is one's "grandparent in the saint." The godparent's other godchildren become one's "siblings in the saint." Esteemed ancestors or founders of the lineage become one's ritual ancestors. Santeros recall all of these connections every time they recite the moyubá invocation, as examined in chapter 6.

In addition, the initiation ceremony requires a second godparent, called the *ayugbón* or *ayugbona*, a Lucumí term santeros translate as "assistant godparent" or "godparent to raise (the child)." This second gloss reflects the role of the *ayugbón*, which is to nurture the new initiate, who is treated like a helpless newborn baby during the larger part of the initiation ceremonies. Together, the two godparents become the ritual parents who metaphorically bear and raise their initiating godchild. In another divine parallel, the initiate also gets an oricha "father" and "mother": if the principal oricha is male, a female oricha will be identified through divination as the "mother," whereas if the principal oricha is female, a male will be identified as the "father." Santeros might say, for example, that their "mother" is Yemayá and their "father" is Obatalá. Given the pervasive parenting metaphors of initiation, it is not surprising that the santeros often compare the *recién iniciado* (new initiate) to a *recién nacido* or newborn.

Initiation

Indeed, the elaborate and expensive week-long initiation ceremonies bear all the marks of classic rites of passage: the initiate is removed from his or her ordinary context and, under the control of his or her godparents and the officiating santero or oriaté, lives for a week in a space circumscribed by the mats that make up the altar space. The initiate is stripped of clothes, bathed, shaved, re-dressed entirely in white, and even renamed, all as part of a process of spiritual purification.[3] For the rest of the ceremony and, indeed, for the entire year to follow, the initiate must wear only white clothes, must keep his or her head covered, and must answer only to the special Lucumí name for new initiate, "iyawó."[4]

Throughout the initiation ceremonies, parts of the religious community are brought into contact with the iyawó, so that at the same time that the iyawó is being incorporated into the religious community as a godchild of a particular lineage, the religious community is reincorporating itself: the lineage members come together to participate, as do other invited santeros. Some rituals during initiation allow the community of participating santeros to shape the iyawó's new identity as a santero.

Others present the iyawó to the broader religious community, cementing his or her new religious identity. An example of the latter is the "Day of Presentation," in which the iyawó is dressed in a specially made outfit akin to a wedding dress in that it will be worn only on this one day. The outfit, always in the colors and style of the iyawó's principal oricha, will be saved so that when the iyawó someday dies, the outfit will be buried with him.[5] On the Day of Presentation, the iyawó sits on the altar receiving visitors, who in turn salute their saints and leave an offering of money and perhaps some advice for the iyawó.

A crucial example of the former ceremony where the community shapes the iyawó's new identity occurs the morning following the Day of Presentation on the "Day of Itá."[6] The Itá is a special divination ceremony in which an *oriaté*, or "officiating priest," throws the cowrie shells for each of the orichas whom the iyawó has received. That is, in addition to the iyawó's own principal oricha, he or she will, at a minimum, receive the orichas known as the Guerreros or Warriors (including Eleggua, Ogún, and Ochosí) and those known as the Corte or Court (including Yemayá, Changó, Ochún, Obatalá, and Oyá). All of these orichas will "speak" to the iyawó during the Itá divination, in order to give advice, warnings, prohibitions, and encouragements. As santeros like to explain, the Itá sets down the regulations according to which the iyawó must now live. The regulations form an individualized Regla that will continually remind the new initiate to respect and obey the orichas. Certain foods, drinks, and behaviors will be forbidden: Perhaps the iyawó may no longer eat goat or squash or drink dark beverages like coffee or Coke; Perhaps he may no longer be permitted to wear black clothes or drink alcohol or fight with his spouse; Perhaps she should beware of going out in groups of three or more and must take care of her vision lest she develop a problem. The prohibitions and warnings may range from the utterly mundane to the most dramatic, as when Emilio was told in his Itá that a grave was open for him or a family member (see chapter 1).

The Itá ceremony requires the presence of a number of witnessing santeros beyond the oriaté, iyawó, and the two godparents. The oriaté (also called the "italero") runs the Itá, which means that he leads the liturgy, throws the cowries, and interprets the results. Other santeros, especially the principal godparent, may also contribute their interpretations of the divination results. While it is from santeros' mouths that the advice and rules for the iyawó are uttered, santeros credit themselves (or each other) only with inspired interpretation. It is the orichas themselves who send the advice and dictate the rules when they "speak" through their cowries. Thus, while santeros' overt metapragmatic understanding of Itá is that the orichas "speak" directly to the iyawó, their practice of Itá implicitly emphasizes the importance of religious community participation in the ritual as witnesses to and mediators of the orichas' will.

Ritual hierarchy

In their cumulative effects, the ceremonies of initiation establish a clear boundary between before and after and between santeros and everyone else. Santeros have a number of Lucumí terms for themselves, as individual santeros or as a community: *oloricha, omo oricha, iguoro.* There is also a Lucumí term for noninitiates: *aleyo.* While the word refers to any religious outsider, santeros typically use it to refer to noninitiates who are present in a ceremony. For example, I have heard frustrated santeros attempt to control a rowdy tambor by hollering that all aleyos must leave the room to make room for santeros to dance close to the drums. Thus, being designated an aleyo already moves a person out of the general population and into a contrastive position with santeros around the pivot point of initiation.

Becoming a santero means joining a ritual lineage and family as the most junior member. Only with time and, perhaps, after initiating one's own god-children, does one gain status, including the designation of *babalocha* or *iya-locha*, "father-of-the-oricha" or "mother-of-the-oricha." A few santeros—men only—move even higher up the ladder of ritual status by completing other rituals and developing special expertise as officiating priests, whom santeros refer to by any of three interchangeable Lucumí titles: oriaté, italero, *obbá*.[7] The second term, "italero," is a hispanicization of Itá meaning "one who does Itá," which is indeed one of the duties of the officiating priest. One final layer of ritual authority is represented by those men initiated as babalawos, priests who master the complex system of Ifá divination. Babalawos comprise a relatively autonomous caste of priests, since some are initiated without first becoming santeros, and since they perform their rituals and maintain their lineages sepa-rately from santeros (D. H. Brown 2003, Dianteill 2000).

Whether santero or babalawo, a priest gains seniority over time and with increased status according to his standing among other santeros. A santero's standing generally improves with more godchildren and more ritual expertise. Upon dying the santero joins the ancestors, to be invoked by descendants of his lineage. A few exceptional individuals, especially those who initiated large numbers of godchildren, will be invoked by many santeros across multiple lin-eages. Since the orichas are, in some sense, understood to be deified ancestors, all santeros can, in theory at least, approach the asymptote of divinity. Figure 7.1 places all of the roles described along a single continuum where the arrows move from aleyo across the boundary of initiation to ever more senior ritual status, then across the boundary of death toward divinity.

By connecting these ritual roles with arrows, I suggest that the ritual hi-erarchy is also a ladder of sorts, a progression one follows to get closer to the authority of the deities. In practice, a santero may also gain ritual authority by filling in the ranks behind him with godchildren who will seek out his advice and expertise. These same godchildren will someday, ideally, keep the santero's memory alive by invoking his or her name in the moyubá. One very senior

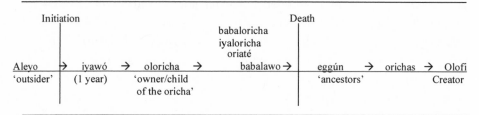

Figure 7.1. Diagram of ritual hierarchy in Santería.

santera I interviewed who is getting older frequently voiced her concern about how she would be remembered by wondering aloud whether anyone would bother to *moyubar* or "pay homage" to her.

As I described above for the Itá divination, more senior santeros mediate ritual communications between the orichas and more junior religious participants. This principle of mediation is also apparent in how santeros first placate the ancestors before communicating, in words or offerings, with the orichas. The orichas, in turn, are the ultimate arbiters between humans and Almighty God, known in Santería as Olofi.

In this overview of ritual kinship, I have described how santeros organize an idealized ritual hierarchy of roles across which individuals seek to move ever closer to the divine. I hasten to caution that my various descriptions and diagrams of ritual kinship and hierarchy should be taken as abstractions, articulated by santeros, as well as by the anthropologist, who precipitate them out of all the activities through which santeros create and reinforce social bonds. I have briefly indicated some of the ways santeros come together as a moral community to initiate new members, while simultaneously reinforcing their own lineages and alliances—in other words, how the moral community is organized in part through normative ritual activity. The next sections examine two cases in which tensions over who has claim to a potential new initiate play out during Itá divinations. My goal is to show how the schema of ritual hierarchy I have outlined also gets enacted through critique and controversy, such that these activities, too, organize the moral community of Santería.

The ethnographer as aleyo (religious outsider and potential initiate)

The Itá divination

In the course of my fieldwork, I was frequently invited to various iyawós' presentation days, although most of the other rituals of initiation are secret and closed to aleyos. Once, however, I was invited to attend an Itá divination. Emilio and I had gone to pay our respects to an iyawó Emilio's friend Roberto was initiating on his Day of Presentation. To my surprise, Roberto invited us both to return the following morning for the Itá divination. As we left, Emilio explained to me that he thought that Roberto had made an exception because he assumed I would soon be initiated myself. I might have been an aleyo, but I was close to crossing that boundary, and perhaps needed only a small push. As it turned out, Roberto's Itá ceremony provided a push of sorts. It also exposed the ways in which introducing new members reinforces the existing moral community, not least by providing the lens through which to reflect upon the Regla that santeros revere in common.

I only briefly describe the events of the Itá, which I was not allowed to record. I will instead focus on how Emilio and I later discussed those events. Emilio engaged in exactly the sort of critical commentary on Roberto's ceremony that is so prevalent among santeros. He detected many ritual errors, some of which he found quite shocking. At the same time, he reiterated his respect for Roberto, who had been initiated since childhood and was well respected among santeros in Santiago and elsewhere on the island. Months later, Emilio revisited his critiques of Roberto's ceremony with his godparents when we visited them, and on another occasion he brought them up with his godfather's *ayugbona* (assistant godmother). All three elders agreed with Emilio's assessment.

In discussing Emilio's critiques of Roberto, I would like to focus on what Emilio accomplished by making his critique—first with me and then with his godparents and his "grandmother in the saint." Much of his critique of Roberto invoked normative notions of the role of religious community in an initiation, especially the adherence to hierarchy and inclusion of proper witnesses. He made his critiques before an audience of his own ritual lineage, and his critiques served to reinforce the ritual ties binding this lineage and to advance claims about its propriety.

Aleyo goddaughter—**Santero**—Godparents—Grandmother in saint
Kristina   Emilio   Teodoro & Tania   María

Despite all that Emilio's critiques did accomplish, they did not and could not pass a certain point, because he did not have any evidence that the orichas were displeased with Roberto. His unwillingness to second-guess the orichas (even as he critiqued the santero) was perhaps the most telling evidence Emilio presented that he lives correctly as a santero who obeys the Regla.

When Emilio and I arrived at Roberto's on the day of the Itá, Roberto, the iyawó, and a few other santeros were waiting for us. The iyawó was a young man, barely twenty, who had traveled from Havana to undergo initiation with Roberto. After some preliminary rituals, the Itá divination itself began when we all gathered around Roberto, who sat on a mat in his living room, with all of the plates of the different saints the iyawó had received sitting lined up next to him. Each plate had on it the cowrie shells that would allow that oricha to speak. The shells still bore the traces of blood and herbs from having been ritually "fed" the previous day. Offerings of sacred herbs, animals, and other valued substances made to the orichas are necessary to activate the aché or sacred energy of the cowries so that they will "speak." As the Itá proceeded, Roberto had each set of cowries brought to him in turn to conduct a divination for that oricha: Eleggua, Obatalá, Oyá, Yemayá, Changó, and finally Ochún, who was the iyawó's principal oricha. For each set of cowries, the iyawó was brought forward from where he sat at the far end of the mat to sit before Roberto, who threw and interpreted them on the iyawó's behalf. A young santero sitting to the side somewhat lackadaisically recorded the divination results and Roberto's advice in a notebook, the iyawó's "notebook of the saint."

As Roberto began to interpret the results from the first oricha, Eleggua, he warned the iyawó to stay on the straight and narrow and to avoid partying. He also spoke of the iyawó's mother, whose dissolute example he must not follow. Tears sprang to the iyawó's eyes, and he nodded furiously throughout all that Roberto said. Later, during the lunch that followed the Itá ceremony, the iyawó told me that everything that had been said was the truth and that he had never told Roberto anything about his life or family beforehand. I believed it, given that Roberto did not even know the iyawó's name when I later asked him for it.

During the course of the divination for Obatalá, Roberto looked up from one throw of the cowries, an "osogbo" or "bad letter," to pronounce that someone in the room would have to be initiated. The santeros looked around at each other, then all looked at me, obviously the only noninitiate in the room. I would have to undergo initiation, Roberto explained to Emilio and me. I would also have to receive the Warriors very soon and also receive Olokun, all because of problems associated with travel and with my family. He did not go into any more detail, instead returning to the divination for the iyawó.

Witnessing ritual violations, offering critiques

The next day, Emilio and I sat down for a class. He began by asking me whether I had noticed all the ritual errors Roberto had made. I reached over and turned on my tape recorder as he began to enumerate them.[8]

> 1   Emilio: First of all, I didn't like that the self-same godfather was also the italero of the ceremony.

Emilio explained that even a knowledgeable godparent like Roberto, who was often hired as an oriaté or italero (officiating priest) could not fill that role for his own godchild's initiation. The italero's role was to officiate over all of the special ceremonies of initiation to ensure that everything was done correctly. By filling the role himself, the godfather short-circuited this important check and balance and thus committed a violation.

2   E: I respect him very much because he has a great deal of knowledge, many years of experience, but for me, for **me**—later we'll verify this with other santeros—(KW: Yes)—for **me** it is a violation.

His next criticism was that Roberto had not "raised" enough additional santeros. We went through who had been present at the Itá—only about five or six additional santeros, all of them godchildren of Roberto. This was a problem in Emilio's judgment.

3   E: Because the witness must be a person who certifies that individual was initiated in the religion. So, if all are his own godchildren, perhaps they could cov—they could cover for their godfather; they could say, "no, everything was fine, there were no problems." That is, that when there is a witness, that witness warns, "this is being done badly, that is not done this way, this we have to do in this way." That's how the witness can say it.

4   KW: But you were one of the witnesses

5   E: Who, me?

6   KW: For two, yes, two days

7   E: But I was not, I was not invited

8   KW: Ah!

9   E: I was not "raised" as a santero to work there

10   KW: Uh-hmm

11   E: I was not, because if one raises me, one has to put, that is another thing that I will tell you now. One has to go before my Ochún to ask permission of my Ochún. That is, my saints, and then deposit a *derecho*, so that I will be able to go to that ceremony.

12   KW: Uhm-hmm

13   E: I participated, but as a friend.

The basis for Emilio's criticism is that rituals such as initiations require the participation of a broad cross section of the religious community. In this way, members of more than one lineage are there to witness that the rituals are correctly carried out and to raise objections if they disagree with anything. But his own presence at Roberto's ceremony did not mitigate his criticism that only Roberto's godchildren were present: Emilio had been present, yes, but he had not been ritually *levantado*, raised. He thus denied having responsibility for correcting Roberto, because he did not have his own saint's permission to participate as an official witness.

Emilio then went on to comment that the iyawó's ayugbona or "assistant godparent" should have been present for the entire Itá, when instead she had come in quite late. She should have had the responsibility of writing down the Itá results in the notebook, a job which instead went to a rather bored young santero who barely wrote down anything. He then summed up his critique thus far:

> 14 E: That is, that we could see (1 second) that there were several viola-
> tions. That one is the second, that is, that there were not many wit-
> nesses.

Those who did participate as witnesses were all godchildren of Roberto and thus were unlikely to criticize him. When a lineage adds new members, santeros from other lineages serve as witnesses for the entire moral community that rituals are done correctly and that the new initiate is legitimate.[9]

Roberto and his godchildren, in contrast, were too informal about everything. Emilio went on to point out that the young ayugbona was herself still an iyawó. She was still completing her first year of being a santero and was thus "too young" to "give birth" to another santero yet. He reminded me that the iyawó must complete one full year from initiation before becoming an *oloricha*. Only then could a santero be godparent to a new iyawó.

Emilio then brought up yet another "violation": he had noticed only a few animal hides in the yard, whereas a typical initiation required a dozen animals or so. When we had come for the Day of Presentation and been offered "food of the saint" prepared from the offerings, there had been only a few dishes. These observations suggested to Emilio that the iyawó had not made all the required offerings. Another thing wrong was that Roberto had not been paying his godchildren their *derechos*, fees, for performing various tasks during the Itá, a few coins or peso notes which the oriaté usually hands out throughout the ceremony. It looked as if Roberto were cutting corners; Emilio suggested that Roberto had been trying to help the iyawó save some money, perhaps because of his urgent need to undergo initiation. And such a young man, barely twenty years old, would surely find it difficult to scrape together the thousands of pesos needed for all the expenses of an initiation. By using only his own godchildren as participants, Roberto might have been simply saving the iyawó's money. While this motive was not as morally suspect as outright commercialization of the religion, the glaring fact of the ritual errors remained.

Note that in all of Emilio's critiques thus far, he has positioned himself in the evidentiary stance of a witness: he continually references what we saw or did not see as the basis for his ability to critique Roberto's ceremonies. This stance becomes even more important in the final critiques he offers. A few minutes later, after recounting an incident from his own initiation in which his godfather made a ritual error with serious consequences, Emilio returns to critiquing Roberto's ceremony, this time speculating on a ritual we had not been present to see. I present the transcript here in much greater detail than above for two reasons: first, Emilio offers herein his most devastating critique of Roberto, and second, there are important implications of this critique for our relationship as godfather and goddaughter, implications embedded in the subtleties of our discursive positioning.

15 E: I did not participate . . . I don't know how they would do the masses.

16 That is, the <u>ebbó</u> *de entrada* (sacrifice of entrance), I don't know how it went.

17 I can not give an opinion because. we were not there.

18 KW: Hmm

19: E: But it seems that it was correct. (1.5 seconds) Why?

20 Because at any rate when the saint is not being—is not coming out well, the dead spirit stalls,

21 it doesn't permit them to continue the ceremony, it provokes some accident,

22 some incident and it does not permit the ceremony to continue.

23 KW: Uhm-hm

24 E: For this reason I say that he must have explained everything very well.[10]

In his speculations, Emilio takes the footing of a witness to events. He first emphasizes that he cannot comment on the *misa*, the spiritual mass for the dead, or the *ebbó de entrada*, the first stage of initiation in which a divination decides the iyawó's principal oricha, because he was not present. But he then goes on to consider indirect evidence: during the Itá he *did* witness, he saw no problems. I know from many other occasions and conversations what Emilio means by problems coming up or accidents happening: perhaps an animal dies before it can be offered or the police show up and demand to see a permit, disrupting proceedings by carting everyone off to the police station. Or perhaps a bad divination result keeps coming up, forcing the santeros to deal with its implications before proceeding. In his comments in lines 20–22, Emilio focuses on the cause of such an incident or accident: the spirits of the dead stir up a problem in order to register displeasure about earlier ritual errors or omissions. Note that Emilio pairs the dead's potential to provoke an accident with the verb "permit." Permission in this context is denied by physical interference in the course of ritual events rather than by verbal prohibition. The spirits are silent but no less potent. However, the conditions for asking and receiving permission are set by the santero's acts of speech, implicitly directed to the spirits, which Emilio refers to in line 24 when he concludes that Roberto "must have explained everything very well." That bad happened, Emilio reads as evidence that Roberto must have done the initial rituals correctly and communicated his intentions clearly to the spirits.

25   E: Because, well, in no—and I watched, I was always relying on the shell.

26   I always watched the shell to see if .. if it was giving well,

27   and the shell indeed said all that he claimed is true, the shell said it (repeatedly).

28   Everything he claimed, the shell said.

29   I saw no .. no problem of

30   KW: That is to say that almost all was <u>iré</u>?

31   E: <u>Iré</u>

32   KW: Uhm-hm

33   E: And without <u>osogbo</u>. Without <u>osogbo</u> are the bad signs that they give you.[11]

Emilio again emphasizes his footing as witness: he repeats three times in this section that he watched the cowrie shells carefully during the Itá. He distinguishes sharply between the divination signs, what the "shells said," and Roberto's interpretation, "what he claimed," which allows him to regard the shells as providing independent evidence of Roberto's assertions. In framing Roberto's speech as a "claim," Emilio expresses doubt about what Roberto knows. The speech of the oracle, however, can independently confirm or deny the truth of the diviner's claims. This distinction between the participant roles of Roberto and the shells-as-orichas continues to be important, as Emilio questions Roberto's performance during the Itá.

I respond to Emilio by attempting to specify how it is that the cowries speak by equating the shells speaking well with a good divination result, *iré*. Emilio responds to this Lucumí term with its antonym, replying: "and without osogbo," (meaning without bad divination results). He goes on to give "bad signs" as a gloss for "osogbo," thus maintaining his teacherly stance toward me, his student, even though my use of "iré" suggests that I already know these Lucumí terms. In the following section, he manages to turn the orichas' and spirits' seeming approval of Roberto's ceremony into a backhanded compliment. Bold type indicates words Emilio stressed.

34   E: Or that is that it **seems ..** or that his saints are (ha-ha) accustomed (ha-ha) to working this way already.

35   Or that he has established his thing very well.

36   Or **prepared** his **house** very well so that there will be no problem.

37   Because that is another thing, the santero has to **know** how to prepare his house, so that there will be no problem at the time of the saint.[12]

Emilio suggests, with a laugh that softens the accusation, that perhaps Roberto's saints are used to the ritual shortcuts he takes, implying that Roberto habitually engages in violations (line 34). He then offers the more generous explanation that Roberto has prepared everything thoroughly in line 35. In lines 36–37 he moves back into a more pedagogical mode, summing up the general importance of knowing how to ritually prepare one's house for ceremonies. He then introduces another topic, still in teacherly mode, as if he will now leave off critiquing Roberto to teach me about something I saw at his ceremony.

38   E: Well, you **saw** a ceremony .. that—it is not **usual** . to see

39   KW: Uhm-hm

40   E: that is the <u>ñangareo</u>. I did not talk to you about this ever.

41   K: Hmm

42   E: I never talked to you about the <u>ñangareo</u> because it is a secret ceremony.

43   But ok, now that you have already seen it I have to tell about it.[13]

In launching this lesson as my teacher, Emilio simultaneously contrasts his position as a santero to mine as an aleyo (noninitiate): he is privy to secret knowledge, whereas I am not. It is only by accident that I now know of this ceremony. His final two lines, 42–43, are markedly faster and softer than the surrounding lines, presenting an audible icon of "telling secrets." Santeros are not supposed to share secret ceremonies with aleyos. As a good teacher, however, he will meet the needs of his researcher-student. I pick up on his implication that it was improper for me to see the ñangareo ceremony and ask a question that derails his lecture and switches us back to critiquing Roberto one final time.

44   KW: And—, ah, .. ah, . Were you, ah, ah, .. surprised that they allowed me . to see?

45   E: Yes, yes, yes, yes, because that is not-

46   Ok, it's that we have a good relationship of friendship
47   and he **knows** that definit—
48   He **thinks**, it's not that he knows.
49   He **thinks** that you will definitely have to be initiated.
50   He you—(laughter) you saw—Did you realize?
51   He **believes** that you will be initiated because I told him,
52   No, she is **my** goddaughter.
53   KW: Uh-huh
54   E: So then he has this stuck in his head and **it came out**.
55   Didn't you see?[14]

Emilio answers my question about whether he was surprised that Roberto let me see the secret ñangareo ceremony with a second "whispered" critique of Roberto that trails off, "Yes, yes, yes, yes, because that is not-" (line 45). He interrupts this train of thought to instead attribute a series of thoughts to Roberto. Roberto, according to Emilio, violated secrecy because he believed that I would soon be initiating. The pattern of words in bold traces Emilio's superimposition of stresses on a series of thought-verbs in lines 47–54: first, Roberto "knows"; then he "thinks"; then he "believes"; and finally, in line 54, he "has this stuck in his head and it came out." The progression reveals Emilio's doubtful attitude toward what Roberto thinks he knows. Why does Roberto have this idea that I must be initiated? Because, Emilio suggests, he himself planted the idea by introducing me to Roberto as his goddaughter. Roberto interpreted this relationship between us to mean that I would soon cross the boundary between aleyo and iyawó. This, in itself, was a common enough assumption, one that Emilio encouraged people to make as he took me around. But in this case, it formed the basis for a serious critique of the Itá results, because Emilio was denying that the result calling for me to undergo initiation truly came from the orichas.

Emilio's choice of the verb *salir*, "to come out" in line 54 is intriguing, because santeros frequently use it to express how the cowries produce a divination result: *salió*, "it came out," they will say, meaning that the oracle has given a surprising or unexpected result, something the diviner might not have previously known. This use of the verb, especially when contrasted with verbs of speaking like "it said," displaces agency and responsibility, allowing what Du Bois (1992) describes as an intentionless message. In Emilio's usage in line 54, what came out (in divination) was what Roberto had "stuck in his head." Emilio is thus implying that the result that I must undergo initiation was not the speech of the orichas through the cowries, but Roberto's projection of something he believed into his interpretation of the cowries. To put plainly what Emilio has only hinted, Roberto at best misread and at worst faked divination results, seeing what he wanted to see in the divination signs. Without lingering, Emilio then switched from the topic to a futile search for a scrap of paper on which Roberto had written down what I needed to do, "lo que te salió" or "what came out for you," as Emilio put it. His critique made, he then launched directly into a lecture on the ñangareo ceremony.

Tracing the circulation and effects of a critique

What did it mean that Emilio questioned Roberto's divination results? This critique capped an entire list of critiques Emilio had made. His skepticism, his concern with ritual detail, and indeed his emphasis upon the importance of witnessing in rituals are all common enough among santeros to qualify as religious virtues. But in making his critiques, and especially in questioning Roberto's results for me, Emilio was also putting into play our religious role alignments. Emilio and Roberto were both santeros, and I was Emilio's godchild, a potential iyawó. By channeling the oricha's claims on me during the Itá divination, Roberto had set up a momentary interactional structure that suggested how it would be if I were to undergo initiation. I was receiving Roberto-the-oriaté's interpretation of my Itá results while my godfather stood by. The results suggested a future repetition of this interactional alignment, in which Emilio and I would come to Roberto, who would oversee my initiation as an iyawó. Alternately, I could replicate the situation of the current initiation, bypass Emilio, and have Roberto initiate me as both godparent and officiating priest. In either case, Emilio's final critique of Roberto suggested that he, too, saw these suggestive role alignments and intervened to cast doubt on Roberto's motives and his ritual correctness. Each time he critiqued Roberto, he implicitly positioned himself on the moral high ground of one who knows and respects the Regla.

This example of how Emilio critiqued Roberto illustrates how such critique works, and especially how it effects its own context by mobilizing ritual roles and relationships in both the narrative of the critique and in the interactional context of its retelling. Within this dynamic, some claims to ritual authority and relationships get advanced, while others get challenged. In this specific instance, Emilio offered his critiques in the context of our dual religious and secular relationship as professor lecturing student and godparent preparing godchild.

On several later occasions, sometimes months later, Emilio revisited parts of his critique of Roberto when we were with other, more senior members of his ritual lineage. The day after our own conversation, Emilio brought up his concerns about Roberto's ritual errors with his godparents, Teodoro and Tania. He had brought me to their home that day to have Teodoro do a consultation for me. The results did not in any way echo Roberto's call for me to undergo initiation, which Emilio told me confirmed his suspicions about Roberto's results. What did come up in Teodoro's divination was the repeated warning that I not go off with just anybody to participate in rituals. Emilio looked at me significantly each time, knowing as he did that I followed up every possible lead in my fieldwork. Afterward, Emilio had Teodoro and Tania sit down in the living room to listen to his account of Roberto's many ritual violations. Shocked, they agreed that each of the critiques he made was valid: the initiation had been ridden with violations. Emilio had his godparents' validation to back him up in his critiques. He had demonstrated his conscientiousness before them and me. Teodoro's divination results for me implicitly confirmed that Roberto's results had been false and that I should not stray from Emilio's lineage. At a different level, and most significantly for my argument, Emilio brought his ritual family together to reinforce their sense of being knowledgeable and respectful in contrast to someone outside the lineage, who was sloppy and disrespectful of ritual rules. Just like the santero family in the chapter's opening anecdote, Emilio and his ritual kin sat critiquing everyone else and promoting their own religious propriety, thereby reinforcing their lineage as the core of their moral community. Note, however, that santeros are only in a position to make such critiques to the extent that they continue to participate in and witness rituals held by others.

Emilio recounted Roberto's ceremony on at least two other occasions half a year later. Both were interviews I recorded with him and two different senior santeras he counted in his ritual lineage. One was Teodoro's godmother (and so Emilio's grandmother-in-saint) and the other had been a major participant in Emilio's initiation ceremony, even though she was not actually his godmother.[15] On both occasions, Emilio brought up Roberto by name and recounted two or three of his ritual errors, receiving the santeras' vigorous agreement that Roberto had committed serious violations. Once again, a critique of Roberto's ritual violations fueled a discussion of the Regla and their own allegiance to it.

This story of how Emilio critiqued Roberto's ritual performance cannot do more than suggest what effects his critiques have had over time. Nor is there any evidence that Emilio's critiques ever made it back around to Roberto (although if he continues to share his opinions with people, the religious community is intimate enough that Roberto will probably hear something eventually). The second and final case study of the chapter focuses on the broader effects of circulating evaluations, appraisals, and critiques of rituals and their participants to show how critiques, paradoxically, create community even as they establish competing factions. Emilio's critiques are extraordinarily ordinary: I cannot count the number of times I heard santeros critique other santeros. It was especially common for santeros within a single ritual lineage or family to disparage other lineages, in particular or in general, for "una falta de respeto" (a lack of respect) of the religion. In doing so, those present reinforced their own sense of being in a superior lineage.

When foreign aleyos like me were added into the mix, the critiques often became even more volatile, as santeros accused other santeros of initiating foreigners for profit. Below I explore how the charge of "commercializing the religion" (the ultimate act of disrespect) played out as the ultimate challenge to another santero's claims to religious propriety.

The Dutch iyawó

Only santeros may participate in the Itá divination

Months after my participation in Roberto's Itá ceremony, I was again invited to attend an Itá by a santero whose godfather was initiating a foreigner from the Netherlands. Difficult as it was to gain access to this semisecret ceremony, I happily accepted the invitation.[16] The Dutch man, whose name I never learned because people referred to him solely by this epithet, had come to Santiago at least once before, had been quite taken with the religion, and had arranged to return in order to be initiated as both a santero and a babalawo. My friend knew him because the foreigner had become close to my friend's godparents, a married couple. The foreigner had also met a young babalawo, Pedro, who lived nearby. He had arranged with Pedro that Pedro would serve as his godfather in Ifá and that he would undergo initiation as a babalawo just as soon as he completed his initiation as a santero. The foreigner thus had two godfathers. This often happens when a santero later goes on to become a babalawo, although not all babalawos are first initiated as santeros. Later, several santeros commented to me that the foreigner's planned schedule of back-to-back initiations was a bit rushed and that it is better to wait between these initiations. But coming from abroad as he did, it must have been more expedient for the man to complete both ceremonies during a single two-week trip.

In any case, I attended his very festive Day of Presentation one afternoon, then returned the next morning hoping that my santero friend had succeeded in convincing his godfather to let me sit in on the Itá. All initiation ceremonies were being held at the house next door to where the godparents lived. The house's living room had been taken over as the "cuarto de santo" or "room of the saint," the sacred space in which the altar with its living space for the iyawó was set up and where most of the rituals would be performed. Outside in the large courtyard, the place was abustle. Along the walls hung the hides of any number of goats, sheep, and other animals sacrificed the previous day to the iyawó's new saints. There was even a tortoise shell. A small army of santeras commanded the outdoor kitchen. At least a dozen other santeros and santeras milled about, chatting. Many of them had been *levantado* (raised) to serve as witnesses during the Itá divination. Among them I recognized several senior santeras. An oriaté, or officiating priest, had been hired to perform the actual Itá in which each of the iyawó's saints would "speak" directly to the iyawó through its cowrie shells. One of the "raised" santeros would be charged with recording the divination results and the specific advice of each saint in a special notebook for the new initiate and his godparents.

After the initial, secret ceremonies of the morning got under way inside, those present reassembled outside to participate in a ritual invocation of Olorun, understood to be the sun in Santería.[17] During this ritual, called the "ñangareo," Pedro, the babalawo-godfather of the Dutch iyawó, arrived. Afterward, all the santeros filed inside for the Itá, and Pedro followed. I waited outside until my friend emerged to tell me that I would not be allowed to enter because I was not initiated. I remained outside in the courtyard for awhile, hoping that I might chat with someone in the kitchen. For this reason, I was still there when the first controversy erupted. Voices were suddenly raised inside, then Pedro the babalawo emerged, looking very disgruntled. Inside, the oriaté had noticed his presence and interrupted his invocatory prayers to question why he was there. Although Pedro was a babalawo, the oriaté insisted to the assembled santeros that he could not stay, because he had never been initiated as a santero. If Pedro wanted to hear the Itá, he could sit outside the room and do his best to listen in, but more. Pedro left in a huff and joined me outside, where we could just barely hear what happened next.

According to a transcription I made from someone else's tape recording inside the room, the oriaté proceeded with the divination for a minute or so, then interrupted himself a second time to castigate the other santeros, saying: "You know that it is permitted when it is a relative in the saint, but otherwise it cannot be. (16 seconds) You people have to learn, gentlemen."[18] Another santero spoke up in defense of the santera who had apparently invited Pedro to come in: "Juana knows. What happened is that she respects him." This exchange prompted a brief general discussion among the participants, which the oriaté cut off by pointing out that babalawos never would let santeros into their sacred room during their rituals: "We santeros cannot enter into the room of Orunmila (oricha of babalawos) for anything. . . . In the same way the room of the saint has to be respected." This imbalance, wherein often young, twenty-something babalawos pulled rank on even senior santeros by denying them entrance to the proceedings of their ceremonies was a sore spot for many santeros, especially senior santeros such as the oriaté and several of the older santeras present. Now they were repaying the insult by demanding equal respect for their rituals. They banned Pedro because he had skipped over the step of being initiated as a santero before becoming a babalawo, a sort of "social climbing" that also rankled senior santeros.

Pedro stomped angrily around outside for a few minutes, trying to hear what was being said inside, then left in a huff. When a friend and I met up with him a week later to visit a ceremony for babalawos, he told us as we walked that he had had every right to be present as the godfather in Ifá of the Dutch iyawó. That is, when the oriaté declared that only a "relative in the saint" could be present in the Itá, he was splitting hairs in not considering Pedro's role to count. It was apparent to everyone I talked with later, whether present or not, that the oriaté had been reacting to a perceived lack of respect from babalawos in the city toward santeros. On this all agreed, differing only in whether they saw the oriaté's reaction against Pedro's presence as justified or not.

An osogbo, or bad letter, is blamed on the babalawos

Toward the end of the Itá divinations, a bad letter (osogbo) called "Arayé" came up. When the oriaté asked the oracle whether the osogbo pertained to the Dutch iyawó, the answer came back "No." Next he began asking who it might pertain to. Was it directed at him, the oriaté? No. The iyawó's sister, back in Europe? No. The iyawó's godmother? No. The oriaté tried a different tack with his next question to the oracle: did the bad letter have to do with the house in which they sat? Yes. He called for the owner of the house to come forward while he did further divination steps to figure out which saint was offended. Was it Olokún, Yemayá, those who speak through this particular sign? No. Was it perhaps Eleggua? Yes.

Recall that all of these affirmatives and negatives are decided in a cowrie divination by giving the client, or in this case the iyawó, two objects to hide in his hands (all such objects are known as *ibo* or *ibú*). The oriaté casts the cowries once or twice, depending upon the first letter he gets, and this sign determines whether he asks to see the iyawó's right or left hand. If the chosen hand holds the large snail shell, the answer is "Yes." If the small, dark pebble is revealed instead, then the answer is "No." Those assembled occasionally declare "yes" or "no" aloud when they see the object, thereby translating the chosen object into a verbal response from the oricha.

In any case, after the suspenseful process of deciding that it was Eleggua who was angry at the owner of the house, the oriaté suggested that the problem must have arisen during the *matanza* or "killing ceremony" of the animals that he had missed the previous day. He suggested that the Eleggua of the house had been neglected during the offerings, and that this made Eleggua "uncomfortable." At this, the woman who owned the house asked the oriaté's permission to speak and suggested that something had happened: during the matanza, an unspecified "they"—those officiating—had neglected to feed and cleanse her Eleggua in its place behind the door. At this, the oriaté began to fume:

1   Oriaté: But look, thank God and Eleggua and all the saints

2   Thank God and Eleggua and all the saints that I left,

3   because all the atrocities that (you/they) say that (you/they) did here, get out, I would have had to take out a gun and shoot myself.

4   I would have had to take out a gun and shoot myself,

5   because that I do not understand and I do not want to talk more

6   lest people take offense.[19]

The oriaté's furious outburst does not make clear who he is blaming for the ritual lapses. From his elision of the subjects of "say" and "do" in line 3, he could be holding the assembled santeros or other parties responsible. In the acrimonious debate that followed, the defensive responses of the owner of the house, my friend's godfather, and the oriaté's own godmother, a very senior santera, suggest that they felt that the oriaté was holding them responsible at least in part for violating the Regla and offending the Eleggua of the borrowed house. But the other responsible parties were not present to defend themselves—indeed, I understood that the babalawos were involved in the error of overlooking the house's Eleggua only when my friend, reviewing the transcript with me, commented:

Now [the oriaté] begins to make a complete analysis, because it happens that when the matanza was done—as it is an outside house, see, that the house does not belong to my godfather or anything. They made the saint in a house. When the babalawos made the offerings of food [to the saints], they did not feed the Eleggua of the house. So that's where the problem comes, because everyone is asking themselves where the Eleggua was fed, and so from there a complete argument about that problem [starts], because if the babalawos did it badly, because if they did it like this, what do I know? From there it sheds light on another thing, that you are going to hear all this debate [about].[20]

It transpired that the oriaté had left the matanza ceremony because Pedro and a group of his fellow babalawos had come to participate. By virtue of being babalawos, they were senior to all the santeros present and so, apparently, had taken over running the ceremony. When I suggested to my friend that the babalawos had forgotten to feed the Eleggua of the house, he retorted: "It's not that they forgot, it's that the babalawos, when they did not become initiated as santeros, don't know!"

Here too, bad feelings between santeros and babalawos in the city underlay the controversies infecting these ritual events. Santeros felt that the babalawos, even the young and inexperienced ones, condescended to them even though they actually knew very little about rituals. Indeed, they had blundered badly enough in this case to offend an oricha by making a mistake that, the santeros implied, no one properly initiated as a santero would ever make.

What is interesting about this moment of critique is that it occurred during a ritual and referred to an earlier ritual in the same initiation ceremony. While there was nothing "sacred" about the nasty finger-pointing that ensued after the oriaté's furious comment (which I will spare my readers), these arguments fed directly into the interpretation of the bad sign during the Itá divination. Indeed, when the oriaté was finally able to get a word in edgewise, he seamlessly began to give the owner of the house his interpretation of her bad sign, explaining that in that sign "Eleggua comes telling you" warnings about upcoming problems and ways to protect herself and undo the damage. But let us reexamine how these pointed critiques of a previous ritual came up to begin with. The oriaté arrived at his initial suggestion that Eleggua had been neglected during the matanza only after a bad sign came up and only after he had taken further steps to define the source and target of the bad sign. Any Santería practitioner would quickly point out that it was the saints themselves who were bringing up the problem, explaining such a situation by saying that ritual errors are bound to have consequences by "coming up" in the divination.

Nor was this the end of the santeros' critique of the babalawos. But before proceeding to act 3 of the Dutch iyawó's Itá, I wish to compare the first two instances of critique that arose within the ritual. First, the oriaté took it upon himself, as the officiating priest, to throw out Pedro the babalawo because he was not initiated as a santero. His justification was that it was incumbent on him, as the senior priest, to avoid violating the Regla by having a noninitiate present at a "secret" ceremony. The oriaté couched his comments as a critique of the santeros present for allowing Pedro in. Throwing out Pedro opened up a discussion in which the oriaté aired the santeros' grievances against the babalawos, who did not respect them and therefore did not respect the Regla de Ocha. In the second event, the saints, via the cowrie divination, were the arbiters who pointed out a ritual error. The oriaté merely interpreted their message, which again led to his initial critique of the other santeros (namely the iyawó's godfather and the oriaté's godmother), who then fought it out among themselves about who was responsible for allowing the babalawos to skip feeding the Eleggua.

These examples show how important critique is, not only when it happens after the fact as commentary on a ritual, but when it becomes part of the ritual itself and thus gains additional moral authority from the ritual context and the presiding orichas. Even as things seem to be flying apart, the santeros who gathered for this Itá ritual are negotiating and co-constructing the boundaries and norms that unite them as a moral community. The babalawos, in the santeros' retelling of events, are portrayed as an arrogant, ignorant, and disrespectful out-group against which the assembled santeros define themselves as the truly religious followers of the Regla.

The saints forbid the iyawó from becoming a babalawo

One final event during the Itá surpassed the previous two in impact. While it followed logically from the earlier critiques of the babalawos, its ramifications exceed even those of kicking Pedro out. At the very end of the Itá divinations, just before the oriaté was about to close the communication channel with the final saint, the iyawó's godfather spoke up. He asked the oriaté for permission to speak. Yes, yes, yes, said the oriaté somewhat impatiently. The godfather then spoke quietly, directly addressing Eleggua, and explaining that the iyawó wanted to continue on to receive Ifá and become a babalawo. He then asked Eleggua's permission for this step, saying, "If you permit him to, he will continue, or if you do not permit him then he will not."[21] The room was for once utterly silent. Then, the oriaté held up the snail shell and pebble to be used in divining Eleggua's answer, saying: "Here is the *ibú*. This one says 'Yes,' look at it, that one says 'Yes,' (unclear) that (other) one says 'No.'"[22]

Since, during the course of the previous hour, he had used the shell and pebble in this standard way dozens of times, pointing out the yes-no possibilities to the assembled santeros before the question had been asked carried a special significance. The oriaté was, in essence, stating for the record that it was the saints who would answer through these divination objects, not him. Disclaiming responsibility in this dramatic way made an impression great enough for my santero friend to clearly recall the moment two years later. The oriaté then handed the shell and pebble to the iyawó to hide in his palms and threw the cowries, leading the crowd in the Lucumí call and response:

> Oriaté: ¡Ochareo!
> Santeros: ¡Adaché!
> Oriaté: ¡Ochareo!
> Santeros: ¡Adaché!

We can imagine that all leaned forward to watch, as the oriaté counted the face-up cowries and declared, "Obbara, six face up," then tossed them again to produce Ogunda, three face up. Silently, he indicated which hand the iyawó was to open (it would have been the right hand for this sign, 6–3), and then, showing what must have been the pebble all around, he asked, "Is that clear?" Ten seconds of silence passed, then he added:

> Oriaté: I don't say this, Eleggua said it, got it? And (unclear) from his
>   hands. You can make what you will of that, ok? With that may
>   all <u>ba binu</u> with Olofi, <u>Ochareo</u>![23]

With that, the oriaté washed his hands of the matter, letting the godfather decide how to respond to Eleggua's "no." Lapsing into the Lucumí formula for closing a divination, he drew a final "Adaché" from the assembled santeros and threw the cowries for the closing divination that ensured that the saints had said all they wished to say.

How controversy shapes community

And what did the godfather's final question and its answer mean? He asked Eleggua directly whether he gave permission for the Dutch iyawó to be initiated as a babalawo in Ifá. The final divination result was "No." The oriaté took pains to distance himself from responsibility for this answer, making clear that it was the cowries that spoke, and not him. He also refrained from interpreting the result, instead saying that the other participants should make their own decision about what to do.

Why all the drama? By posing the question, the iyawó's godfather "in the saint" was challenging Pedro's right to be his second godfather of Ifá. Pedro had already been kicked out of the ceremony. Now the godfather would have to go to him and explain that a divination result had forbidden the iyawó from initiating as a babalawo, not next week, not ever. He did go to tell Pedro, who brought in other babalawos, and there were apparently a number of visits back and forth between the santero participants and the babalawos. Of course, Pedro and the other babalawos were furious. Wherever I went during the next few weeks, I heard about the acrimony, the accusations of impropriety from all sides. The topic came up spontaneously, whether I was walking with two santeros or interviewing a babalawo or just sitting in the kitchen with a santera friend who happened to be a close friend of the oriaté and had heard about the situation from him. Everyone, even santeros and babalawos who had not been present for the Itá, had opinions about what had happened. Those who had been present or who were directly involved, like Pedro, had even stronger feelings. As my santero friend rather mildly summed it up for me a month later: "That was a huge problem afterward, but a huge problem! Many problems, many arguments. That took about ten or fifteen days of wrangling."

Amidst all the discussion, two positions solidified: that of the babalawos and that of the santeros. The babalawos felt that the iyawó's godfather had no right to ask such a question. As Pedro explained to me and a sympathetic santero friend one day while we were walking with him to another ceremony, the matter had already been settled before the Itá, indeed before the santero initiation had even begun. Pedro himself had already done an Ifá divination in which the result was that the Dutch iyawó would have to receive Ifá. For the other godfather to ask the question again during the Itá was incorrect, a ritual violation even. Worse yet, Pedro couldn't be there to protest because they had kicked him out. The other godfather was looking to start trouble, he concluded.

The santeros, on the other hand, felt that the godfather was justified in posing the question, given all the trouble that the babalawos had already caused. Why, just within the Itá ceremony, one uninitiated babalawo had to be removed and their earlier ritual errors had offended an oricha and come back as a bad sign on the house. Given these and other (usually unspecified) problems the babalawos had caused, the godfather was right to seek to protect his godchild by making sure the godchild's principal saint gave his blessing. When the answer came back "No," that only confirmed the godfather's suspicions. One santero, a godchild of the Dutch iyawó's godfather, pointed out to me one day about a month later while I was interviewing him that the iyawó's principal saint, Eleggua, seldom allows his "children" to become babalawos for esoteric reasons derived from and supported by various legends involving Eleggua and Orunmila, the oricha of Ifá divination.

Presented thus, both sides of the debate found support in ritual protocol and religious doctrine for their positions. However, while each side clung to its version of the moral high ground, they each lambasted the other side for "commercializing the religion." The babalawos sadly said that the godfather in the saint was greedy and jealous, afraid to share a foreign godchild with anyone else. He "stole" the iyawó away from Pedro by posing a faulty Itá question that should never have been asked. The santeros accused the babalawos of the very same pecuniary interest: hadn't the iyawó paid Pedro $1,000 (a small fortune when Cubans were lucky to earn maybe $25 a month) for his Ifá initiation? And the babalawos didn't want to give the money back. Some said that they had already spent some of it preparing for the initiation that never happened. It was the babalawos who were out to steal away the iyawó and make money off of him. Several santeros I spoke with echoed the critiques the oriaté had made during the Itá divination: these young men became babalawos because they hoped to make lots of money charging exorbitant rates for Ifá divinations. The proof was that they were in too big a hurry to become babalawos to be initiated as santeros first and really learn the religion. They went straight to being initiated as babalawos and then thought they were better than anyone else!

Round and round went the debate, braiding together religious error and bald commercial interest. Two years later, when I revisited some of the same santeros, they themselves brought up the situation and rehashed the old arguments. Several new babalawos (and many new santeros) had been initiated in the meantime, but the fault lines separating santero and babalawo had not changed. What is fascinating about the debate, hinging as it did on criticizing the other position for a lack of religious propriety, was that no one, not once, questioned that Eleggua, when asked, had said "No." It may or may not have been wrong to ask the question, but no one would contradict what the saint had answered. The Dutch iyawó, in the meantime, quietly accepted Elegguá's verdict. He went home without becoming a babalawo.

Conclusion: Rituals, recriminations, and emergent moral community

This story, which I have told at length, illustrates several more general points about the role of rituals and of reflective discourses about rituals in the making of religious community. This particular controversy, which served as a lightning rod for deep-rooted concerns about babalawo-santero relations and problems of commercialization, is perhaps unusual in its scale, but not atypical in its outlines. Like countless other less dramatic encounters, critiques, and debates, the controversy over the Dutch iyawó throws into sharp relief both the outlines of the religious community of Santería and the fissures within it. Participation in the debate, even among those at several degrees of remove from the actual ritual participants, indicates who is included in this particular moral community. The positions taken in this controversy, and in other instances of critique, gossip, and so forth, inevitably fall out along the lines separating ritual lineages and distinguishing babalawos from santeros; but santeros and babalawos alike, most of whom had not been present during the ritual itself, were drawn into the discussions and were thereby clearly participating in a common moral community.

The evidence in this and previous chapters illustrates that an essential part of the dynamics of religious community in Santiago is wrapped up in competition over prestige, deference, and recognition. The recognized markers of cultural capital among members of this community are numerous godchildren—especially foreign godchildren, invitations to participate in numerous rituals, signs that one is consulted by others for one's ritual knowledge, an ability to display such ritual knowledge (as in speaking Lucumí and knowing the ritual songs), and even recognition by folkloric and other cultural and scholarly institutions of the state, as described in chapter 3. Amid all of the individual strategizing, alliance-building, self-advancement, and lineage-promotion that santeros (and babalawos) find to be necessary to advance their "religious" capital, consider more closely what it is that makes religious community. Throughout the chapters, I have emphasized the crucial interrelationship between rituals and reflective discourse about rituals, especially because Santería does not have centralized institutions or membership rolls. It is through participation in rituals *and* evaluations of rituals that santeros enter into a religious community. The religious community consists of that unbounded and porous, but still recognizable, group that comes together around a common set of religious practices, including discursive practices. But that consensus is not stable: it is better characterized as a shared interpretive focus on continuities and norms that masks ongoing struggles and negotiations over what constitutes religiously correct tradition, what is within the Regla of the orichas, and what evinces respectful religious propriety.

Before rituals, during rituals, and after rituals, religious participants come together to plan, discuss, teach, witness, help, evaluate, critique, and engage in all the activities that advance both personal and collective religious agendas. Rituals are the grist of the mill, where events happen that are noteworthy, newsworthy, and in need of discussion, evaluation, and critique. Rituals, we have seen, also can provide space for discussion, evaluation, and even critique of outside events. They can also provide frames for understanding events that happen elsewhere and serve as clearinghouses for consensus, as when the oriaté articulated many santeros' feelings of hostility toward babalawos from his "bully pulpit" as the officiating priest of the Itá divination. Rituals themselves provide opportunities to comment on and reach (or not reach) consensus on other rituals, past or future. The Itá divination events examined above illustrate three of these evaluative possibilities in critiquing outside events, previous rituals, and planned future rituals. Figure 7.2 below illustrates these moments of reflective discourse within the sequence of rituals that occurred for the Dutch iyawó.

Starting with "Ritual Event 1" during the Itá divination, the oriaté justified throwing out the babalawo on the grounds that babalawos do not show the proper respect for santeros and their rituals. In the second ritual event I examined (Ritual Event 2), the oriaté interpreted a bad sign to refer back to a previous, botched ritual conducted by the babalawos. In the third ritual event, the

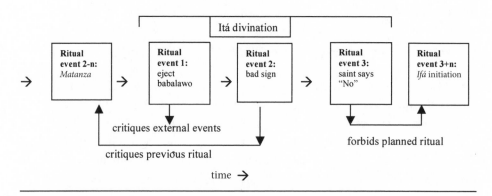

Figure 7.2. Diagram of how moments in the Itá divination comment upon other ritual and non-ritual events, past and future.

godfather posed a question to the oracle about whether a future ritual could occur, receiving a negative response.

Such ritual-internal commentary may be formal or informal to different degrees. Sometimes a participant may break from formula to enforce a particular rule, as when the oriaté declared that noninitiates could not stay. Sometimes a critique arises out of divination results which prompt those assembled to examine what rules or ritual details may have been neglected and to assign blame. What have you done, and was it done correctly? What should you do next? Of course, such commentary can and does happen outside of ritual as well, whenever santeros assemble. But what makes rituals so important is that they project the weight of moral authority. We have seen how ritual structures of participation model proper relations with the divine, including an emphasis on respect, divine causation, and attention to detail. Rituals perform sacred communications and demonstrate patterns of sacred significance that participants may then apply to other life events. In rituals, the voices of the orichas are established to be tangible: as tangible as the cowries, the Lucumí invocations, the divination signs—all of which invoke the voice of the orichas. Rituals establish patterns of sacred significance by linking events into sequences of cause and effect: A ritual error during one ceremony brings out a bad divination result in a later ceremony. A piece of advice during a divination suggests how a person should conduct themselves thereafter in life, with dire consequences for failure to heed the advice.

The progression of ritual events diagramed in figure 7.2 also reminds us that santeros agree in regarding the orichas as the final arbiters, to be consulted in divinations and obeyed. Controversies like the one simmering between santeros and babalawos in Santiago do tend to culminate (but not necessarily end) with what the orichas have to say on the subject. Their word on things is taken as final, or at least accorded the respect of never being directly challenged, even if santeros sometimes find room for differing interpretations of the orichas' messages. How different this is from the skeptical stance santeros often take with regard to each other's religious activities and motives. And yet, it is in santeros' reflections on ritual performances and other religious activities, in discursively sifting the sacred wheat from the chaff of human foibles and interferences, that santeros construct their moral community.

8

Conclusion

The Promise

Babalú/ Babalú	*Babalú/ Babalú*
Babalú Ayé	*Babalú Ayé*
Babalú Ayé/ Babalú	*Babalú Ayé/ Babalú*
Tá empezando lo velorio	*The mass is beginning*
que le hacemos a Babalú	*that we do for Babalú*
Dame diez y siete velas	*Give me 17 candles*
pa' ponerle en cruz	*to put them in the shape of a cross*
Dame un cabo de tabaco Mayenye	*Give me a cigar, Mayenye*
y un jarrito de aguardiente	*and a small bottle of cane liquor*
Dame un poco de dinero Mayenye	*Give me a bit of money Mayenye*
pa' que me dé la suerte—yo quiere pedí	*so that I'll have luck—I wants [sic] to request*
que mi negra me quiera	*that my black woman will love me*
que tenga dinero	*that I will have money*
y que no se muera	*and that I won't die*
Ay, yo le quiero pedí Babalú	*Oh, I want to request of Babalú*
na negra muy	*black woman so*
Santa como tú que no tenga	*Beloved like you that she not*
otro negro	*have another black man*
pa' que no se fuera	*so that she won't leave*

—Margarita Lecuona

Desi Arnaz, costar of the 1950s television sitcom *I Love Lucy*, sang Margarita Lecuona's song "Babalú" as his signature tune. "Babaloooo!" his character, Ricky Ricardo, would exclaim when something surprised or impressed him. Born in Santiago de Cuba, Arnaz did what Cuban musicians and singers have done before and since: he drew upon the Afro-Cuban cultural motifs that surrounded him in his music and lyrics (Isabel Castellanos 1983). Unbeknownst to the vast majority of his U.S. audience, Arnaz's signature tune and trademark interjection invoke the name of a fearsome oricha, Babalú Ayé, deity of leprosy and other contagious diseases. Nor is Babalú Ayé the only oricha to find his way out of religion's sacred sphere into popular song lyrics: Cuban popular music has long been full of songs such as "Que Viva Changó" ("Long Live Changó") and "Una Flor Para Ochún" ("A Flower for Ochún").[1] The names of these deities, like other elements of Lucumí praise songs—rhythms, phrases, melodies—are cultural forms that circulate widely in Cuban society. Similarly, bits of other rituals of the popular religious complex, like the Spiritist *velorio* (mass for the dead) described in "Babalú," also get recirculated in nonreligious contexts like popular song, although perhaps not to the extent that Santería's emblems do. Sometimes their very presence conveys a sacred stance, but sometimes they are reinterpreted as folklore or superstition. Arnaz's lyrics, with their colloquial and even bozal inflections, caricature a poor, uneducated, and superstitious Afro-Cuban man who offers a ritual to his santo, Babalú, in hopes of improving his circumstances. Although playfully rendered, the song portrays its character's religious stance as simpleminded and slightly ridiculous. In doing so, it implicitly squeezes the sacred stance into a broader interpretive frame that associates that kind of religiosity with that kind of social persona.

But this interpretive "squeeze" on the sacred is not the end of the story, nor are manifestations of popular religiosity like Santería diminishing under contact with the folkloric stance. Even when co-opted into other interpretive frames, religious interpretations have a way of infiltrating along with the borrowed cultural forms. Daniel (1995) and Hagedorn (2001) have documented how folkloric drummers, singers, and dancers performing sacred rhythms, songs, and dances of the orichas for tourists sometimes seem to allow the "hierophany" of the music and movements to carry them away, blurring the lines between sacred and folkloric stances. While Daniel reports on how a dance troupe's officers reprimand dancers for such slippages, Hagedorn describes a more complicated interpenetration of the sacred and the folkloric (aligned with what I describe in chapter 3) in which she argues that the combined "intent" of performers and audience ultimately shapes the meaning of the performance. The Cuban notion of doble moral should remind us that intent is neither clear cut nor ever completely knowable. Nor is a performance's meaning necessarily fixed or unitary. I have shown that even when ritual participants share a sacred stance, their interpretations of the ritual vary and even shift over time with further reflection. Like santeros who critically analyze each ritual, we can seek clues about a performance's motivations and effects, clues we pursue by reading into the stances and role alignments different participants take, both as events unfold and later, with hindsight. Thus far, I have considered Arnaz's song only from the point of view of the singer, who takes a parodic position in relation to the figure he animates in the lyrics. But Hagedorn reminds us that the audience, too, has agency to accept or to challenge and reframe the implicit framing of the performance.

I once witnessed Desi Arnaz's popular number reclaimed and reframed within the sacred stance in a startling way. A Cuban santero swore to me that Desi Arnaz chose his signature tune to fulfill a "promise" he made to Babalú Ayé back in Santiago in his youth. In Cuban popular religiosity, a "promise" is a vow one makes to a particular deity or spirit in return for receiving that entity's help in resolving some problem or achieving some goal. People may promise the patron saint of Cuba, the Virgen de La Caridad del Cobre, that they will visit her shrine in the town of El Cobre on her saint's day. They may promise Eleggua, an oricha sometimes portrayed as a child, that they will thank him by having a party for all the children in the neighborhood. They may promise the muerto who is their spiritual protector that they will throw a tambor every year in his or her honor. As a general rule, the more desperate the plea, the more grandiose the promise. Indeed, La Caridad's shrine in El Cobre is filled with relics left by grateful supplicants: crutches, war medals, photographs. And pilgrims to the church of San Lázaro (identified with Babalú Ayé) in Rincón, outside of Havana, may crawl the distance on his feast day, December 17th (Ayorinde 2004: 127; Ramos, Orejuelos, and Gray 1995/1993). Desi Arnaz, according to the story I was told, promised Babalú Ayé that he would dedicate a song to him if the saint would help him become successful. Arnaz did achieve fame, and so he chose his signature tune so as to praise and thank his saint on the show.

The historical truth of this claim is obviously not my concern here. What interests me is that a santero was proposing a sacred interpretation for a T.V. sitcom song, in which the song's lyrics signal the singer's dedication to a fearsome and powerful oricha. Why else would a singer risk invoking the name of Babalú Ayé, oricha of gruesome diseases? The logic makes sense only within a framework in which deities' names are powerful, songs are prayers that open communications with the divine, and people make and keep promises to the deities. In this interpretation, Arnaz was not voicing the words of a "black witch" with ironic detachment but was taking on this religious persona in order to covertly praise a saint or oricha. Doing so is, in fact, a well-worn trope in Cuban popular music, in which the singer may well intend the song to praise an oricha as well as to entertain the human audience. (Celina González's "Que Viva Changó" is one well-known example, as she was known to be a santera.)

By attaching the interpretation of "promise" to as catchy and well-known a cultural icon as Arnaz's "Babalú," the santero was, whether aware of it or not, promoting the further circulation of this genre of religious activity. The song, in the santero's interpretation, stands as a comprobación (proof) of Arnaz's religiosity and, less directly, of Babalú Ayé's potency. Now that I, in turn, have repeated the story, we see how well it worked. To fill in details that supplement the santero's account, we know of "Babalú" because Arnaz became famous, which, in the logic of the story, suggests that his "promise" worked. Who knows what else we might reinterpret as a sign of a private act of bargaining with Higher Powers! What else might be revealed as a "promise?" It seems that the sacred can squeeze back!

Metaphysical and metacultural squeezes

Throughout this book I have argued that the interactions among interpretive stances—the ways in which they converge or compete, co-opt one another or simply coexist—are what generate Santería as a tangible and widely recognized cultural product. It is both part and parcel of Cuba's popular religious complex and, in large part because of interpretive discourses among practitioners and folklorists alike, it is polarized relative to other traditions within that complex, so that it emerges most sharply as the paragon of Afro-Cuban religiosity.

Although I have made only passing references to other practices in Cuba's popular religious complex, these, too, emerge as more or less well-defined "religions" by the same kinds of interactions among interpretive discourses and practices that may reinforce or blur boundaries among them. Whether distinct communities of Espiritismo, Palo, popular Catholicism, and Muertería are shaped by similar dynamics of community-through-controversy remains an open question, although my guess, based on my admittedly limited empirical data for these cases, is that these practitioners form much smaller, more localized groups that are more fragmented, more likely to be connected into the better-defined networks of Santería, and less well integrated into larger-scale communities on their own merits. The recent scholarly recognition of the entity tentatively called Muertería makes this an especially interesting case to watch, in order to see whether this scholarly-folkloric category takes hold among practitioners and leads to a growing sense of being a community of practice. Even if so, Santería's case may be distinct because of how santeros' own emphasis on community, coupled with their dynamics of competitiveness and skepticism, interacts with folkloric interpretations that highlight Santería as an emblem of national Euro-African cultural synthesis.

These dynamics were the subject of part 1, on religious histories. I examined how alternate, even competing construals of Santería made by others outside of the religion put a squeeze on santeros' own sacred stance. Santería itself emerges from this swirling mass of discourse as a particular sort of cultural form, or rather, as several strikingly different cultural forms, depending on one's interpretation. It is as if, in the course of this book, I have cut through onion-like layers of discourse only to find that the onion consists of and in those layers.

Of course, santeros construct their sacred stance through their ritual and other discursive practices, as fractious and skeptical as these can sometimes be. And yet, out of the controversies and conflicting interpretations emerges a coherent metaphysical order and a recognizable moral community. Detailed ethnographic examples have illustrated how santeros' religious practices provide both distinctive phenomenological experiences that cry out for interpretation and frames for interpreting those experiences. Simply put, it is in the bright light of metacultural attention that Santería emerges as a coherent community of practice. That attention comes from both intrinsic interpretive frames of rituals and explicit discourses of reflection and evaluation.

Throughout this book, I have shown the ways in which santeros, individually and as a community, engage in religious activities to elicit particular sacred experiences, make sense of them, and impose sacred order on their lives. In doing so, they continually recreate Santería as a living religion. In part 2 I considered the nature of religious experience in Santería, showing how santeros evaluate and retell experiences through the lens of hindsight. Rituals provide many potential experiences of the sacred and even provide implicit interpretive models for those experiences. But ultimately, it is through discursive processes of retrospection and reflection on events that santeros decide on their religious value.

Finally, I examined in part 3 how religious community is built out of participation in both rituals and the reflective, often critical, discourses that surround rituals. These two poles of discursive activity together promote shared meanings and ritual goals, even when santeros seem to be working for personal goals of "advancement in the religion." Indeed, it is through the very channels of gossip, critique, and controversy that santeros continually reconstitute the social boundaries and moral contours of their religious community. Rituals provide a necessary center, but surrounding discourses give definition to that center.

In the course of chopping this onion first one way and then another, there are many aspects of Santería that I have not touched or have mentioned only in passing en route to some other point, even though these may be primary in other published descriptions (the "pantheon" of orichas and their *patakines* or legends, the key rituals of initiation, the notion of aché and associated herbal lore and sacrificial practices, and so forth). I have cited many other treatments of Santería, from scholarly books that provide greater historical and folkloric context, to scholarly and popular discussions of rituals and religious lore by santeros themselves, to manuals for practitioners.[2] Likewise, I have referred to boundary-blurring practices across the popular religious complex—divination techniques, bembés, initiation procedures, ritual kinship, liturgical registers of speech, and performative genres like "making a promise"—without dwelling on all of the details of the standard distinctions made among the ostensibly different religions.

My approach, in many ways, has mirrored my argument about the interplay of experience and interpretation: I have on the one hand presented detailed analyses of religious activity as I experienced and recorded it in my role as participant-observer. On the other hand, I have sought to bring into focus my own and other possible interpretive frames by asking how practitioners, through religious activity, constitute Santería as a religion and themselves as a moral community.

During a tambor ceremony I witnessed, the oricha Ochún had possessed a young santero and was giving advice to another young santero who had spon-sored the ceremony. This encounter between the divine presence of Ochún and the young santero was mediated by an older santera who stood between them and translated what Ochún was saying. The Lucumí speech of the santero pos-sessed by Ochún necessitated an experienced translator, a santera who could give the message to its intended recipient. In that moment of ritual, the triad of participants enacted the ritual hierarchy, with a more senior priest mediating between the oricha and the recipient of her advice.

As their encounter proceeded, Ochún reminded the santero of all she had done to help him, then asked whether he had completed what he was sup-posed to do. After a few attempts at interpretation, aided by additional, cryptic comments by the oricha, the translating santera was able to make this rather vague question explicit: had he made a pilgrimage to the shrine at El Cobre? He hadn't. Ochún and the translating santera then reminded him that he had made a silent promise to do so. By claiming to know about this presumably se-cret intention, and by calling it a promise, the descended oricha and the senior santera proposed an emplotment of events that would reveal a sacred meaning—namely, the give-and-take relationship between a santero and an oricha. The oricha, echoed and magnified by the senior santera's translation, raised the stakes by threatening to withhold her support in the future if the young santero did not acknowledge her past support by respecting his promise. If the young santero accepted this plot, then their very words would become a "proof" of Ochún's omniscience in knowing of his promise and an impetus for him to carry through the plot by making his pilgrimage to El Cobre. If, as a result of completing his end of the bargain, the santero experienced the good fortune he hoped for, then the stage would be set for him to retroactively regard the entire series of events reaching back to his initial silent promise before the ritual as a sacred experience. This example, together with the host of other examples I have examined, illustrates how rituals seek to induce religious experiences of this sort in participants, by producing intense experiences during the ritual itself that then pull events of everyday life into their orbit.

As essential as ritual performances are in establishing religious order, they are not the only activity that matters. Throughout the book, I have also examined the reflective practices in which santeros engage: indeed, discourses of reflection, interpretation, and critique surround rituals and occur whenever santeros get together. The moral community of Santería emerges because the same people participate in both rituals and reflective practices. We have seen how santeros' reflective practices encourage skepticism and how their skepticism serves to draw their attention to ritual details. Attention to ritual details, in turn, reinforces the sense of a Regla, a sacred Law and tradition to which practitioners adhere. Skeptical reflective practices, thus, focus practitioners' attention on a set of cultural practices that looks, to them and to those of us observing from outside, like tradition.

For example, the very idea of the "promise" as a category of religiously relevant activity circulates because religious practitioners persist in identifying certain of their own and others' acts as being promises. The two examples above illustrate that a promise is a religious interpretation of an act that, on the surface, may not appear to be religious (or that may even have been silent and hidden until being revealed as a promise). To label something a promise reinforces the idea of divine communication at the core of Santería and related practices, because it is keeping one's own end of a bargain, presumably after the divine being has kept its end too. Promises aren't in themselves experiences, but are about narrativizing a series of experiences to become a sacred story: An intractable problem presents itself, so the victim makes a promise to an oricha. If the problem gets resolved then the promise must be fulfilled lest another, worse problem return. The promise as a genre takes on its own circulation, as something we can apply to a situation in order to construe the actors' intentions in a religious sort of way. The promise, as a cultural act and as a meaningful interpretive category, is about faith.

Enacting faith

Perhaps the most startling moment of my fieldwork was also the moment that I most viscerally understood what a religious experience, a moment of deep faith, might feel like. What an indelible image Graciela made: my seventy-something hostess lay prone on the hard cement floor of her house before her Eleggua and banged her forehead on the ground. "Eleggua, please open the way," she cried. Then she made him a promise.

Graciela did this on my behalf. My grandmother had died, and I had to interrupt my fieldwork in Santiago de Cuba to attend the funeral. The trouble was that it was Saturday and my husband and I had encountered a major obstacle to getting to the funeral: we needed permission from Cuban Immigration to leave, and we needed it before noon, when the office would close until Monday. Without permission, we would miss our flight—the only one we had been able to find on short notice that would get us out in time. Our host family mobilized to help us. Graciela's son, Maceo, took my husband off to get the necessary papers and rush everything over to a friend of a friend in Immigration—a classic case of Cuban "socio-lismo," or drawing upon one's social network to circumvent the impenetrable Socialist bureaucracy. Meanwhile, Graciela sat with me, nervously watching the clock. At 12:05 p.m., Maceo called to tell me that things were still in process and gave me the cryptic message that Graciela should "attend to the thing at the door," meaning the Eleggua. A conical cement head with cowrie shell eyes and mouth, Eleggua can be found behind the front door of many Cuban households, often seated in or on a small wooden box, which is his "house" (see figure 2.5). Eleggua is the oricha who "opens and closes the way," as Cubans say, the keeper of doors, crossroads, and journeys. When Graciela got Maceo's message, she ran to light a candle for Eleggua, then lay on the floor before him and performed her extraordinary supplication.

Maceo and my husband returned a while later with our exit permits in hand, and everyone declared that it was a miracle, a literal miracle, that we had run the gamut of Cuban bureaucracy in time. Graciela's young grandson, as it happened, was celebrating his birthday later that afternoon, and Graciela explained that she had promised Eleggua that she would turn the party into a *don de gracias* (thanksgiving offering) to him for opening the way. Because Eleggua is personified as, among other things, a small child, it would please him if we invited all the neighborhood children to come share the birthday cake.

The events of this extraordinary day were suffused with religious meanings, with signs of divine intervention and human reliance upon it. Immersed as I was in grief and desperation to reunite with my family, I came as close as I ever have to experiencing events as a miracle of divine intervention. I felt immense gratitude and relief as I handed cake out to some 20 children and their mothers who crammed into the kitchen later that afternoon. The joyful, tearful faces of Graciela and Maceo, in particular, suggested that they had lived the day's events as a religious experience.

Looking back on the day with the benefit of some distance, I still wonder at the cultural forms of meaning-making through which events can become religious experiences. Our success in getting exit visas in time was noteworthy, but what made it miraculous was the religious activity surrounding it, namely Graciela's acts of faith. Her dramatic way of getting Eleggua's attention should focus our attention on the plot she set in motion in that moment of making a "promise." By these means, our human efforts to get the exit visas became contingent upon divine intervention. Our success obligated us to make our return offering to Eleggua, which we did that same afternoon by adding a new purpose to the birthday party. Such acts of faith originate in the deployment of religious labels and genres like the "promise" and, whether successful or not, become "telling moments" that generate further reflective discourse that keeps religious participants focused on their search for communion with the divine.

Coda: "Una Flor Para Ochún"

I close with one more telling moment about Santería's resilience as a religion. Emilio once invited me to see a cabaret show he had choreographed. Such shows are important tourist attractions and revenue-generators, and the state lavishes resources on these showcases of tropical beauty and exoticism. Being a folklorist as well as a choreographer, Emilio had chosen to develop his show around folkloric themes, and so he featured elements of Santería's sacred songs, in addition to Carnival details, Jamaican and Haitian influences, and so forth. Tucked into this folklore-meets-glitz extravaganza was a short number featuring an old popular song, "Una flor para Ochún." The dancers emerged dressed as flowers, and by the end of the number they had arranged themselves around one dancer clad in an enormous, shimmering golden cape that rose behind her in a sunburst. Emilio, who had joined me at my table after the opening, leaned across to tell me that this number was his special *don de gracias* to Ochún for giving him the opportunity to direct the cabaret production. I looked up again at the stage and it hit me: Emilio had choreographed an altar to Ochún, complete with an offering of flowers and a resplendent, golden Ochún herself at the center (see figure 8.1). As much as secular stances of suspicion and folklore might put a squeeze on the sacred, as much as santeros find themselves and their traditions co-opted into folkloric and commercial ventures, the sacred interpretive frame of Santería also has potential to circulate beyond the moral community of practitioners and to make an appearance where one least expects it. Aché!

Figure 8.1. Tropicana dancers create a living altar to Ochún to fulfill the choreographer's promise to her.

Notes

Preface

1. I thank Matt Tomlinson for reminding me of their discussion.

2. In particular, see the exemplary work in Bauman and Briggs (1990) Bauman and Sherzer (1974) Goffman (1981), Gumperz and Hymes (1972), Hill and Irvine (1993), Parmentier (1997), Silverstein and Urban (1996), Urban (1991), and Wortham (2001).

3. From the Oficina Nacional de Estadísticas estimate, December 31, 2001. This figure includes the metropolitan area. The estimate for the urban center itself was 454,000 (2002).

4. Farnell and Graham's (1998) excellent treatment of research methods in discourse-centered approaches emphasizes the importance of naturally occurring discourse.

5. One of the issues Farnell and Graham (1998) raise concerns local sensibilities about nonrecordable events. This was one of my key concerns, because many rituals in Santería are secret, and many older santeros forbid cameras even during more public ceremonies. I usually found that an audio recorder was more acceptable than a camcorder, although I was careful to always ask permission of my hosts. In some cases I was permitted to attend secret ceremonies, but without recording. In these cases I wrote extensive field notes afterward. In another case, I was not allowed to attend, but a santero was permitted to enter with a tape recorder and record events for me. It was sometimes a struggle to balance my research needs with santeros' sensibilities, especially when the lines of the permissible were constantly shifting, depending upon whom I asked and when. I always tried to err on the side of respecting the wishes of my hosts, recognizing the ethical struggle in which many santeros found themselves between a long-standing code of silence and secrecy and new pressures to tell all and reap the pecuniary benefits of attracting foreign friends and godchildren. My approach proved its benefit as I came to realize how fast gossip travels, especially when it concerns disrespect to the religion.

Chapter 1. Introduction: Telling Moments

Author's note. Translations from the original Spanish, French, or Yoruba are mine unless otherwise indicated.

1. Emilio, recorded March 21, 2000, in Santiago de Cuba: "¡Vaya! Yo tengo experiencias increíbles en el santo. Por eso yo creo tanto en mi santo. . . . Y respeto tanto, porque son vivencias que uno ha tenido. (laughs, 2 seconds) Parece mentira, parece cuento de Aladino."

2. All names are pseudonyms unless otherwise noted.

3. Some good entry points into this extensive literature are Bell (1992), Desjarlais (1992), Drewal (1992), Hanks (1996), Keane (1997), Tambiah (1979), Turner (1967), and Whitehead (1987). In addition, Bloch (1974), Briggs (1993), Feld (1982), Schieffelin (1985), and Urban (1991, 1996) provide important discussions of how ritual speech and song, in particular, both create and evoke metaphysical orders.

4. To use more Michael Silverstein's more recent but abstruse terminology, rituals, like any other sign-events, convey an intrinsic metapragmatic regimentation, or set of semiotic clues to their own interpretation (1992: 70–71; 1993). Because rituals are so highly entextualized, which is to say easily recognized and replicated as cohesive units, their metapragmatics may more readily be replicated in later events or even transposed into other kinds of events, like narratives about ritual events.

5. Bakhtin's (1981) classic work on voicing and dialogicality provides the original insight motivating this sort of analysis.

6. Original Spanish text of Emilio's narrative of the warning, recorded June 19, 1998, in Santiago de Cuba:

Emilio: No es fanatismo. No es fanatismo, es realidad porque yo no soy fanático. Yo, sí, tengo mí-, y yo soy religioso y tengo mi creencia pero no soy fanático. Yo te dije que cuando en Itá .. a mí me salió, a mí hubo que darme Olokun, urgente, el día del Itá mío. O sea, el tercer día, cuando me dijeron todo eso dentro de las cosas que me dijeron, me dijeron, el hoyo está abierto. El hoyo en el cementerio está abierto para uno de la familia. Y rápidamente, para salvar al iyawó, o sea, para salvarme a mí, había que darme Olokun. Porque Olokún es muerto, Olokún protege de los muertos. Como es muerto, protege de los muertos. O sea, mi padrino tuvo que salir rápidamente a buscarme Olokún, hacer la ceremonia en el mar, porque hacer la ceremonia en el mar lejísimo, a buscar todas la herramientas, buscar todas las cosas, todos los pañuelos de Olokún, todas las cosas y darme Olokún para que el hoyo no estuviera abierto por mí. Cuando hay un hoyo abierto para la familia en el cementerio, porque alguien se va a morir. Cuando me dieron Olokún, que buscaron todo rápidamente, todo, todo, todo, buscar la máquina, rápidamente, al mar, buscar todas las cosas, Eh, bueno. Salvamos al iyawó. O sea, me salvaron a mí. Ya no soy yo, pero ahora hubo alguien de la familia se va, se iba a morir. Hay que investigar quien es y empezaron a preguntar, pero no decían quien era. No dijo. El santo no dijo en ningún momento quien era.

Es alguien de la familia, pero no dijo quien es. ¿Y bueno, que decisión se tomó? Proteger a las personas de la familia que estuvieron más enfermas, mi mamá, mi hermano Pedro, que siempre estaba enfermo, y un tío mío, que siempre estaba, que como tomaba tanto, siempre estaba enfermo tambien. Empezamos a cuidar a esas personas, hasta dependiente de yo, su medicina. Si tenían algo rápidamente para el médico.

KW: ¿Ellos tenían, podían ir a—?

E: ¿—A la ceremonia mía del santo?

KW: Sí, o al, a: , algún—

E: —lugar para, para protegerse? No. El santo no dijo que protegiera a toda la familia. Que estuviera pendiente a las fami-, a las personas que más enfermas estuvieron dentro de la familia. Y eso fue lo que hicimos estar pendiente a mi mamá, a mi hermano Pedro, a mi tío Marcos, que son las personas que, porque Pedro siempre estaba enfermo, ¿que toque en [nombre del grupo folklórico]?

KW: Anja

E: El siempre se ha operado, y mi mamá es hipertensa y siempre tenía la presión alta, y siempre así, muy viejita. Actualmente tiene 89 años. Muy mayor, muy mayor. Y mi tio Marcos, como tomaba tanto, siempre estaba en la calle. Se quedaba a dormir, se daba golpes, se caía, un carro le estropeó una vez. Entonces, pensabamos que una de estas tres personas podía estar la muerte porque yo lo estaba bien hasta que hubieron vuelto, no se cerraba. Entonces empezamos a cuidar estas tres personas. En el que menos pensamos queda mi hermano Jorge .. fue que se murió a los tres meses justo. Me habían dicho, a los tres meses justo. Le cayó un aguacero, estaba tomado, se mojó. Se fue para la casa y se acostó . mojado, con la ropa mojada, se tiró en la cama y se quedó dormido. Al otro día amaneció con una fiebre fulminante, y no fue al médico. Empezó a tomar él mismo medicarse, y no fue al médico. Le cayó una broncho-pulmonía fulm-fulminante. A los dos días murió. Así fue rápido así, rápido. Lo que menos pensamos nosotros. (pausa) A los tres meses. (pausa) Que la muerte de verdad estaba allí, y era mi familia, una de familia llevaron, mi hermano. Terrible, terrible el caso. Y me lo advirtió. Eso lo avisan los santos.

Chapter 2. "All the Priests in the House": Defining Santería

Epigraph. My translation is based on santeros' glosses and one possible Yoruba back-translation (based on etymological reconstruction of a Lucumí term's possible Yoruba derivation) of the Lucumí sections (with Spanish words in parentheses): "Mo júbà (all the) ọmọ òrìṣà (and) bàbálóṣà, gbogbo àwòró kí ó wà ilé."

1. I am drawing upon Urban's theorization (2001) of metaculture as culture interpreting other culture. In focusing attention on a particular strand of culture, metaculture creates and recreates the cultural object of its attention. One of Urban's key insights is that metacultural reflections determine which cultural forms persist

through time, in part by drawing attention to them and pointing out recognizable instances of a type. He argues that metaculture, like culture, circulates in the world, has a history and trajectory, and is reproduced through particular institutional nodes.

2. See Silverstein (2003) for a similar point about how the sum of such characterizations is a dynamic folk-interpretive framework through which we carve up our world and charge each chunk with social value. (Silverstein coins the descriptive, if unwieldy, term "ethno-metapragmatics.")

3. A few examples include Alcaraz (2000), Argüelles Mederos and Hodge Limonta (1991), Barnet (1995), Bolívar Aróstegui (1994), Cabrera (1996), Canizares (1993), González-Whippler (1992), and Mestre (1996). It is illustrative to compare these to actual manuals, such as the classic ones by the highly respected Havana santero Nicolás Angarica (n.d.a, n.d.b).

4. See examples listed in n.3 above and also more sophisticated and textured accounts in Barnet (1995), Brandon (1993), James Figarola (1999), M. A. Mason (2002), and Murphy (1994).

5. See especially Cuban folklorist Fernando Ortiz's influential early discussion (Bronfman 2002; Ortiz 1973/1906).

6. "Magic" usually appears as a modifier in Cuban scholarship to mark some kinds of religious practices as "magico-religious," with an implied comparison to "proper" religions like church Catholicism or Protestantism that presumably are not focused on possibilities of supernatural manipulation.

7. Where I am differentiating between matters Cuban and matters Yoruba I use two different word forms: "Oricha" and "Orisha." "Oricha" is the Cuban spelling and pronunciation. "Orisha" is the English spelling, which is also closer to the Yoruba spelling and pronunciation: òrìṣà.

8. But see D. H. Brown's historical analysis (2003) of how European images of royalty have been incorporated into Santería ritual aesthetics at a number of levels.

9. On the ethnogenesis of the Yoruba, see Doortmont (1990), Kopytoff (1965), Law (1997), and Peel (1989).

10. White, elite observers in the late nineteenth and early twentieth centuries tended to lump all of this noninstitutionalized, folk religious activity together as an undifferentiated mass of "witchcraft" and superstition (Ortiz 1995/1906; Urrutia y Blanco 1882). They linked these religious practices with the largely black underclass, even though it is likely that many whites and even white elites also participated (see for example Barnet 1994: 27; Palmié 2002a: 197–98, 337 n.60; Román 2002).

11. I use "popular" in the Cuban sense meaning "of the people," a widespread term among Cuban scholars that captures the official socialist promotion of "popular culture." The notion of popular religion is officially deployed to distinguish what the Revolutionary State regards as valid forms of folk or "popular" culture from counterrevolutionary religious institutions—namely the Catholic Church, which clashed

with Fidel in the early days of the Revolution (Ayorinde 2004; Betto 1985; Kirk 1989; Millet, Brea, and Ruiz Vila 1997: 53–54).

12. Muertería has received very little scholarly attention, even within Cuba. To the extent that a general description can be applied to this unformalized set of practices, muerteros describe themselves as working with spirits of the dead, spirits that bear affinities to those of Palo and Spiritism. Self-identified muerteros I met often engaged in very similar practices of divination, card-reading, maintaining altars, and sponsoring bembés to other practitioners of popular religions, as I describe below.

13. She also utilized ritual utterances she described as "Haitian French" underscoring the historical influence of Haitian immigrants on Santiago's religious culture, another topic sorely in need of scholarship.

14. See Pérez Jr. (1995a, 1995b) on the history of Protestantism in Cuba and Kirk (1989) and Betto (1985) on relations between the Catholic Church and the Revolution.

15. It would be quite difficult for a foreign researcher, especially one from the United States, to get permission to do even a neighborhood survey of the sort that ethnographers frequently do (which would need to be conducted with the consent and cooperation of the neighborhood-level Comité en Defensa de la Revolución (CDR).

16. The researchers sampled 21 microregions of the neighborhood to build a representative sample of 133 households (Millet et al. 1997: 28).

17. I avoid using social class because it is very problematic in the context of Cuba, and in any case I do not have data that would allow me to make well-supported class designations. Cuba had a class system prior to the Revolution, such that class designations would have been strongly predictive of family income, economic status, neighborhood, and access to privileges such as education and health care. The Revolution has spent forty years dismantling the class system and officially speaking insists that class has been abolished. Government policies have sought to decouple variables such as family income, educational attainment, profession, and even neighborhood from vestigial social class. Of course, remnants persist, especially in how people view themselves and others. Certainly, Santiagueros (residents of Santiago) perceive that denizens of a neighborhood like Los Hoyos are poorer, blacker, and less educated than those who live in other, formerly middle-class or upper-class neighborhoods.

18. It is telling that these researchers, who are affiliated with the Casa del Caribe, a center for cultural research in Santiago, would be met with suspicion. Although the current climate has opened toward religion, some wariness obviously remains. Although they do not specify what they sought, the researchers would have looked for evidence such as bead necklaces and bracelets signifying different orichas, as well as altars, statues of saints, or other religious objects. Such a methodology is obviously problematic, not least in counting only what is seen, while saying noth-

ing about which household members are religious or what labels they would give to their religiosity.

19. We can take these data as rough indications only: the sample sizes for some groups were quite small, and the authors neither specify how they identified an entire household's race or educational level nor did they attempt any multivariate analyses that would indicate the relative importance of these and other variables examined.

20. One explanation for the dominance of santeros among applicants might be that their ceremonies often require drumming and can also last several days. Both features could serve to draw more attention from neighbors and officials, necessitating the trouble of getting licensed in lieu of conducting ceremonies quietly in hopes that no one checks for licensure. See Ayorinde (2004) for a discussion of Cuban laws controlling religious expression.

21. I do not have statistics for other religious traditions listed in table 2.1.

22. Arará is related to Santería and Vodú, but is localized to western Cuba (Matanzas in particular).

23. For more information on Ifá practices and continuities in West Africa and Cuba see Abimbola (1976), Bascom (1969), Bolívar Aróstegui (1996), D. H. Brown (2003), Fuentes Guerra and Gómez (1994: 39–63), Matibag (1997), and Otero (2002).

24. Matibag (1996) also describes the use of shells in Palo divination. I can make no claims about the directionality of any borrowing that occurred or whether the two methods are a case of convergence of widespread divination techniques across Africa (Peek 1991; Pemberton 2000).

25. Cuban scholars use Fernando Ortiz's term "transculturation" to describe the productive amalgam of European and African influences that characterizes Cuban culture and Cuban national ideology (see Ortiz 1970/1947).

26. Excellent discussions of the general Latin American context include Rahier (2003), Wade (2001), Williams (1991), and Wright (1990). For discussions of the Cuban case, see Daniel (1995), C. Moore (1988), R. Moore (1997), and Palmié (2002b).

27. See Wedel (2004: 53–56) for a description of links between Palo and witchcraft. Cuban folklorist Ernesto Armiñán Linares described to me three sects of the Regla de Palo: La Kimbisa, which works only for good; La Mayombe, which includes good and evil rituals; and La Briyumba, which practices evil.

28. Houk (1995) describes similar spatial and temporal boundaries that religious practitioners in Trinidad maintain between Spiritual Baptist, Orisha, Hindu, and Kabbalah traditions, which many combine, while maintaining separate altars and rituals for each.

29. See Johnson's 2002 study of Brazilian Candomblé for a compelling account of the role of what he calls secretism in African diasporic religions—an account that generally matches my observations of Santería.

Chapter 3. Competing Histories and Dueling Moralities

1. Note that dialogicality does not imply cooperation or equality among voices, a point made by Urban and Smith (1998).

2. The show was entitled *Fifi Okkan: Pintura sobre la cabeza* by Omar Enrique Moya Moya.

3. Alternately, one could put a positive spin upon this historical consciousness and read it as an emphasis upon preserving tradition, in Urban's sense of a "metaculture of tradition" that prioritizes exact replication of religious culture (2001: 43, 83). I choose to emphasize the struggle against loss because I situate sacred practice in relation to hegemonic processes that have, until very recently, forced practitioners underground.

4. If we were to trace the suspicious stance back further in time, I suspect that it would resonate less with secular scientific beliefs and more with popular Catholic notions of witchcraft and paganism. Catholicism had been a major tool of Spanish cultural hegemony, although colonial-era attempts to replace African practices with Catholicism were seldom successful. Here I merely pick up on evidence of the suspicious stance as it was configured at the turn of the twentieth century.

5. In Spanish the phrase reads: ¿Y no hay río en Santiago? ¿No hay hierbas? ¿Y entonces, por qué no se hace santo aquí? Millet's consultants attribute the phrase to Aurora Lamar, known as La China (2000: 112).

6. Matt Tomlinson (n.d.: 157–58) examines the widespread phenomenon of nostalgia and distinguishes between nostalgic discourses highlighting loss of power and discourses of moral decline. In the case of Santería, santeros link their concerns about moral decline to efforts to preserve powerful ritual knowledge.

7. Vicente, *ibayé ibayen tonú* (rest in peace), passed away in 2001. The santeros who gave me the news told me they were very sad to lose such a prominent santero and palero, especially because he represented a storehouse of knowledge direct from Reynerio. They did not see a clear descendent of this direct, ritual genealogical line from Reynerio through Vicente.

8. Consider the following bembé songs as examples:
   (1) Saca lo' sombre pa' 'fuera / A do' a do'
   [Throw the men outside / Two by two]
   (2) <u>Omo</u> <u>patele</u> / <u>Omo</u> <u>patele</u> / <u>Omo</u> <u>patele</u> pa' <u>Changó</u> / <u>Omo</u> <u>patele</u>
   [(No translation) / . . . / . . . for Changó / . . .]
   Notice that these simple lyrics are largely in Spanish and that they border on the nonsensical, which makes them distinct from Lucumí songs, which have as their matrix a garbled, half-remembered Lucumí. Sometimes, as in example 2, singers will convert the unintelligible lyrics into something similar sounding, like "He ate sweets" (Comió pasteles) for "Omo patele." It may be that Spanish lyrics like those in example 1 arose that way, too. Other bembé songs seem to have Lucumí lyrics and so blur the lines and may more readily be accepted in Santería ceremonies:

(3) <u>Mai</u> <u>mai</u> <u>soló</u> / <u>Ra</u> <u>koso</u> / <u>Mai</u> <u>mai</u> <u>soló</u> / Pa' <u>Changó</u>
Even in example 3, Emilio told me that people often sing "maíz" (corn) for "mai."

9. My translation of Ortiz's original Spanish: "La brujería es el caldo de cultivo para el desarrollo del microbio criminoso contenido en la psiquis del brujo."

10. The metaphor of contagious culture is quite common in historical and contemporary accounts of the threats posed by diasporic Africans and African culture (Borges 1993; Browning 1998; Graham 1990).

11. Fernández Robaina (1994) and Helg (1995) forcefully argue this point, although 1912 did not quell ongoing Afro-Cuban political mobilizations by other means as de la Fuente extensively documents.

12. Racial terminologies of mestizaje and *mulataje* have notoriously variable meanings across Latin America. In Cuba, "mestizaje" primarily refers to African and European hybridization. Elsewhere, "mestizaje" means the racial mixing of Europeans and indigenous peoples, while the Cuban situation is described as "mulataje" (Rahier 2003: 42, 45–46).

13. De la Fuente points out that elite attempts to present a safely folklorized Afro-Cuban presence in national culture were contested by at least some Afro-Cubans, although Afro-Cuban elites largely concurred, being anxious to distance themselves from the Afro-Cuban masses (2001: 183–87, 154–55).

14. Erwan Dianteill recounts the naming controversy between Ortiz and Lachatañeré (1995: 40–50). Lachatañeré attacked Ortiz's use of the pejorative and overly general term "witchcraft," instead advocating "Santería." Dianteill argues that each claimed to take his preferential term from popular usage, but that both fell into ethnocentric traps intrinsic to their different social positions—Ortiz as a member of the white elite intelligentsia and Lachatañeré as a privileged mulatto intellectual struggling for elite membership.

15. See Isabel Castellanos (1996) for an etymological account of the ethnonym "Lucumí."

16. I am grateful to Licenciada Zoe Cremé Ramos at the Centro Cultural Africano "Fernando Ortiz" in Santiago de Cuba for the detailed biographical information on Lachatañeré.

17. Lydia Cabrera's introductions to *El Monte* (1993/1954) and *Anagó* (1958) are especially telling. She begins *Anagó* by asserting her familiarity with Lucumí speech and thus her ability to gain her informants' trust, but she also references her social distance from her informants by referring to "the folklore of our blacks" (13).

18. Dianteill reproduces Ortiz's article (1995: 133–46), which originally appeared in the July 1937 issue of the journal *Ultra* 3(13), 77–86.

19. Recall the use of this term (*iguoro*) in the moyubá invocation discussed in chapter 2.

20. See Ayorinde (2004) for a useful history of the Revolution's evolving attitudes and policies toward Afro-Cuban religions.

21. Daniel (1995) and Hagedorn (2001) also make this point.

22. For more on the special period and informal economy, see Fernandez (2000), Henken (2000 and 2002), and other articles in the economic journal *Cuba in Transition*. Also see Palmié (2002a).

23. While the Revolution never outlawed religion, my consultants made clear that it did marginalize religious practitioners and try to discourage young people from being religious—by banning the initiation of children for example. See Ayorinde for more on the Revolution's discouragement of religion (2004: 125–32).

24. Interview with santero, audio tape 12, October 1999, Santiago de Cuba:

> Hubo una época anterior a mi iniciación como santero en la cual aquí en Cuba en mi país, se practicó el culto a los hombres . por sus ideas y por sus historias y yo como todos los que pertenecen a mi generación me asumé a esa corriente en creer en los hombres hasta un momento que dejé de creer en los hombres, y tuve la necesidad de buscar en quien creer. Y entonces llegué a esta religión. Me gustó, empecé a creer en los dioses y aquí estoy.

25. Stephan Palmié's field consultant in Havana used the evocative term "santero jinetero" for someone who "prostitutes" their religion for cash (2002a).

26. Interview with Carmen and family, video recording 5, December 17, 1999, Santiago de Cuba.

Chapter 4. From Skepticism to Faith: Narratives of Religious Experience

Epigraph. The Euripides quote came to my attention as an epigraph in Guthrie (1993: 11).

1. Interview with Mayeya, audio tape 50, April 1, 2000, Santiago de Cuba.

2. He and others frequently related aspects of my personality and profession to Obatalá, and various ritual events such as divination results seemed to reinforce their supposition that Obatalá "owns my head."

3. Critical reappraisals of Geertz's definition of religion, notably by Asad (1983), have problematized his overly cognitive, ahistorical account of religious belief and his somewhat mysterious orchestration of belief through symbols deployed in ritual. The notion of religious experience, another presumably cognitive process, shares in some of the thorny problems of belief. My path through the thicket is to focus on performance, whether in ritual or in other more mundane interactions, because what people say and do is directly accessible in a way internal mental states are not. But people can and do represent their beliefs and experiences in discourse and act upon them; they align themselves according to particular interpretations of events and cite these interpretations to explain their choices, such as deciding to undergo religious initiation (see Kirsch 2004; Pigg 1996).

4. I say this in full awareness that it has become almost de rigueur for ethnographies of African diasporic religions like Santería and Vodú to adopt sacred as well as secular-analytical metacultural stances toward their religious material, even

when the scholars do not profess to be religious practitioners. Hagedorn (2001: 16) recounts a dream-visitation from the oricha Ogún in a brief personal vignette following her introduction. Murphy recounts his experience being possessed by the oricha Changó (1988: 98), and K. M. Brown details her initiation into Vodou (1991: 317–27). Even Palmié, who positions himself as merely a sympathetic student of Afro-Cuban religion, opens his prologue by introducing his muerto, Tomás, the spirit of a nineteenth-century slave (2002b: 1–14). Such movement across multiple stances and attention to polyvocality are of course in keeping with the reflexive turn in writing anthropology (Clifford 1986; Marcus and Fischer 1986), and in particular the recent calls for a dialogical anthropology that attends to culture's character as dynamic, fluid, and emergent in interaction (Tedlock and Mannheim 1995; Yelvington 2001: 204–42). Moreover, as Trouillot points out, and as illustrated in the previous chapter, it is no easy matter to disentangle the scholarly and popular discursive fields, particularly in the Caribbean (1992: 25).

5. Emilio, audio tape 1, October, 3, 1999, Santiago de Cuba:

Dentro de la Santería . se dicen pellizquitos de Ochún. Esos son pellizquitos porque ella te hace una maldad para que tu reacciones. . . . Ochún dice así cuando ella dice, tú eres mi hijo. Tarde o temprano tú tienes que hacer santo. . . . siempre le pone [a sus hijos] trabajo, trabajo, trabajo hasta que hace el santo.

6. Interview with Rey, audio tape 5 October 12, 1999, Santiago de Cuba.

7. Excerpt from Emilio's lecture to visiting folklore students, audio tape, January 7, 1998, Santiago de Cuba:

Yo . no creí en nadie, porque bueno, yo casi . me desarrollé con el proceso revolucionario, y al principio de la Revolución, al principio de la Revolución aquí, la, la religión no era bien visado. Al principio, en el ambiente porque había problemas con la gente religiosa. Y yo como me inicié, con el proceso de poco a poco, no creía en la religión. Y tení-, tenía una tradición de familia religiosa pero viví en una nueva generación. No creía, era comunista. (ha-ha) No creí.

8. I am grateful to Susan Harding's excellent *Book of Jerry Falwell* (2000) for bringing this James passage to my attention.

9. Emilio, audio tape, June 18, 1998, Santiago de Cuba. Bold type indicates emphasis; em dashes indicate no break between phrases, and a forward slash mark (/) indicates finger taps on the table:

(Section A) **Pero**, eh, yo confronté un problema de que cuando empecé a viajar en el extranjero, los ladrones me perseguían **mucho**—me perseguían **mucho**. Y **siempre** yo estaba, **siempre** se me perdían cosas—se me perdían cosas, me **robaban**—me robaban. (Section B) Y la **policía** . **encontraba** los **ladrones** pero no **podía** sancionarlos, ni lo **podía** hacer **nada**, porque (2-second pause) nada. (Section C) Y **entonces**, yo **empecé** a **consultarme**, y era que **Ochún** me estaba **pidiendo** la **cabeza**, se dice así. Y que hasta que **yo** no hiciera santo, no **iban**, no iban a parar los róbos. (Section D) Y yo no lo creí, **estuve** como **cinco** o **seis años** en **eso**, y eran **robándome, robándome, robándome, robándome**. (Section E) Hasta que me dieron una **prueba final**, que me dijeron, Si no haces **santo** . en el **próximo** viaje que tenga lo **vas** a **perder todo**. . . . **Así** me **dijeron**, lo **vas** a **perder todo**. (Section F) Y yo no lo hice así. Yo voy a hacerme **santo**, no se preocupe padrino, porque **entonces** yo le decía **ya** al **padrino**. No, yo voy a hacer **santo**. Pero, . ptch .. vino el **viaje**, y se me olvidó y no hice **nada**. (Section G) Y como a los **cinco meses** me llovar-, me llevaron **todo, todo**, lo perdí **todo, todo, todo, todo**. **Todo, todo, todo, todo**. Me **dejaron** una casa **vacía**. (Section H) (2-second pause, table drumming: // /// // // /// //). Y **tuve** que hacer **santo** por ese **problema**. (Section I) Mira, a partir de allí nada no sucedió **nada más**, ¿no? Así. Y todo me ha ido muy **bien**.

10. Indeed, on other occasions, he pointed out to me signs that an oricha was claiming my head for initiation. One particularly dramatic "little pinch" he noted occurred a few days after a divination in which I had received a very bad sign relating to my travel plans. Emilio accompanied me to the airport for my departure and so witnessed my astonishment when the airline clerk informed me that my flight off-island had been precipitously canceled. There was no information about when the flight might be rescheduled, and I was told that I should come back in a few days, maybe. To my supreme annoyance at the time, Emilio's face was almost gleeful as he declared this a "proof" of the divination results and therefore a sign of an oricha making trouble for me.

11. Note, however, that a fracture line runs through current studies of religious experience, largely separating psychologists and neurologists who focus on the phenomenological angle of religious experience from anthropologists who are more likely to study its interpretive or epistemic angle.

12. Schleiermacher was a German philosopher at the turn of the nineteenth century who wrote *On Religion* (1799). James was an American psychologist at the turn of the twentieth century whose *Varieties of Religious Experience* (1922/1902) stands as the cornerstone of the literature on the psychology of religion. Both imbued their definitions of religious experience with European Christian traditions of mysticism and individual contemplation.

13. See H. Burhenn for excerpts from Friedrich Schleiermacher and Rudolf Otto (1995: 146–47).

14. This stance is evident in everything from neurological studies of perception and cognition (Azari et al. 2001) to historiographic arguments about the inherent structure of historical events (Carr 1986) to the insights of Sapir and Whorf's linguistic relativity hypothesis about how language organizes thought (Boas 1889; Lucy 1992a, 1992b; Sapir 1949/1921; Whorf 1997/1956).

15. See reviews in Hood (1995), Hood et al. (1996), and Newberg et al. (2001).

16. Newberg and coauthors describe four related "transcendent" states, which

they distinguish according to autonomic nervous system arousal: hyperarousal, hyperquiescence, or either one with breakthrough of the other. Briefly explained, our autonomic nervous system, operating largely below any level of conscious awareness or control, contains two pathways, the sympathetic and parasympathetic. These coordinate a wide range of bodily functions, with the sympathetic pathway stimulating organs and blood flow to contribute to alert activity (e.g. increased heart rate) and the parasympathetic pathway stimulating more vegetative activities, such as digestion. These two pathways usually operate with negative feedback, so that the arousal of the sympathetic pathways inhibits arousal of the parasympathetic pathways, and vice versa. Under certain conditions, however, both systems can be simultaneously aroused, and the sensations correspond variously to mystical bliss, flow state, ecstatic trance, or oceanic tranquility (2001: 40–42). The researchers also looked at prefrontal lobe and limbic system activity that they postulate involves distinct cognitive elements of spatial orientation, emotion, attention, and abstract verbal conceptualization to produce mystic states (27–32).

17. This evocative tendency of some discourse and the action to organize what follows it is what Mattingly, following Ricoeur, calls "emplotment" (1998). She describes how clinical encounters between occupational therapists and their clients are subject to emplotment, both because of the ritualized structure of such encounters and because of efforts by one or both parties to organize the encounter according to a guiding narrative. Whenever the therapist or the patient is working toward some outcome or seeking to elicit a particular conversational direction, emplotment is at work. Not surprisingly, Mattingly looks to ritual as a metaphor for the clinical encounter, in that both promote a telos and lend themselves to narrativization. That is, rituals may be "emergent stories"—Victor Turner's "social dramas"—that unfold according to well-established tropes of interaction (1974).

18. Rituals are at the highly entextualized and entextualizable end of a spectrum of human interaction (Bauman and Briggs 1990; Kuipers 1990; Silverstein and Urban 1996). That is, the degree and density of internal structuring in rituals makes them recognizable as chunks to be transmitted whole. Ritual performances additionally "may create events worth telling stories about" (Mattingly 1998: 162), in part because of their capacity to envelop bodies and senses in "heightened, multisensory experience" or to delineate temporal and spatial boundaries that set them apart from ordinary events (Bell 1997: 160; Bloch 1974).

19. Santeros' normative understanding of rituals as communication coincides with anthropological definitions of ritual that focus on its performative and communicative functions (Rappaport 1999; Robbins 2001).

20. Rituals encourage participants to interact according to particular structures of participation, at least for the duration of the ritual activity. For example, *tambor* (drumming) rituals encourage participants to adopt a sacred stance to interpret the behavior of those who fall into trance as being possessed by an oricha. Occupying a

stance temporarily but repeatedly serves as a mode of learning and thus can potentially move a person toward more readily transferring that stance to other situations and even adopting it as a long-term, stable way of being in the world.

21. Santería emphasizes authorization over inspiration, and mediumship is a matter of inspiration. This means that it would violate the canons of hierarchy in Santería by promoting a more charismatic style of authority that is anathema to the rules of seniority and authorization regulating the Santería community.

Chapter 5. Skepticism in Faith: Evaluating Religious Experiences in Rituals

1. Robbins (2001), developing Rappaport's thesis (1999), suggests that rituals are fundamentally communicative events, in which certain kinds of messages are conveyed in semiotically dense ways that bypass mere denotation. The ambiguities, indeterminacies, and unintelligibilities so common to rituals require explanation not as breakdowns in communication, but as necessary components of how ritual communication occurs, as Malinowski first pointed out (1966/1935, 2: 218). Trawick (1988) argues that ambiguities intrigue people and encourage them to continue to circulate the texts, both by duplicating the originals and by reentextualizing them in exegeses whose open-endedness makes them endlessly adaptable to new contexts and new situations (see also Wirtz 2005).

2. Conversation with ritual singer (Desi) and Emilio, audio tape 46, March 25, 2000, Santiago de Cuba.

> Desi: Porque hay veces los tamboreros que salen con un toque .. y te están probando. Te están probando para ver si hay conocimiento. Ellos te salen ¡kum-kum-ba! ¡Tun-ba, bi-bi Tun ba, bi-bi! Y tú debes saber que eso es el rezo de Eleggua, que te están tocando la entrada para que tú le cantes a Eleggua. Yo puedo ir ahora a La Habana y si me quieren probar allá, algunos tamboreros—
>
> Emilio: [Que eso se lo hacen
>
> KW: [Ha-ha. Entonces, ?no es verdad que los cantantes también hacen pruebas a los bail—
>
> D: —¿A los tocadores?
>
> KW: ¿A los tocadores, y a los santeros que vienen a bailar?
>
>   [Porque Emilio me ha contado unas historias
>
> E: [ha-ha
>
> D: Sí, sí. En la religión, más bien todo es una competencia. La religión es una competencia de: , y en realidad una competencia favorable. Porque es una ayuda para mi que yo descubra que hay tantos cantos allí que yo no sé. Que a tocarme algo que yo no sé ya me preocupo por eso, y aprendo, y debo aprender esa cosa.

3. Conversation with ritual singer (Desi) and Emilio continued. (See n.2 above.)

> D: El trabajo del cantante es . hacerle saber al santo lo que, pedirlo que tú

quieres al santo, y a través de tu conocimiento, de tu conocimiento, tratar de: darse cuenta si está el santo en realidad o no está. Porque puede dar un santo, pero algunos llegan y no está el santo. Eso también ocurre en la religión.

E: ¿Qué fin tiene eso?

D: Hacen muchas cosas. Entonces—

E: —El santero tiene que comprobar lo que dice, tiene que comprobar si es verdad que hay un santo o no

KW: ¿Y cómo se, se sabe?

E: A través de los tratados   [de ese

D: [de los tratados.

4. Conversation with ritual singer (Desi) and Emilio continued. (See n.2 above.)

D: Porque bueno, ah: , .. el santo .. y el santo puede tener eh: un plato de miel, y decirle al santo iyalode, que quiere, gran señora, iyalode, gran señora. Wole die mi, que me escuche. Emi ni eyeumo ni, yo le estoy pidiendo que me escuche a mí como cantante, y que quiero comer miel, o tomar miel. Y él no me da esa miel, no está el santo.

5. Batá drums can undergo initiation ceremonies much like those santeros go through, in which they are dedicated to the oricha Aña (Ayan) and receive a "secret" that is placed inside them. Only a few sets of drums are consecrated in this way, and only drummers who undergo their own ceremony to Aña and become "omo aña" may play these drums, which also require other kinds of special treatment.

6. "Ayé Aranlá" is a Lucumí phrase that can be translated from Yoruba to mean "the world of great beings," or "heaven." Most santeros would not be able to give this translation. Many know that *orun* (song) is a Lucumí word derived from the Yoruba *orin*, also meaning "song."

7. The Spanish part of the song says, "I am alone, what are we going to do for you."

8. And, indeed, I follow Kirsch (2004) in rejecting an understanding of beliefs as (unknowable) internal states (also see Palmer et al. 2005)

9. See Isabel Castellanos (1990), Ortiz López (1998), Schwegler (2006), and Wirtz (2005) for further discussion of bozal in contemporary Cuban speech.

10. Germán: Yemayá, yo soy yo soy religioso, pero así no puede seguir cantando, porque la gente me tiene que ayudar. No puede seguir cantando. Estamos con los tambores de fundamento.

Chapter 6. Respecting the Religion, Advancing in the Religion

1. M. at her *don de gracias*, author's field journal 8 (pp. 10–11), March 10, 2000, Santiago de Cuba.

2. As commentators on the Gluckman-Paine debate have pointed out, there is likely truth in both positions, not least because gossip is a complex and highly ambivalent social practice—or rather, a set of social practices that may take different forms in different settings (Stewart and Strathern 2004).

3. While most of this section remains unintelligible to me, whether as Lucumí or as Yoruba, Maura's reply seems likely to be derived from the Yoruba salutation, "A kú èyin," meaning "We greet you (plural)."

4. Other santeros spell out the sign for eight variously as *iyonle* or *elliunle*.

5. Without getting mired in all the complexities, suffice to say that each of the 16 possible numbers, from one to all sixteen cowries face up, is considered either a "major" or a "junior" sign. Generally speaking, the eleven major signs call for the left hand, and the five junior signs call for a second throw and then generally for the right hand.

6. To be strictly accurate, some of the signs are dead ends, cutting down on the possibilities somewhat. For example, signs for 12 to 16 cowries landing face up are automatic referrals to babalawos, who use the even more complex Ifá system of divination.

7. Alberto: . . . donde dice Eleggua, "<u>Iré</u>, <u>arikú</u>, <u>moyale</u>." Dice Elegba que trae <u>iré</u> con <u>Iroso</u>, y el <u>arikú</u> lo trae con <u>Oddí</u> <u>Obbara</u> . y <u>moyare</u> <u>Ojuani</u> <u>Oddí</u>. Dice Eleggua que Ud. nació para cabeza. Que Ud. nació para una gente intelectual, una gente inteligente, una gente capaz de . profundizar cualquier sabiduría, o preocupaciones por saber ¿no es verdad? Tu interés propio ¿no? en como llegar a la cosa para despues que se conozca todo el paso que quiera dar ya no tiene . duda ¿verdad? Porque ya aprendido y ya tiene el paso determinado para el día de mañana que Ud. acepte el santo, ya tú sabe todo el manejo no el secreto pero sabe ya por donde defenderte para el día de mañana.

8. Alberto: Ahí es donde, ahí es donde Santa Bárbara bendita, Changó le ponen cabeza. ¿Para que? Cabeza para que piense, cabeza para que analice y obselve. O sea muy observadora dentro de todo lo que tú te relaciona dentro del campo espiritual y el campo santorial que fé es la que te puede (1 second) eh .. <u>iré</u>. Me refiero por ejemplo, tú tiene tus mayores, tiene tus padrinos ¿verdad? Y hasta ahora ¿ellos te han hecho algo que tú has visto resultado?

9. Maura: El motivo ¿por qué? Sí tú tienes que darte paso, pero ¿por qué? Que este paso te va a traer la vida, te traerá prosperidad, ¿no? Pero aquí dice Eleggua que Ud. nació para ser rey, Ud. nació para buscar dinero, Ud. nació para buscar desenvolvimiento y más que desenvolvimiento.

10. Alberto: Pero dice Changó que por tu propio mano, con santo hecho Ud. puede resolver muchas cosas en la vida.
Maura: Y tiene conocimiento.
Alberto: Y tiene conocimiento ¿por qué? Porque tú puede traer gente de allá para acá y puede aumentar tu presupuesto de dinero. No es que tú va a hacer negocio, es que Changó te va a poner esa evolución en tu mano.

11. The derivation of "moyubá" is clearly the Yoruba phrase "mo júbà": "I" + "give homage." In Lucumí, the first-person declaration has been generalized to mean "give homage." Indeed, the phrase is one of the few from Yoruba to have been lexified

and hispanicized into a regular -ar verb that follows Spanish rules of conjugation and nominalization: *moyubar* = to pay homage; *moyubación* = the act of saying the moyubá; *moyubando* = doing the moyubá, and so on.

12. The polarity of hot and cold in Santería is an example of a broad metaphysical principle across parts of West Africa and its diaspora, in which coolness is necessary for ritual efficacy (Abrahams 1977; Laguerre 1987; Voeks 1995).

13. The Lucumí *tilla tilla* may derive from the Yoruba ideophone *tiya tiya*, meaning fiasco or failure.

14. My Cuban transcriber, who was not at all involved in Santería, did not segment the Spanish word "todo" (all), abbreviated as "to'" out of Alberto's repeated phrase "to' eggún." She treated the entire unit as unintelligible Lucumí.

15. One possible Yoruba derivation is "ìbà ayé, ìbà èyin tí ọrun," meaning "homage to the world, homage to you (plural) of heaven." The verb derivation, "ìbà," "to give homage," seems likely. The lexeme "onu" appears in other contexts in Lucumí, where it also seems likely to derive from ọ̀run, "heaven." (Thanks to Dr. Yiwọla Awoyale, of the Linguistic Data Consortium at the University of Pennsylvania whose help was instrumental in deciphering possible Yoruba derivations of this and other Lucumí phrases.)

16. A likely derivation of "kinkamaché" in Yoruba is "kí ikú má ṣe!," meaning "may death not get you" (literally "that death not act"). Note that the word meaning "death," *ikú*, is identical in Yoruba and Lucumí, but in this phrase, with its changed pronunciation and collapsed segmentation, *ikú* is not recognizable.

17. "Ochareo" may derive from a Yoruba invocatory exclamation, "òòṣà, iré o," which addresses an oricha to call for good fortune: "oricha, goodness!"

Chapter 7. Building a Moral Community out of Critique and Controversy

1. Santería was established in Santiago much later than in its Cuban "birthplaces" of Matanzas and Havana. The oral history of Santería's arrival in the city is discussed in chapter 3.

2. When, inevitably, some godparents and godchildren have fallings out, other santeros regard these conflicts as especially problematic and are quick to blame the godchild for "a lack of respect." Santeros frequently admonish their own and others' godchildren to respect their elders, especially their godparents.

3. For extensive descriptions of the rituals of initiation in Santería, see Mason (2002: 57–83) and Cabrera (1996: 128–234). See also video recordings of initiation rituals by Gleason and Mereghetti (1992) and Drufovka and Stanford (1996).

4. This Lucumí word is equivalent to *iyàwó*, "wife" in Yoruba. The valences of becoming like a wife to one's principal oricha are discussed below.

5. For gorgeous examples of these initiation outfits, see Flores-Peña and Evanchuck (1994) and D. H. Brown (2003).

6. Although Cuban santeros use Itá to mean the special divination done on this day of initiation, the Lucumí word likely derives from Yoruba *ę́ęta* (three) or *mę́ta* (third), referring to the third day of the sequence.

7. D. H. Brown provides a detailed explanation of rituals for higher degrees of initiation, such as *pinaldo*, and the controversies surrounding them (2003: 109–11, 333 n.182, n.184).

8. Conversation with Emilio, audio tapes 2 and 4, October 11, 1999, Santiago de Cuba. The entire dialogue in its original Spanish follows.

1 Emilio: En primer término, no me gustó que el mismo padrino fuera el italero de la ceremonia.

2 Yo lo respeto mucho porque él tiene mucho conocimiento, muchos años de experiencia . pero para mi, para **mi**—eso después lo vamos a comprobar con otros santeros—(KW: Sí)—para **mi** es una violación.

3 Porque el testigo tiene que ser una persona que certifique, que ese individuo se inició en la religión. Entonces si todos son ahijados de él, a lo mejor por cubri—por tapar a su padrino, pueden decir, "no, todo estuvo bién, no hubo ningún problema." O sea que cuando hay un testigo, ese testigo advierte, "esto se está haciendo mal, esto no es así, esto tenemos que hacerlo así." El testigo puede decirlo.

4 Kristina: Pero estuviste uno de los testigos

5 E: ¿Quién, yo?

6 KW: Para dos, sí, dos días

7 E: Pero no fui, yo no fui invitado

8 KW: ¡Ah!

9 E: Yo no estaba levantado como santero, para trabajar allí

10 KW: Anja

11 E: Yo no estaba, porque si se me levanta hay que poner, esa es otra cosa que te voy a decir ahora. Hay que ir delante de mi Ochún, pedirle permiso a mi Ochún. O sea, mis santos y entonces depositar un derecho, para que yo pueda ir a esa ceremonia.

12 KW: Anja

13 E: Yo participé pero como amigo

14 O sea que pudimos ver (1 second) que hubo algunas violaciones. Esa es la segunda, o sea que no habían muchos testigos.

9. See D. H. Brown (2003: 94) for an example of the lengths to which santeros and babalawos may go to ensure that their initiations are regarded as legitimate.

10. 15 E: No participé . . . No sé cómo se harían las misas.

16 O sea, el ebbó de entrada, no sé cómo fue..

17 No puedo dar opinion porque .. no estabamos allí.

18 KW: Hmm

19 E: Pero parece que fue correcto (1.5 seconds) ¿Por qué? ..

20 Porque de todas formas cuando el santo no está sien—no está saliendo bien, el muerto se para,

21 no permite que continuen la ceremonia, provoca cualquier accidente,

22 cualquier incidente, y no permite que se- que se- que siga la ceremonia.

23 KW: Uhm-hm

24 E: Por eso es que yo digo que todo él tiene que haberlo explicado muy bien.

11. 25 E: Porque, bueno, en nin—y yo miré, siempre estaba pendiente al caracol.

26 Yo siempre miré el caracol para ver si .. si estaba dando bien,

27 y el caracol sí dijo todo lo que él planteó es verdad, lo decía el caracol. .

28 todo lo que él planteó lo decía el caracol. .

29 no vi ninguna .. ningún problema de .

30 KW: ¿Es decir que casi todo fue <u>iré</u>?

31 E: <u>Iré</u>

32 KW: Anja

33 E: Y sin <u>osogbo</u>..Sin <u>osogbo</u> son las letras malas que te dan.

12. 34 E: o sea que **parece** .. o que los santos de él están (ha-ha) acostumbrados (ha-ha) a trabajar así ya.

35 O que, él ha planteado muy bien su cosa.

36 O **preparó** muy bien su **casa** para que no haya ningún problema.

37 Porque esa es otra cosa, el santero tiene que **saber** preparar su casa, para que no haya problema a la hora del santo.

13. 38 E: Bien, **viste** una ceremonia .. que: no es **habitual** . que se vea

39 KW: Anja

40 E: que es el <u>**ñangareo**</u>. Yo no te hablé nunca de esto.

41 KW: Hmm

42 E: Nunca te hablé del <u>ñangareo</u> porque eso es una ceremonia secreta.

43 Pero bueno, ya que la viste te la tengo que decir.

14. 44 KW: Y: ah, .. ah . ¿Estabas ahm, ah .. sorprendido que me permitieron . ver?

45 E: Sí, sí, sí, sí, porque eso no: -

46 Bueno, es que nosotros tenemos buena relación de amistad

47 y él **sabe** que en defini—

48 él **piensa**, no es que el sabe.

49 Él **piensa** que en definitiva tu vas a hacer santo.

50 Él ti—(ha-ha-ha) tu vi—¿te diste cuenta?

51 Él **cree** que tu vas a hacer santo porque yo le dije,

52 No ella es ahijada **mía**.

53 KW: Anja

54 E: Entonces él tiene eso metido en la cabeza y **salió**.

55 ¿No lo viste?

15. Interviews with Emilio and senior santeras, audio tapes 41, 45, 48–50, March 21 and March 27, 2000, Santiago de Cuba.

16. I have changed trivial details of the event to protect the identities of those involved, while striving to stay true to the underlying dynamics of the situation. The event occurred early in 2000 in Santiago de Cuba.

17. For Cuban and comparative perspectives on the deity Olorun, see Bolívar Aróstegui (1990: 66–69) and Díaz Fabelo (1960).

18. The relevant excerpt of the original transcript follows, in which lined up brackets indicate overlapping speech (Itá recording, audio tapes 43 and 44, early 2000, Santiago de Cuba).

1   Oriaté: Uds. saben que se permite cuando es familiar en santo, mientras tanto no puede ser. (16-second pause)

2   Uds. tienen que aprender señores, si Uds no aprenden
                [(can't be heard)

3   Santero: [No, Juana lo sabe. Juana sabe. Lo que pasa que ella
                        [le respeta

4   Oriaté: [Pero el respeto no impide el ubicar las cosas como son
                        [(can't be heard)

5   Male voice: [(can't be heard)

6   Santera 2: Sí, pero el problema
                        [(can't be heard)

7   Many voices: [(can't be heard)

8   Male voice: [Uds. saben quien tiene la culpa—

9   Oriaté: Nosotros los santeros no podemos entrar al cuarto de Orunmila a buscar nada—

10   Female voice: —Así sea—

11   Oriaté: Por tanto el cuarto de santo hay que respetarlo.

12   (11-second sound of cowries, then Oriaté resumes speaking in Lucumí, invoking Eleggua)

19. 1 Oriaté: Pero mira, gracias a Dios y a Eleggua y a to' los santos.

2   Gracias a Dios, a Eleggua, y a todos los santos que yo me fui,

3   porque todas las atrocidades que dicen que se hicieron aquí, vaya había que sacar un revolver y matarme.

4   Había que sacar un revolver y matarme,

5   porque yo eso no lo entiendo y no quiero hablar más

6   para que la gente no se ofenda.

20. Santero's interpretation of Itá, CD 31 (track 9), April 6, 2000, Santiago de Cuba.

21. Padrino: Es para Eleggua: se sabe que hay una situación pero no hay nada que (too quiet to hear) que quiere pasar por el Ifá, el iyawó. Si lo permite, él pasa, si no lo permite, no pasa.

22. Oriaté: Ahi está ibú. Esto dice que sí, míralo, eso dice que sí, (unclear) eso dice que no.

23. Oriaté: No lo digo yo, lo dijo Eleggua, ¿claro? Y jamateando(?) por sus ma-

nos. Ud. hace lo que Ud. entienda con eso, ¡eh! Con eso que to' ba binu con Olofi, ¡Ochareo!

Chapter 8. Conclusion: The Promise

Epigraph. Song lyrics from Tropicana Nightclub Web site <http://members.tripod. com/TropicanaNightclub/babalu.html>, and *Babalu: Desi Arnaz and his Orchestra*, Audio CD, released June 4, 1996, RCA. See Isabel Castellanos (1983) for an account of Afro-Cuban religious motifs in Cuban popular music, including "Babalú."

1. Although often referred to as "Que Viva Changó," the song's actual title is "A Santa Bárbara."

2. Some important scholarly sources include Argüelles Mederos and Hodge Limonta (1991), Barnet (1995), Bolívar Aróstegui (1994), Brandon (1993), Castellanos and Castellanos (1988), Fernández Robaina (1997), Hagedorn (2001), James Figarola (1999), Lachatañeré (1992), Murphy (1994), and Palmié (2002b). Especially interesting santero-scholar accounts include Canizares (1993), González-Whippler (1992), M. Mason (2002), J. Mason (1985, 1992), and Pedroso (1995). Actual manuals include Angarica (n.d.a, n.d.b), Cabrera (1996), Mestre (1996), and Valdés Garriz (1991).

References

Abimbola, W. 1976. *Ifa: An Exposition of Ifa Literary Corpus*. Ibadan: Oxford University Press Nigeria.

Abrahams, R. 1977. The West Indian tea meeting: An essay in civilization. In *Old Roots in New Lands: Historical and Anthropological Perspectives on Black Experiences in the Americas*, ed. A. M. Pescatello, 173–208. Westport, Conn.: Greenwood Press.

Agha, A. 2003. The social life of cultural value. *Language and Communication* 23(3–4): 231–73.

———. 2005. Voice, footing, enregisterment. *Journal of Linguistic Anthropology* 15(1): 38–59.

Aguirre, S. 1974. *Eco de los Caminos*. Havana: Editorial de Ciencias Sociales.

Alcaraz, J. L. 2000. *Santería Cubana: Rituales y Magia*. Barcelona: Tikal Publications.

Alonso, G., and A. L. Fernández, eds. 1977. *Antología de lingüística cubana*. Vol. 1. Havana: Editorial de Ciencias Sociales.

Angarica, N. V. n.d.a. *Lucumi al alcance de todos*. Cuba: n.p.

———. n.d.b. *Manual de Orihate: Religion Lucumi*. Cuba: n.p.

Argüelles Mederos, A., and I. Hodge Limonta. 1991. *Los llamados cultos sincreticos y el espiritismo*. Havana: Editorial Academia.

Argyriadis, K. 2000. Des Noirs sorciers aux babalaos: Analyse du paradoxe du rapport a l'Afrique a la Havane. *Cahiers D'Etudes Africaines* 160(XL-4): 649–74.

Asad, T. 1983. Anthropological conceptions of religion: Reflections on Geertz. *Man* 18:237–59.

Austin-Broos, D. J. 1997. *Jamaica Genesis: Religion and the Politics of Moral Orders*. Chicago: University of Chicago Press.

Ayorinde, C. 2004. *Afro-Cuban Religiosity, Revolution, and National Identity*. Gainesville: University Press of Florida.

Azari, N. P., J. Nickel, G. Wunderlich, M. Niedeggen, and H. Hefter. 2001. Neural correlates of religious experience. *European Journal of Neuroscience* 13:1649–652.

Bakhtin, M. 1981. *The Dialogic Imagination: Four Essays by M. M. Bakhtin*. Austin: University of Texas Press.

Barber, K. 1981. How man makes god in West Africa: Yoruba attitudes towards the Orisa. *Africa* 5(3): 724–45.

———. 1990. Oriki, women, and the proliferation and merging of Orisa. *Africa* 60(3): 313–37.

Barber, K., and P. F. de Moraes Farias. 1989. *Discourse and its Disguises: The Interpretation of African Oral Texts.* Birmingham, England: Centre of West African Studies, University of Birmingham.

Barnet, M. 1994. *Biography of a Runaway Slave.* Willimantic, Conn.: Curbstone Press.

———. 1995. *Cultos Afrocubanos: La Regla de Ocha, La Regla de Palo Monte.* Havana: Artex y Ediciones Union.

Barreal, I. 1992. Prólogo to *El Sistema Religiosa de los Afrocubanos.* Havana: Editorial de Ciencias Sociales.

Barth, F. 1969. Introd. to *Ethnic Groups and Boundaries: The Social Organization of Cultural Differences,* ed. F. Barth. London: Allen and Unwin.

Bascom, W. R. 1969. *Ifa Divination: Communication Between Gods and Men in West Africa.* Bloomington: Indiana University Press.

———. 1971 (1950). The focus of Cuban Santería. In *Peoples and Cultures of the Caribbean,* ed. M. M. Horowitz, 522–27. New York: Natural History Press.

———. 1980. *Sixteen Cowries: Yoruba Divination from Africa to the New World.* Bloomington: Indiana University Press.

Bauman, R., and C. L. Briggs. 1990. Poetics and performance as critical perspectives on language and social life. *Annual Review of Anthropology* 19:59–88.

Bauman, R., and J. Sherzer, eds. 1974. *Explorations in the Ethnography of Speaking.* 2nd ed. Cambridge: Cambridge University Press.

Bell, C. 1992. *Ritual Theory, Ritual Practice.* New York: Oxford University Press.

———. 1997. *Ritual: Perspectives and Dimensions.* Oxford: Oxford University Press.

Berhenn, H. 1995. Philosophy and religious experience. In *Handbook of Religious Experience,* ed. R. W. Hood, 144–60. Birmingham, Ala.: Religious Education Press.

Betto, F. 1985. *Fidel y la Religión: Conversaciones con Frei Betto.* Havana: Oficina de Publicaciones del Consejo de Estado.

Bhabha, H. 1994. *The Location of Culture.* New York: Routledge.

Bloch, M. 1974. Symbols, song, dance and features of articulation. *Archives Europeennes de Sociologie* 15:55–81.

Boas, F. 1889. On alternating sounds. In *The Shaping of American Anthropology,* ed. G. Stocking, 72–77.

Bolívar Aróstegui, N. 1990. *Los Orichas en Cuba.* Havana: Ediciones Unión, UNEAC.

———. 1994. *Opolopo Owó.* Havana: Editorial de Ciencas Sociales.

———. 1996. *Ifá: Su Historia en Cuba.* Havana: Ediciones Unión.

Borges, D. 1993. "Puffy, ugly, slothful, and inert": Degeneration in Brazilian social thought. *Journal of Latin American Studies* 25:235–56.

Brandon, G. 1993. *Santería from Africa to the New World: The Dead Sell Memories.* Bloomington: Indiana University Press.

Brenneis, D. 1984. Grog and gossip in Bhatgaon: Style and substance in Fiji Indian conversation. *American Ethnologist* 11(3): 457–506.

Briggs, C. L. 1993. Generic versus metapragmatic dimensions of Warao narratives: Who regiments performance? In *Reflexive Language: Reported Speech and Metapragmatics*, ed. J. A. Lucy, 159–212. Cambridge: Cambridge University Press.

———. 1994. The sting of the ray: Bodies, agency, and grammar in Warao curing. *Journal of American Folklore* 107(423): 139–66.

———. 1996. The politics of discursive authority in research on the invention of tradition. *Cultural Anthropology* 11(4): 435–69.

Briggs, C. L., and R. Bauman. 1992. Genre, intertextuality, and social power. *Journal of Linguistic Anthropology* 2(2): 131–72.

Bronfman, A. 1998. "Unsettled and nomadic": Law, anthropology, and race in early Twentieth-century Cuba. Latin American History Workshop. Princeton University.

———. 2002. "En plena libertad y democracia": *Negros Brujos* and the social question, 1904–1919. *Hispanic American Historical Review* 82(3): 549–88.

Brown, D. H. 2003. *Santería Enthroned: Art, Ritual, and Innovation in an Afro-Cuban Religion*. Chicago: University of Chicago Press.

Brown, K. M. 1991. *Mama Lola: A Vodou Priestess in Brooklyn*. Berkeley: University of California Press.

Browning, B. 1998. *Infectious Rhythm: Metaphors of Contagion and the Spread of African Culture*. New York: Routledge.

Burhenn, H. 1995. Philosophy and religious experience. In *Handbook of Religious Experience*, ed. R. W. Hood, 144–60. Birmingham, Ala.: Religious Education Press.

Cabrera, L. 1958. *Anagó, Vocabulario Lucumí*. Havana: Ediciones C. R.

———. 1993 (1954). *El Monte*. Havana: Editorial Letras Cubanas.

———. 1996. *Yemaya y Ochun: Kariocha, Iyalorichas y Olorichas*. Miami: Ediciones Universal.

Canizares, R. 1993. *Walking with the Night: The Afro-Cuban World of Santería*. Rochester, Vt.: Destiny Books.

Carr, D. 1986. *Time, Narrative, and History*. Bloomington: Indiana University Press.

Castellanos, Isabel. 1976. The use of language in Afro-Cuban religion. PhD diss., Georgetown University.

———. 1983. *Elegua Quiere Tambo: Cosmovision Religiosa Afrocubana en las Canciones Populares*. Cali, Colombia: Universidad del Valle.

———. 1990. Grammatical structure, historical development, and religious usage of Afro-Cuban bozal speech. *Folklore Forum* 23(1/2): 57–84.

———. 1996. From Ulkumí to Lucumí: A historical overview of religious acculturation in Cuba. In *Santería Aesthetics in Contemporary Latin American Art*, ed. A. Lindsay, 39–50. Washington, D.C.: Smithsonian Institution Press.

Castellanos, Israel. 1926. El apodo de los delincuentes en Cuba. *Revista Bimestre Cubana* 21:346–589.

Castellanos, J., and Israel Castellanos. 1988. *Cultura Afrocubana*. 4 vols. Miami: Ediciones Universal.

Centro de Investigaciones Psicológicas y Sociológicas (CIPS). 1998. *Panorama de la religión en Cuba*. Havana: Editorial Política.

Clifford, J. 1986. Partial truths, introd. to *Writing Culture: The Poetry and Politics of Ethnography*, ed. J. Clifford and G. E. Marcus. Berkeley: University of California Press.

———. 1988. *The Predicament of Culture: Twentieth-Century Ethnography, Literature, and Art*. Cambridge: Harvard University Press.

Comaroff, J., and J. L. Comaroff. 1993. *Modernity and its Malcontents: Ritual and power in postcolonial Africa*. Chicago: University of Chicago Press.

Corin, E. 1998. Refiguring the person: the dynamics of affects and symbols in an African spirit possession cult. In *Bodies and Persons: Comparative Perspectives from Africa and Melanesia*, ed. M. Lambek and A. Strathern, 80–102. Cambridge: Cambridge University Press.

Crapanzano, V. 2003. Reflections on hope as a category of social and psychological analysis. *Cultural Anthropology* 18(1): 3–32.

Creed, G. W. 2004. Constituted through conflict: Images of community (and nation) in Bulgarian rural ritual. *American Anthropologist* 106(1): 56–70.

Csordas, T. J. 1994. *The Sacred Self: A Cultural Phenomenology of Charismatic Healing*. Berkeley: University of California Press.

———. 1997. *Language, Charisma, and Creativity: The Ritual Life of a Religious Movement*. Berkeley and Los Angeles: University of California Press.

Cutie Bressler, A. 2001. *Psiquiatría y religiosidad popular*. Santiago de Cuba: Editorial Oriente.

Daniel, Y. 1995. *Rumba: Dance and Social Change in Contemporary Cuba*. Bloomington: Indiana University Press.

Darwin, C. 1964. *On the Origin of Species*. Fascimile of 1st ed. Cambridge: Harvard University Press.

de la Fuente, A. 1998. Raza, desigualdad y prejuicio en Cuba. *América Negra* 15:21–39.

———. 2001. *A Nation for All: Race, Equality, and Nation in 20th century Cuba*. Chapel Hill: University of North Carolina Press.

Desjarlais, R. R. 1992. *Body and Emotion: The Aesthetics of Illness and Healing in the Nepal Himalayas*. Philadelphia: University of Pennsylvania Press.

———. 1996. Presence. In *Performance of Healing*, ed. C. Laderman and M. Roseman, 143–64. New York: Routledge.

Dianteill, E. 1995. *Le savant et le santero: Naissance de l'etude scientifique des religions afrocubaines (1906–1954)*. Paris: L'Harmattan.

———. 2000. *Des dieux y des signes—Initiation, ecriture et divination dans les religions afro-cubaines*. Paris: Editions de L'Ècole des Hautes Etudes en Sciences Sociales.

Díaz Fabelo, S. T. 1960. *Olorun*. Havana: Centro de Estudios Folklóricos, Teatro Nacional de Cuba.

Doortmont, M. R. 1990. The invention of the Yorubas: Regional and pan-African nationalism versus ethnic provincialism. In *Self-assertion and Brokerage: Early Cultural Nationalism in West Africa*, ed. P. F. de Moraes Farias and K. Barber, 101–8. Birmingham: Centre of West African Studies, University of Birmingham.

Drewal, M. T. 1992. *Yoruba Ritual: Performers, Play, Agency*. Bloomington and Indianapolis: Indiana University Press.

Drufovka, I., and R. Stanford. 1996. *Yo Soy Hechicero (I am a Sorcerer)*. DVD. Dir. R. Stanford. Stanford Creative and Bilingual Media Co.

Du Bois, J. W. 1992. Meaning without intention: lessons from divination. In *Responsibility and Evidence in Oral Discourse*, ed. J. H. Hill and J. T. Irvine, 48–71. Cambridge: Cambridge University Press.

Durkheim, E. 1995 (1912). *The Elementary Forms of Religious Life*. New York: The Free Press.

Eliade, M. 1959. *The Sacred and the Profane: The Nature of Religion*. New York: Harcourt, Brace, and World.

Evans-Pritchard, E. E. 1937. *Witchcraft, Oracles, and Magic Among the Azande*. Oxford: Clarendon Press.

Farnell, B., and L. R. Graham. 1998. Discourse-centered methods. In *Handbook of Methods in Cultural Anthropology*, ed. H. R. Bernard, 411–57. Walnut Creek, Calif.: AltaMira.

Feld, S. 1982. *Sound and Sentiment: Birds, Weeping, Poetics, and Song in Kaluli Expression*. Austin: University of Texas Press.

Fernandez, D. J. 2000. *Cuba and the Politics of Passion*. Austin: University of Texas.

Fernández Robaina, T. 1994. *El Negro en Cuba, 1902–1958*. Havana: Editorial de Ciencias Sociales.

———. 1997. *Hablen Paleros y Santeros*. Havana: Editorial de Ciencias Sociales.

Ferrer, A. 1999. *Insurgent Cuba: Race, Nation, and Revolution, 1868–1898*. Chapel Hill: University of North Carolina Press.

Flores-Peña, Y., and R. J. Evanchuck. 1994. *Speaking Without a Voice: Santería Garments and Altars*. Folk Art and Artists Series. Jackson: University of Mississippi Press.

Fuentes Guerra, J., and G. Gómez Gómez. 1994. *Cultos Afrocubanos: Un estudio etnolingüístico*. Havana: Editorial de Ciencias Sociales.

Fuentes Guerra, J., and A. Schwegler. 2005. *Lengua y ritos del Palo Monte Mayombe: Dioses cubanos y sus fuentes africanas*. Madrid: Iberoamericana Vervuert.

Geertz, C. 1973. *The Interpretation of Cultures*. New York: Basic Books.

Geurts, K. L. 2003. *Culture and the Senses*. Berkeley: University of California Press.

Gleason, J., and E. Mereghetti, producers. 1992. *The King Does Not Lie: The Initiation of a Priest of Shango*. Video recording. New York: Filmakers Library.

Gluckman, M. 1963. Gossip and scandal. *Current Anthropology* 4(3): 307–16.

Goffman, E. 1981. *Forms of Talk*. Philadelphia: University of Pennsylvania Press.

González Huguet, L., and J. R. Baudry. 1967. Voces "bantú" en el vocabulario "palero." *Etnología y Folklore* 3:31–64.

González-Whippler, M. 1992. *The Santería Experience: A Journey into the Miraculous.* St Paul, Minn.: Llewellyn Press.

———. 1995. Santeria: Its dynamic and multiple roots. In *Enigmatic Powers: Syncretism with Africa and Indigenous People's Religions among Latinos,* ed. A. I. Pérez y Mena and A. M. Stevens-Arroyo, 99–112. New York: Bildner Center for Western Hemispheric Studies.

Graham, R., ed. 1990. *The Idea of Race in Latin America, 1870–1940.* Austin: University of Texas Press.

Guillén, N. 1972. *Obra Poética.* Havana: Instituto Cubano del Libro.

Gumperz, J. J., and D. Hymes. 1972. *Directions in Sociolinguistics: The Ethnography of Communication.* New York: Holt, Rinehart, and Winston.

Guthrie, S. E. 1993. *Faces in the Clouds: A New Theory of Religion.* New York: Oxford University Press.

Hagedorn, K. J. 2001. *Divine Utterances: The Performance of Afro-Cuban Santeria.* Washington, D.C.: Smithsonian Institution Press.

Hanks, W. F. 1996. Exorcism and the description of participant roles. In *Natural Histories of Discourse,* ed. M. Silverstein and G. Urban, 160–202. Chicago: University of Chicago Press.

Harding, S. 1992. The afterlife of stories: Genesis of a man of God. In *Storied Lives,* ed. G. Rosenwald and R. Ochberg, 60–75. New Haven: Yale University.

———. 2000. *The Book of Jerry Falwell.* Princeton: Princeton University Press.

Hay, D. 1982. *Exploring Inner Space: Scientists and Religious Experience.* Harmondsworth: Penguin.

Helg, A. 1990. Race in Argentina and Cuba, 1880–1930: Theory, policies, and popular reactions. In *The Idea of Race in Latin America, 1870–1940,* ed. R. Graham, 45–69. Austin: University of Texas Press.

———. 1995. *Our Rightful Share: The Afro-Cuban Struggle for Equality, 1886–1912.* Chapel Hill: University of North Carolina Press.

Henken, T. 2000. Last resort or bridge to the future? Tourism and workers in Cuba's second economy. *Cuba in Transition* 10:321–36.

———. 2002. "Vale todo" (anything goes): Cuba's *paladares. Cuba in Transition* 12:344–53.

Hill, J. H., and J. T. Irvine, eds. 1993. *Responsibility and Evidence in Oral Discourse.* Cambridge: University of Cambridge Press.

Hinton, L. 1980. Vocables in Havasupai song. In *Southwestern Indian Ritual Drama,* ed. C. J. Frisbie, 275–306. Albuquerque: University of New Mexico Press.

Hood, R. W., ed. 1995. *Handbook of Religious Experience.* Birmingham, Ala.: Religious Education Press.

Hood, R. W., B. Spilka, and R. L. Gorsuch. 1996. *Psychology of Religion: An Empirical Approach.* 2nd ed. New York: Guilford Press.

Houk, J. 1995. *Spirits, Blood, and Drums: The Orisha Religion in Trinidad.* Philadelphia: Temple University Press.

Idowu, E. B. 1962. *Olodumare: God in Yoruba Belief.* Ikeja, Nigeria: Longman Nigeria Ltd.

Irvine, J. 1982. The creation of identity in spirit mediumship and possession. In *Semantic Anthropology*, ed. D. Parkin, 241–60. London: Academic Press.

Jackson, M. 1996. *Things As They Are: New Directions in Phenomenological Anthropology.* Bloomington: Indiana University Press.

James, W. 1922 (1902). *Varieties of Religious Experience.* New York: Longmans, Green and Co.

James Figarola, J. 1999. *Los Sistemas Mágico-religiosos Cubanos: Principios Rectores.* Caracas: UNESCO.

Johnson, P. C. 2002. *Secrets, Gossip, and Gods: The Transformation of Brazilian Candomble.* Oxford: Oxford University Press.

Keane, W. 1997. Religious language. *Annual Review of Anthropology* 26:47–71.

Kelly, J. D., and M. Kaplan. 2001. *Represented Communities: Fiji and World Decolonization.* Chicago: University of Chicago Press.

Kirk, J. M. 1989. *Between God and the Party: Religion and Politics in Revolutionary Cuba.* Gainesville: University Presses of Florida.

Kirsch, T. G. 2004. Restaging the will to believe: Religious pluralism, anti-syncretism, and the problem of belief. *American Anthropologist* 106(4): 699–709.

Kopytoff, J. H. 1965. *A Preface to Modern Nigeria: The "Sierra Leonians" in Yoruba, 1830–1890.* Madison: University of Wisconsin Press.

Kuipers, J. 1990. *Power in Performance: The Creation of Textual Authority in Weyewa Ritual Speech.* Philadelphia: University of Pennsylvania Press.

———. 1993. Obligations to the word: Ritual speech, performance, and reponsibility among the Weyewa. In *Responsibility and Evidence in Oral Discourse*, ed. J. H. Hill and J. T. Irvine, 88–104. Cambridge: Cambridge University Press.

Lachatañeré, R. 1992. *El Sistema Religioso de los Afrocubanos.* Colección Echú Bi. Havana: Editorial de Ciencias Sociales.

Lago Vieito, Á. 2001. El espiritismo en la región oriental de Cuba en el Siglo XIX. *Del Caribe* 35:72–79.

LaGuerre, M. 1987. *Afro-Caribbean Folk Medicine.* Massachusetts: Bergin and Garvey Publishers.

Larduet Luaces, A. 1999. Presencia de los bantú en las creencias populares de base africana en Cuba. Unpublished manuscript in preparation for *Del Caribe*.

———. 2001. Reynerio Pérez en el panorama de las creencias de origen bantú en Santiago de Cuba. *Del Caribe* 34:114–15.

Laviña, J., ed. 1989. *Doctrina Para Negros.* Barcelona: Sendai ediciones.

Law, R. 1997. Ethnicity and the slave trade: "Lucumi" and "Nago" as ethnonyms in West Africa. *History in Africa* 24:205–19.

León, A. 1971. Un caso de tradición oral escrita. *Islas (Santa Clara)* 39–40:139–51.

Lipski, J. M. 1998. Perspectivas sobre el español bozal. In *América negra: Panorámica actual de los estudios lingüísticos sobre variedades hispanas, portugueses, y criollas*, ed. M. Perl and A. Schwegler, 294–327. Madrid: Iberoamericana.

Lucy, J. 1992a. *Grammatical Categories and Cognition: A Case Study of the Linguistic Relativity Hypothesis*. Cambridge: Cambridge University Press.

———. 1992b. *Language Diversity and Thought*. Cambridge: Cambridge University Press.

Malinowski, B. 1966 (1935). *Coral Gardens and Their Magic*. 2nd ed. London: George Allen and Unwin.

Marcus, G. E., and M. M. Fischer. 1986. *Anthropology as Cultural Critique: An Experimental Moment in the Human Sciences*. Chicago: University of Chicago Press.

Marin Llanes, M. 2001. Prevention of an infectious disease in Cuba utilizing Afro-Cuban Santeria religious beliefs. Paper presented at the 100th American Anthropological Association Annual Meeting, Washington, D.C.

Martinez Furé, R. 1979. *Diálogos Imaginarios*. Havana: Editorial Arte y Literatura.

Mason, J. 1985. *Four New World Yoruba Rituals*. Brooklyn: Yoruba Theological Archministry.

———. 1992. *Orin Orisa, Songs for Selected Heads*. Brooklyn: Yoruba Theological Archministry.

Mason, M. A. 1994. "I bow my head to the ground": the creation of bodily experience in a Cuban American Santería initiation. *Journal of American Folklore* 107(423): 23–29.

———. 2002. *Living Santeria: Rituals and Experiences in an Afro-Cuban Religion*. Washington, D.C.: Smithsonian Institution Press.

Matibag, E. 1996. *Afro-Cuban Religious Experience: Cultural Reflections in Narrative*. Gainesville: University Press of Florida.

———. 1997. Ifá and interpretation: An Afro-Caribbean literary practice. In *Sacred possessions: Vodou, Santería, Obeah, and the Caribbean*, ed. M. Fernández Olmos and L. Paravisini-Gebert, 151–70. New Brunswick, N.J.: Rutgers University Press.

Matory, J. L. 1994a. *Sex and the Empire That Is No More: Gender and the Politics of Metaphor in Oyo Yoruba Religion*. Minneapolis: University of Minnesota Press.

———. 1994b. Rival empires: Islam and the religions of spirit possession among the Oyo-Yoruba. *American Ethnologist* 21(3): 495–515.

Mattingly, C. 1998. *Healing Dramas and Clinical Plots: The Narrative Structure of Experience*. Cambridge: Cambridge University Press.

Merleau-Ponty, M. 1989 (1962). *Phenomenology of Perception*. London: Routledge.

Mestre, J. 1996. *Santería: Mitos y Creencias*. N.p.: Ediciones Prensa Latina.

Millet, J. 2000. El Foco de la Santería Santiaguera. *Del Caribe* 32:110–19.

Millet, J., R. Brea, and M. Ruiz Vila. 1997. *Barrio, Comparsa y Carnaval Santiaguero*. Santiago de Cuba y Santo Domingo: Ediciones Casa del Caribe y Ediciones Casa Dominicana de Identidad Caribeña.

Montejo Arrechea, C. V. 1993. *Sociedades de Instrucción y Recreo de Pardos y Morenos que Existieron en Cuba Colonial: Período 1878–1898*. Veracruz: Gobierno del Estado de Veracruz.

Moore, C. 1988. *Castro, the Blacks, and Africa*. Los Angeles: Center for Afro-American Studies, University of California.

Moore, R. 1997. *Nationalizing Blackness: Afrocubanismo and Artistic Revolution in Havana, 1920–1940*. Pittsburgh: University of Pittsburgh Press.

Morrison, K. F. 1992. *Understanding Conversion*. Charlottesville: University Press of Virginia.

Morrison, K. Y. 1999. Civilization and citizenship through the eyes of Afro-Cuban intellectuals during the first constitutional era, 1902–1940. *Cuban Studies* 30:76–99.

Mullen, E. J. 1987. Los Negros Brujos: A reexamination of the text. *Cuban Studies* 17:111–29.

Murphy, J. 1988. *Santería: An African Religion in America*. Boston: Beacon Press.

———. 1994. *Working the Spirit: Ceremonies of the African Diaspora*. Boston: Beacon Press.

Newberg, A., E. d'Aquili, and V. Rause. 2001. *Why God Won't Go Away: Brain Science and the Biology of Belief*. New York: Ballantine Books.

Oficina Nacional de Estadísticas. 2002. Anuario Estadístico de Cuba 2001. Havana: Oficina Nacional de Estadísticas.

Ohnuki-Tierney, E., ed. 1990. *Culture Through Time: Anthropological Approaches*. Stanford: Stanford University Press.

Ortiz, F. 1922. Los afronegrismos de nuestro lenguaje. *Revista Bimestre Cubana* 27:321–36.

———. 1924. Vocablos de la economía política afrocubana. *Cuba Contemporánea* 35:136–46.

———. 1970 (1947). *Cuban Counterpoint: Tobacco and Sugar*. New York: Vintage Books.

———. 1973. *Orbita de Fernando Ortiz*. Havana: Colleción Orbita.

———. 1973 (1906). *Hampa afrocubana: Los negros brujos: apuntes para un estudio etnología criminal*. Miami: Ediciones Universal.

———. 1973 (1921). Los cabildos afrocubanos. In *Orbita de Fernando Ortiz*, ed. J. Le Riverend, 121–34. Havana: UNEAC.

———. 1981 (1951). *Los Bailes y el Teatro de los Negros en el Folklore de Cuba*. 2nd ed. Havana: Editorial Letras Cubanas.

———. 1991 (1924). *Glossario de Afronegrismos*. Havana: Editorial de Ciencias Sociales.

———. 1995 (1906). *Los Negros Brujos*. Havana: Editorial de Ciencias Sociales.

Ortiz López, L. A. 1998. *Huellas etnosociolingüísticas bozales y afrocubanas*. Frankfurt and Madrid: Vervuet Verlag.

Otero, S. 2002. Orunile, "Heaven is Home": Afrolatino Diasporas in Africa and the Americas. PhD diss., University of Pennsylvania.

Otto, R. 1958 (1950). *The Idea of the Holy: An Inquiry into the Non-rational Factor in the*

Idea of the Divine and Its Relation to the Rational. 2nd ed. Trans., J. W. Harvey. New York: Oxford University Press.

Paine, R. 1967. What is gossip about? An alternative hypothesis. *Man* n.s. 2:278–85.

Palmer, C. T., L. T. Steadman, and R. L. Wadley. 2005. Commentary on "Restaging the will to believe." *American Anthropologist* 107(2): 319–20.

Palmié, S. 1993. Ethnogenetic processes and cultural transfer in Afro-American slave populations. In *Slavery in the Americas*, ed. W. Binder, 337–63. Wurzburg: Konigshausen and Neuman.

———. 1995. Against syncretism:'Africanizing' and 'Cubanizing' discourses in North American orisa worship. In *Counterworks: Managing the Diversity of Knowledge*, ed. R. Fardon, 73–104. New York: Routledge.

———. 2002a. Fascinans or tremendum? Permutations of the state, the body, and the divine in late twentieth century Havana. Paper presented to the University of Pennsylvania Ethnohistory Workshop, Philadelphia.

———. 2002b. *Wizards and Scientists: Explorations in Afro-Cuban Modernity and Tradition.* Durham: Duke University Press.

Parkin, D. 1991. Simultaneity and sequencing in the oracular speech of Kenyan diviners. In *African Divination Systems: Ways of Knowing*, ed. P. M. Peek, 173–89. Bloomington: Indiana University Press.

Parmentier, R. 1997. The pragmatic semiotics of cultures. *Semiotica* 116:1–42.

Parsons, T. 1979. Religious perspectives in sociology and social psychology. In *Reader in Comparative Religion* 4th ed., ed. W. A. Lessa and E. Z. Vogt, 62–66. New York: Harper and Row.

Pedroso, L. 1995. *Obbedi. Cantos a los Orisha: Traducción e Historia.* Havana: Artex.

Peek, P. M., ed. 1991. *African Divination Systems: Ways of Knowing.* Bloomington: Indiana University Press.

Peel, J.D.Y. 1989. The cultural work of Yoruba ethnogenesis. In *History and Ethnicity*, ed. E. Tonkin, M. McDonald, and M. Chapman, 198–15. London: Routledge.

Pemberton III, J., ed. 2000. *Insight and Artistry in African Divination.* Washington, D.C.: Smithsonian Institution Press.

Pérez Jr., L. A. 1995a. North American Protestant missionaries in Cuba and the culture of hegemony, 1898–1920. In *Essays on Cuban History: Historiography and Research*, 53–72. Gainesville: University Press of Florida.

———. 1995b. Protestant missionaries in Cuba: Archival records, manuscript collections, and research perspectives. In *Essays on Cuban History: Historiography and Research*, 219–34. Gainesville: University Press of Florida.

Perrino, S. 2002. Intimate hierarchies and Qur'anic saliva (*tefli*): Textuality in a Senegalese ethnomedical encounter. *Journal of Linguistic Anthropology* 12(2): 225–59.

Philips, S. U. 2004. The organization of ideological diversity in discourse: Modern and neotraditional visions of the Tongan state. *American Ethnologist* 31(2): 231–50.

Pigg, S. L. 1996. The credible and the credulous: The question of "villagers' beliefs" in Nepal. *Cultural Anthropology* 11(2): 160–201.

Pike, S. M. 2001. *Earthly Bodies, Magical Selves: Contemporary Pagans and the Search for Community*. Berkeley: University of California Press.

Portuondo Linares, S. 1950. *Los Independientes de Color: Historia del Partido Independiente de Color*. Havana: Publicaciones del Ministerio de Educación.

Portuondo Zúñiga, O. 1995. *La Virgen de la Caridad del Cobre: Símbolo de Cubanía*. Santiago de Cuba: Editorial Oriente.

Proudfoot, W. 1985. *Religious Experience*. Berkeley: University of California Press.

Rahier, J. M. 2003. Introd. to Mestizaje, mulataje, mestiçagem in Latin American ideologies of national identities. *Journal of Latin American Anthropology* 8(1): 40–51.

Ramos, J., A. Orejuelos, and J. Gray. 1995. *La Promesa* (*The Promise*). Video recording. Milwaukee: Center for Latin American and Caribbean Studies, Videotape Special Collection, University of Wisconsin.

Rappaport, R. A. 1999. *Ritual and Religion in the Making of Humanity*. Cambridge: Cambridge University Press.

Riverend, J. L. 1973. Fernando Ortiz y su obra cubana. In *Orbita de Fernando Ortiz*, ed. J. L. Riverend, 7–51. Havana: Colleción Orbita.

Robbins, J. 2001. Ritual communication and linguistic ideology: A reading and partial reformulation of Rappaport's theory of ritual. *Current Anthropology* 42(5): 591–614.

Rodríguez, V. E. 1994. Cuban music and ethnicity: Historical considerations. In *Music and Black Ethnicity: The Caribbean and South America*, ed. G. H. Béhague, 91–108. New Brunswick and London: Transaction Publishers.

Román, R. L. 2002. *The routes of Cuban Spiritism: Displining man-gods in town and country*. Cuban Research Institute Conference, Florida International University, Miami.

Romberg, R. 2003. *Witchcraft and Welfare: Spiritual Capital and the Business of Magic in Modern Puerto Rico*. Austin: University of Texas Press.

Rushing, F. T. 1992. Cabildos de Nación, Sociedades de la Raza de Color: Afrocuban Participation in Slave Emancipation and Cuba Independence, 1865–1895. PhD diss., University of Chicago.

Samarin, W. J. 1972. *Tongues of Men and Angels: The Religious Language of Pentecostalism*. New York: MacMillan.

Sapir, E. 1949 (1921). *Language: An Introduction to the Study of Speech*. San Diego: Harcourt Brace.

Schieffelin, E. 1985. Performance and the cultural construction of reality. *American Ethnologist* 12(4): 707–24.

Schleiermacher, F. 1963 (1821). *The Christian Faith*. 2 vols. New York: Harper & Row.

Schwegler, A. 2006. Bozal Spanish: Captivating new evidence from a contemporary source (Afro-Cuban "Palo Monte"). In *Studies in Contact Linguistics: Essays in Honor of Glenn G. Gilbert*, ed. J. Fuller and L. L. Thornburg. New York: Peter Lang.

Silverstein, M. 1985. The functional stratification of language and ontogenesis. In *Culture, Communication and Cognition: Vygotskian Perspectives*, ed. J. Wertsch, 205–35. Cambridge and New York: Cambridge University Press.

———. 1992. The indeterminacy of contextualization: When is enough enough? In *The Contextualization of Language*, ed. P. Auer and A. DiLuzio. Amsterdam: John Benjamins.

———. 1993. Metapragmatic discourse and metapragmatic function. In *Reflexive Language: Reported Speech and Metapragmatics*, ed. J. A. Lucy, 33–58. Cambridge: Cambridge University Press.

———. 2003. Indexical order and the dialectics of sociolinguistic life. *Language and Communication* 23(3/4): 193–229.

Silverstein, M., and G. Urban, eds. 1996. *Natural Histories of Discourse*. Chicago: University of Chicago Press.

Stewart, P. J., and A. Strathern. 2004. *Witchcraft, Sorcery, Rumors, and Gossip*. Cambridge: Cambridge University Press.

Stoller, P. 1995. *Embodying Colonial Memories: Spirit Possession, Power, and the Hauka in West Africa*. New York: Routledge.

Stromberg, P. G. 1993. *Language and Self-transformation: A Study of the Christian Conversion Narrative*. Cambridge: Cambridge University Press.

Stutzman, R. 1981. El mestizaje: An all-inclusive ideology. In *Cultural Transformations and Ethnicity in Modern Ecuador*, ed. N. E. Whitten Jr., 45–94. Urbana: University of Illinois Press.

Tambiah, S. 1979. A performative approach to ritual. *Proceedings of the British Academy* 65:113–69.

Tedlock, D., and B. Mannheim, eds. 1995. *The Dialogic Emergence of Culture*. Urbana: University of Illinois Press.

Tomlinson, M. n.d. Whose waves roared: Christianity, power, and loss in Fiji. Unpublished manuscript in preparation.

Trawick, M. 1988. Ambiguity in the oral exegesis of a sacred text: *tirukkovaiyar* (or, the guru in the garden, being an account of a Tamil informant's responses to homesteading in Central New York). *Cultural Anthropology* 3(3): 316–51.

Trouillot, M.-R. 1992. The Caribbean region: An open frontier in anthropological theory. *Annual Review of Anthropology* 21:19–42.

Turner, V. 1967. *The Forest of Symbols: Aspects of Ndembu Ritual*. Ithaca: Cornell University Press.

———. 1974. *Dramas, Fields, and Metaphors: Symbolic Action in Human Society*. Ithaca: Cornell University Press.

Urban, G. 1991. *A Discourse-Centered Approach to Culture*. Austin: University of Texas Press.

———. 1996. *Metaphysical Community*. Austin: University of Texas Press.

———. 2001. *Metaculture: How Culture Moves Through the World*. Minneapolis: University of Minnesota Press.

Urban, G., and K. Smith. 1998. The sunny tropics of 'dialogue'? *Semiotica* 121(3/4): 263–81.

Urrutía y Blanco, C. de. 1882. *Los criminales de Cuba y d. José Trujillo; narración de los servicios prestados en el cuerpo de policía de Havana*. Barcelona: Establecimiento tipográfico de Fidel Giró.

Valdés Bernal, S. 1987. *Las lenguas de African subsaharana y el español de Cuba*. Havana: Editorial Academía de Ciencias de Cuba.

Valdés Garriz, Y. 1991. *Ceremonias Funebres de la Santería Afrocubana*. Hato Rey and San Juan, Puerto Rico: Sociedad de Autores Libres.

Voeks, R. A. 1995. Candomblé ethnobotany: African medicinal plant classification in Brazil. *Journal of Ethnobiology* 15(2): 257–80.

Wade, P. 2001. Racial identity and nationalism: A theoretical view from Latin America. *Ethnic and Racial Studies* 24(5): 845–65.

Warren, K. B. 1992. Transforming memories and histories: The meanings of ethnic resurgence for Mayan Indians. In *Americas: New Interpretive Essays*, ed. A. Stepan, 189–219. New York: Oxford University Press.

Watts, F., and M. Williams. 1988. *The Psychology of Religious Knowing*. Cambridge: Cambridge University Press.

Weber, M. 1963 (1922). *The Sociology of Religion*. 4th ed. Boston: Beacon Press.

Wedel, J. 2004. *Santería Healing*. Gainesville: University Press of Florida.

Werbner, R. 1973. The superabundance of understanding: Kalanga rhetoric and domestic divination. *American Anthropologist* 75(5): 1414–440.

Whitehead, H. 1987. *Renunciation and Reformulation*. Ithaca: Cornell University Press.

Whitten, N.E.J. 2003. Symbolic inversion, the topology of el mestizaje, and the spaces of las razas in Ecuador. *Journal of Latin American Anthropology* 8(1): 52–85.

Whorf, B. L. 1997 (1956). *Language, Thought, and Reality: Selected Writings of Benjamin Lee Whorf*. Cambridge: MIT Press.

Williams, B. F. 1991. *Stains on My Name, War in My Veins: Guyana and the Politics of Cultural Struggle*. Durham, N.C.: Duke University Press.

Winick, S. D. 1998. The proverb process: Intertextuality and proverbial innovation in popular culture. PhD diss., University of Pennsylvania.

Wirtz, K. 2005. "Where obscurity is a virtue": The mystique of unintelligibility in Santería ritual. *Language and Communication* 25(4): 351–75.

———. 2007. How diasporic religious communities remember: Learning to speak the "tongue of the oricha" in Cuban Santería. *American Ethnologist* 34(1): 108–26.

Wortham, S. 2001. *Narratives in Action: A Strategy for Research and Analysis*. New York: Teachers College Press.

Wright, W. 1990. *Cafe con Leche: Race, Class, and National Image in Venezuela*. Austin: University of Texas.

Yelvington, K. A. 2001. The anthropology of Afro-Latin America and the Caribbean: Diasporic dimensions. *Annual Review of Anthropology* 30:227–60.

Young, I. M. 1986. The ideal of community and the politics of difference. *Social Theory and Practice* 12(1): 1–26.

Index

Kristina Wirtz is an assistant professor of anthropology at Western Michigan University. She has published and forthcoming articles in *American Ethnologist*, *Journal of Latin American Anthropology*, *Language and Communication*, *Text and Talk*, and *Journal of Religion in Africa*, all based on her ongoing ethnographic and linguistic research on religion in Cuba.

DATE DUE
